INSIGHT GUIDES
FINLAND

APA PUBLICATIONS L
Part of the Langenscheidt Publishing Group

INSIGHT GUIDE
FINLAND

Editorial

Managing Editor
Siân Lezard
Art Director
Ian Spick
Picture Manager
Steven Lawrence
Series Manager
Rachel Fox

Distribution

UK & Ireland
GeoCenter International Ltd
Meridian House, Churchill Way West
Basingstoke, Hampshire RG21 6YR
sales@geocenter.co.uk

United States
Langenscheidt Publishers, Inc.
36–36 33rd Street 4th Floor
Long Island City, NY 11106
orders@langenscheidt.com

Australia
Universal Publishers
1 Waterloo Road
Macquarie Park, NSW 2113
sales@universalpublishers.com.au

New Zealand
Hema Maps New Zealand Ltd (HNZ)
Unit 2, 10 Cryers Road
East Tamaki, Auckland 2013
sales.hema@clear.net.nz

Worldwide
Apa Publications GmbH & Co.
Verlag KG (Singapore branch)
7030 Ang Mo Kio Avenue 5
08-65 Northstar @ AMK
Singapore 569880
apasin@singnet.com.sg

Printing
CTPS – China

©2010 Apa Publications GmbH & Co.
Verlag KG (Singapore branch)
All Rights Reserved

First Edition 1992
Fourth Edition 2010
Reprinted 2010

CONTACTING THE EDITORS
We would appreciate it if readers
would alert us to errors or out-
dated information by writing to:
**Insight Guides, P.O. Box 7910,
London SE1 1WE, England.**
insight@apaguide.co.uk

www.insightguides.com

ABOUT THIS BOOK

The first Insight Guide pioneered the use of creative full-colour photography in travel guides in 1970. Since then, we have expanded our range to cater for our readers' need not only for reliable information about their chosen destination but also for a real understanding of the culture and workings of that destination. Now, when the internet can supply inexhaustible (but not always reliable) facts, our books marry text and pictures to provide those much more elusive qualities: knowledge and discernment. To achieve this, they rely heavily on the authority of locally based writers and photographers.

Insight Guide: Finland is structured to convey an understanding of the country and its people as well as to guide readers through its myriad attractions:

◆ The **Features** section, indicated by a pink bar at the top of each page, covers the natural and cultural history of Finland, as well as featuring illuminating essays on subjects including the Finnish character, the Sami, art, architecture and design, food and drink and the wilderness.

◆ The main **Places** section, indicated by a blue bar, is a complete guide to all the sights and areas worth visiting. Places of special interest are coordinated by number with the maps.

◆ The **Travel Tips** listings section, with a yellow bar, provides full information on transport, hotels, restaurants, activities from culture to shopping to sports and outdoor adventures, and an A–Z section of essential practical information. An easy-to-find contents list for Travel Tips is printed on the back flap, which also serves as a bookmark.

LEFT: landscape at dawn, Lakeland.

of the book, most notably the late **Doreen Taylor-Wilkie**, editor of the original *Insight Guide: Finland* and its companion guides to Norway, Sweden and Denmark. **Kristina Woolnough** also contributed to the original guide, using her vast knowledge of the country gained through 25 years of visiting the home of her Finnish-speaking Peruvian husband. She wrote the Defence of Greenness chapter, which highlights Finland's fantastic natural resources.

James Lewis wrote about Finland's history. **Anne Roston** wrote the original piece on Helsinki, and **Sylvie Nickels** wrote on the Great Lakes region, Lapland, and the traditions of the Laplanders, the Sami people. The West Coast chapter was written by **Robert Spark**.

Like all Insight Guides, this book owes much to the superb quality of its photographs, which aim not just to illustrate the text but also to convey the essence of everyday life in Finland. Many of the images were taken by **Gregory Wrona**, a long-standing favourite Insight photographer and an inveterate traveller.

Other major contributors of pictures were **Michael Jenner**, **Robert Fried**, **Jim Holmes**, and **Layne Kennedy**. Picture research was undertaken by **Steven Lawrence** and **Tom Smyth**.

This edition was proofread by **Neil Titman** and indexed by **Helen Peters**.

The contributors

This fully revised and updated edition was managed and edited by **Siân Lezard** at Insight Guides' London office. The entire book was comprehensively updated by **Roger Norum**, a travel writer with a special interest in Finland. Norum first visited the country as a 16-year-old naïf on an extended layover during a winter journey to Russia. The impression those long, dark nights left on him resulted in studies in Finnish language and literature at Cornell, Tromsø, Kuopio and Helsinki universities, followed by later stints as a Finnish–English translator. He now divides his time between his doctoral work in social anthropology and journalism, and leading creative holidays in Scandinavia.

The current edition builds on the excellent foundations created by the editors and writers of previous editions

Map Legend

— - -	International Boundary
— — —	Province Boundary
_•_ _	National Park/Reserve
— — — —	Ferry Route
⊖	Border Crossing
✈ ✈	Airport: International/ Regional
🚌	Bus Station
Ⓜ	Metro
✉	Post Office
❶	Tourist Information
∴	Archaeological Site
✝ ✝ ✝	Church/Ruins
✝	Monastry
☪	Mosque
✡	Synagogue
∩	Cave
𝟏	Statue/Monument
★	Place of Interest

The main places of interest in the Places section are coordinated by number with a full-colour map (e.g. ❶), and a symbol at the top of every right-hand page tells you where to find the map.

Contents

VÄLKOMMEN
TILL FINSTRÖM

LEFT: Helsinki
Cathedral.

THE BEST OF FINLAND: TOP ATTRACTIONS

Discover Finland's unique attractions – exciting adventure activities, absorbing museums, vast empty landscapes, indigenous culture... Here, at a glance, are our recommendations

▽ **Karelia and Russian Orthodox history** – Much of present-day Finnish Karelia was once a part of Russia, and the churches, monasteries, museums and frontier-running bunkers evoke a strong sense of history, beauty and – for Finnish people, at least – immense nostalgia. *See page 273.*

▷ **Snowmobiling along the Russian border** – Lapland is known for three things: Father Christmas, the Sami people, and its amazing, immense wilderness. Get to know the region's furthest reaches by hopping on a diesel-powered skidoo and taking to roads, trails and frozen lakes. *See pages 287 and 303.*

△ **Exploring Lakeland by kayak** – Finland is famous for its lakes, and one of the best ways to enjoy them is by renting a kayak. *See pages 255 and 319.*

▷ **Taking a sauna** – Spending time broiling in a sauna and then cooling off by jumping into a nearby lake or the sea is a Finnish national pastime and favoured tradition. An invitation from a Finn to his or her sauna is not one to turn down – it means you have made headway to a close and lasting friendship. *See page 192.*

◁ **Kiasma Museum, Helsinki** – The cutting-edge art at this excellent museum gives a strong sense of what modern-day Finland is all about. *See page175.*

△ **Jugend architecture in Helsinki** – On the headland of the Helsinki peninsula is Katajanokka, the best known historical part of town, with sights including the Russian Orthodox Uspenski Cathedral and architect Alvar Aalto's most controversial construction. *See pages 161 and 166.*

△ **Exploring the Baltic states** – From Helsinki it's easy to take a ferry to one of the Baltic capitals; Tallin, capital of Estonia, has a fine medieval Old Town, a lively nightlife and the lure of cheap alcohol. *See page 182.*

△ **Biking around the Åland archipelago** – This lush collection of islands off the western coast is one of the most enigmatic and handsome in all of Europe, and is great for exploration by bike. *See page 231.*

▷ **Goldpanning in the far reaches of Lapland** – Lapland once experienced a small but frenzied gold rush along the Ivalojoki river valley in the 1860s, and locals and visitors alike still come to sift for whatever might have been left behind. There's even a Gold Prospectors' Museum. *See page 291.*

△ **Sibelius Hall in Lahti** – Only one concert hall in Finland is named after the country's greatest composer, and Lahti's world-renowned symphony orchestra are resident players here. *See page 265.*

THE BEST OF FINLAND: EDITOR'S CHOICE

Our selection of the most exciting Finnish experiences and adventures, the top cultural and historical sights, the best things to do with the family, and recommendations on eating out and Finland's quirky hotels

BEST FOOD AND DRINK IN HELSINKI

● **Chez Dominique**
One of the best restaurants in the world is located in Helsinki, with Michelin stars, awards and an outstanding menu of Finnish-meets-French cuisine. *See page 311.*
● **Kasakka**
Scrumptious, authentic Russian cuisine served across several gorgeous sitting rooms – think portraits of tsars on the walls – that make you feel as if you have been transported to imperial Russia. *See page 311.*
● **Bali-Hai**
This great down-home eatery is at once irreverent and refined, with retro decor, cool staff and a super location on a quiet central street in Punavuori. Serves the best burgers in the city. *See page 311.*

BEST OUTDOOR ADVENTURE ACTIVITIES

● **Huskies**
Lapland is the place for outdoor adventure experiences – none as thrilling as driving a pack of sledge dogs through the snow and out towards the middle of, well, nowhere. *See page 292.*
● **Kayaking**
Kayaking in Finland is great for both the athletic and the novice. Hiring a kayak or canoe is the best way to see some of the most remote, and otherwise inaccessible, parts of the country. *See pages 269 and 319.*
● **Taking a sauna**
No trip to Finland is complete without experiencing this most Finnish of activities, an invigorating and restorative way to get to know nature – and the locals. *See page 192.*
● **Snowkiting**
Finland's newest sport is set to take the younger generation by storm. Variations include quiet trips across an icy lake and freestyle flying off mountains. *See page 320.*
● **Snowmobiling**
The Sami people have been relying on snow-mobiles since the 1970s, so there are umpteen trails running through forests, across empty tundra and over frozen lakes. *See page 303.*

TOP: sailing round the islands. **LEFT:** sauna bliss. **RIGHT:** huskies.

BEST MUSEUMS

● **Aboa Vetus Ars Nova**
This striking museum in Turku combines city history and modern art and is set right on the Aura River. *See page 211.*

● **Kiasma, Helsinki**
The gorgeous architecture of Finland's premier modern art museum is a top attraction in itself, but venture inside to take in the compelling exhibitions. *See page 175.*

● **Lenin Museum**
The world's only museum on the revolutionary covers his life both during and after he lived in Finland. *See page 222.*

● **Mannerheim Museum**
An immensely engaging museum, with free guided tours filled with historical gems and fascinating anecdotes. *See page 178.*

● **SIIDA, Inari**
An excellently curated museum on Sami history and society – virtually reason in itself to visit Lapland. *See page 293.*

ABOVE: plush interior of the bar at Haven.

BEST BOUTIQUE/UNIQUE HOTELS

● **Haven**
Helsinki's newest hotel is also its most luxurious, with designer linens, leather sofas and an extensive honesty bar attached to the sumptuous lobby. Helsinki's honeymoon haven is definitely Haven. *See page 305.*

● **Kakslauttanen Igloos**
There could be no better place to sleep under the stars and see the Northern Lights than this collection of glass-and-snow igloos tucked away in a far corner of Lapland. *See page 309.*

● **Klaus K**
Quite possibly Finland's best hotel, with a refined designer ethos that is both ultramodern and enduringly classic. Service is top-notch, and they also have two great restaurants and a very hip bar. In the very centre of the capital. *See page 305.*

● **Omena**
These reception-free hotels are sprouting up in cities all around the country, offering minimal service, low prices and an exceedingly high standard of pampered, design-friendly accommodation. *See page 305.*

● **Villa Lanca**
This charming collection of rooms set right in the heart of one of Lapland's most fetching towns is run by a lovely Sami couple who also sell traditional handicrafts. *See page 309.*

BEST FOR FAMILIES

● **Moominworld**
Probably the Nordic countries' best theme park, with a host of rides and attractions based on the beloved characters of Tove Jansson's Moomin books. *See page 214.*

● **Santa Park**
No trip to Lapland with the kids would be complete without a visit to this small theme park inside Santa's home. Don't forget to bring the camera. *See page 290.*

● **Särkänniemi**
Tampere's beloved amusement park also holds a compelling aquarium, planetarium, and a zoo observation tower with a lovely revolving restaurant. *See page 220.*

● **Tietomaa**
Oulu's science museum teaches children technology, physics and the natural world through a series of absorbing exhibits that can easily hold the interest of adults too. *See page 247.*

TOP: Lenin Museum. **ABOVE:** Moominworld is a perennial favourite. **RIGHT:** festive Finnish baking.

A PLACE IN EUROPE

The Finns are among Europe's least understood but most dynamic people, fully confident in their unique position in the world between East and West

While mobile phones weren't quite invented in Finland – the technology was first created in Motorola's offices in New York – they may as well have been. After their invention, they were pioneered, developed and revolutionised by Finns and are currently owned by over 90 percent of them – an unrivalled per capita ratio. The technology is at the heart of Finnish life in the 21st century.

Still, the rampant addiction to the mobile phone and its attendant technology is just one aspect of life that – at least on the surface – tears apart the conventional wisdom about Finns. Reserved and reticent? You'd never guess it from the constant telephone talk. The population's proficiency in tongues other than its own exotic and complex language also means that Finns, especially younger ones, are ever happier to converse in English too. The Finns are now really starting to open up.

Celebrating its 460th birthday in 2010, Finland's capital of Helsinki has burgeoned, maturing into a distinctive and vibrant metropolis with a clear identity of its own. Its restaurant scene has exploded, and startling new buildings have transformed the city's silhouette. In spite of a global downturn, Finnish confidence remains high.

Yet still, the local character is shaped by climatic extremes – long nightless summer days and bitter winter nights – and its moods swing accordingly. From the rocky archipelago of the southwestern coast to the majestic sweep of the lakeland labyrinth stretching to the border with Russia and the sweeping fells of Lapland that traverse the Arctic Circle in the north, Finland's natural environment is one of Europe's wildest and most exotic. And Finns, modern as they are, still claim a special affinity with this landscape, retiring en masse to their lakeside cabins and saunas in the summer, gliding on skis through the snow-smothered woods in winter. The urban scene may have changed recently, but the unparalleled remoteness and tranquillity of Finland's umpteen lakes and forests make them uniquely timeless. ❏

PRECEDING PAGES: Sami life as captured by the Sami artist Andreas Alariesto; shopfront for eager anglers; at the heart of Finland's dense forests.
LEFT: total calm at Puruvesi Lake, Karelia. **ABOVE:** band performing at Esplanade Park, Helsinki; Iittala glassware on sale in Tampere.

A WILDERNESS EXPERIENCE

One of the many advantages of a visit to Finland is that there are relatively few tourists; that said, the vast open spaces and natural splendour attract more and more visitors every year

Finland, often forgotten and sometimes even ignored, is one of the best-kept secrets in Europe. It's a country with few world-renowned attractions: no superlative fjords, no medieval monasteries and few spectacular old towns. Yet Finland maintains an indigenous culture with much regional variety, thousands of lakes, rivers and islands, and unlimited possibilities for a wide range of outdoor – and indoor – activities.

Slowly, the world is taking notice. Finland, a member of the EU and the only Nordic country to use the euro, offers unspoilt wilderness, quaint historical attractions, tranquillity and free access to practically anywhere – all forests are potentially yours for trekking, berry-picking or short-term camping.

Finland has its share of great European legacy – about 70 medieval stone churches, several imposing castles and plenty of old and new art in museums. Its own traditions are preserved in numerous museums around the country – indeed, there may still be more museums than hotels in Finland.

Compared to the other Nordic countries, Finland has always been a quiet place when it comes to tourism. But the past decade has seen a surge in visitors, with many people discovering Finland for the first time – and coming back. Since 2002, the number of foreign visitors to Helsinki has increased by nearly 25 percent.

And Finland challenges the idea of the traditional holiday. While there are plenty of hotels – even a number of five-star boutique places in

LEFT: tranquillity in the Lakeland region. **RIGHT:** spend the night in a comfy, warm, glass-roofed igloo.

KAKSLAUTTANEN IGLOO

There is nothing more memorable than sleeping under the stars, but this is simply not possible in the freezing Finnish winter. The solution is to spend the night in your own personal glass-roofed igloo. The compound at the Kakslauttanen Hotel and Igloo Village features five separate glass igloos, perfect for marvelling at the majesty of the firmament and the Northern Lights in comfort. The grounds, located near the Urho Kekkonen National Park, also feature an ice gallery of art, an ice bar, an ice chapel and the world's largest snow restaurant. The igloos are open from December to April.

the capital – Finland also offers thousands of campsites, lakeside holiday villages, guesthouses, youth hostels, and even the ability to camp privately in the wild.

Local attractions

Over the past decades, the Finnish state has invested in the development of hundreds of museums, churches, parks, installations and traditional buildings into world-class tourist attractions that today have become some of the most interesting and culturally rich places to see in Europe. Add to that literally hundreds of arts, music and culture festivals – plus dozens of off-the-wall festivals such as wife-carrying, high-heel relay and air guitar – and you quickly see that Finland is a unique destination that has turned upside down the idea of what it means to be a tourist. No wonder, then, that traditional tourists are confused.

World-class attractions in the Finnish Tourist Board's top twenty include Kiasma, the Museum of Contemporary Art *(see page 175)* in Helsinki, Bomba House in Nurmes *(see page 277)*, Ateneum Art Museum *(see page 158)* and Soumenlinna, the 18th-century sea fortress sometimes called "Gibraltar of the North" outside Helsinki *(see page 179)*.

SOMETHING FOR EVERYONE

As Finland lacks mass tourism, most visitors have an individual approach to the country, with specific needs. At times, certain cities – such as Rovaniemi or possibly Jyväskylä – may be filled with a group of architecture buffs ogling buildings designed by Alvar Aalto; architecture fans may choose Functionalism, Art Nouveau, modern or neoclassical "tours". Music-lovers may choose among hundreds of small or large festivals, or follow Sibelius's footsteps from Hotel Kämp in Helsinki to Ainola to north Karelia. Visitors interested in design can tour various glass factories, pottery studios and cutting-edge shops. Santa Claus can be visited in Rovaniemi.

Despite a great increase in the number of visitors to their country, you'll still find that Finns – especially outside of Helsinki – can maintain a quirky, almost incredulous attitude towards tourists, as if they can't understand why anyone would come to their country for a visit. They may not always smile at you when you'd expect them to, and do when you wouldn't. They remain silent when you want to hear an explanation, or they speak (in Finnish) when you'd rather enjoy the serenity. Still, in many cases, tourists will experience unconditional warmth and hospitality typical of the Finnish people when invited into a local home, especially in rural towns and in farming communities.

If Finns are eccentrics, so are some of their attractions. The wife-carrying championships are an international media event, as is the mobile phone throwing competition, the annual air guitar festival and the first Kutema-järvi sex festival, exclusively for old and stout people. There are plenty of other weird festivals, offbeat art exhibitions and crazy habits.

Savonlinna, the opera festival held in a medieval castle *(see page 261)*, is one of the most renowned in Europe. In Retretti, a man-made cave becomes an eerie but hectic summer art exhibition *(see page 259)*. Modern architecture shaped the Forest Museum Lusto into an inter-

swimming or skating in winter when ice covers nearly every body of water. Fishing is possible in lakes, rivers and along the seashore, though a permit is required. Moving from one place to another in winter tends to be on skis, dog sleds or snowmobiles in winter, by bicycle or trekking on foot in summer.

Many tourists seek nature experiences in Finnish national parks. Finland's unique network of parks is administered by the Forest and Park Service, which controls 35 national parks, 19 nature reserves and nearly 400 other protected areas. The organisation (www.outdoors.fi) rents interesting accommodation in isolated

esting exhibition on everything wooden – now the region is one of the top destinations in all the Nordic countries.

Nature calls

As Finnish nature is so varied and so accessible, the only limit is imagination. Activity holidays are increasing. Several birdwatching towers have been built near major lakes and bays – the Worldwide Fund for Nature has financed Liminganlahti near Oulu. Individual tourists have about 180,000 lakes to choose from for canoeing,

In the far northeast, the Ranua Wildlife Park is a managed wilderness area containing some 50 species including lynx, elk, brown bear and polar bear (although there are no wild polar bears in Finland).

wilderness cottages, often well equipped and of relatively high quality.

National parks are just the tip of the iceberg. Local municipalities often finance recreational hiking routes for local needs. Many of these can be combined, and thus was born the Karelian Circuit, Finland's longest trekking route, with approximately 1,000km (620 miles) of marked

LEFT: tour guides take groups into the wild. **ABOVE:** an invigorating post-sauna dip. **ABOVE RIGHT:** bears roam in the northeast of Finland.

trails. This circuit offers genuine wilderness routes, variety in four different national parks, and a possibility to combine walking with mountain biking, canoeing and fishing.

Accommodation is possible in bed and breakfasts, free wilderness huts (or ones that have to be reserved in advance) or lean-to structures. Pitching a tent is legal (and free) almost everywhere along this route.

Organised tours

Small service companies are now popping up around Finland. An interesting one is Archtours (tel: 09-477 7300; www.archtours.fi), which

North (tel: 02-034 4122; www.wildnorth.net), an excellent adventure tour company, offering fishing, hunting, husky and reindeer tours, as well as skiing holidays and trips to see the Northern Lights.

Farm holidays

As membership of the EU decreases opportunities for Finnish farmers to earn money from agriculture alone, many families are now turning their estates into guesthouses. Bed and breakfast may be the official term, but most farms provide visitors with a full range of options. It's an experience that will always be

runs trips based on architecture, design and culture. They offer several interesting tours in and around Helsinki. In Nurmes, the Metsän-väki Group (tel: 013-687 2229; www.bomba.fi),

> For the outdoor adventurer, Finland is ideal. Activities may include husky tours or snowshoe treks to the wilderness in winter, canoeing, rafting or trekking in summer.

located at the Safari House near the Bomba tourist centre, provides full-range adventure services, including winter gear for up to 150 visitors. Up north in Rovaniemi, try Wild

unforgettable – bathing in a lakeside sauna, with a dip in the shallow, lukewarm water, riding horses across dirt tracks, paddling in the lake, then savouring an enormous buffet with fresh farm produce, game, fish and wonderful cakes. The opportunity for individual freedom is an experience in itself – nothing is actually forbidden – as you have the forest tracks and lakes to enjoy all for yourself.

Lakeland leisure

Increased tourism along Finland's lake system is bringing the lake steamers back into business. There are now regular passenger routes on several of the lake systems, but the oldest and probably the most romantic are those across Saimaa's vast expanses *(see page 256)*. Steam first came to Saimaa, wheezing and belching its thick black smoke, in the 1830s. It revolutionised the timber business, until then reliant on sailing vessels – and, in turn, their dependence on the vagaries of the wind – enabling easier transport of Finland's "green gold" from forest to factory during the short summer months.

The heyday of passenger steamers was in the early years of the 20th century, when the well-to-do of St Petersburg arrived by the night train at Lappeenranta for a leisurely nine-hour steamer trip to Savonlinna, then a new and fashionable spa. In due course the steamers

Santa Claus at home

At midsummer and midwinter, planes arriving in Rovaniemi bring passengers eager to "meet" Santa Claus on his home territory *(see page 140)*. And it's here that Santa Claus himself may be visited 365 days a year, around an ever-growing tourist village by the name of Napapiiri, in the Arctic Circle. Here you can experience the midnight sun to the north of the Arctic line, which is clearly marked across Napapiiri village. This is the biggest tourist trap in the country, but a nice reminder of the Finnish character – a theme village built around a character who couldn't be more sympathetic to his guests. ❏

covered the four points of the Saimaa compass, picking up and dropping off the lakeland's scattered inhabitants, along with livestock and every imaginable form of cargo, at communities of all sizes or no size at all. One of the great sights of Savonlinna each morning and evening was the Saimaa fleet of wooden double-deckers. Several still survive. Today, many Finns and foreigners alike come to this region to spend a relaxing time in waterfront cabins, steaming themselves in the sauna and then jumping into the cooling waters.

FAR LEFT: dry slope bobsleighing.
LEFT: fishing in the rapids near Viitasaari.
ABOVE: the Northern Lights.

NORTHERN LIGHTS

The aurora borealis, better known as the Northern Lights, is one of the most fascinating phenomena to see while visiting Finland. It occurs all year round but, of course, dark nights are required – so autumn and winter are best. It is a magical experience: a flicker of fire will shine across the sky, sometimes only for a few seconds at most, or a few minutes at longest. These iridescent ribbons of orange and green are created by solar particles crashing against the earth's atmosphere and magnetic field. Auroral activity depends on the amount of solar particles hitting the atmosphere, which is highly variable – but possible to forecast: see http://cc.oulu.fi/~thu/Aurora/forecast.html.

DECISIVE DATES

EARLY HISTORY:
8000 BC–AD 400

8000 BC
Tribes from Eastern Europe (ancestors of present-day Sami) settle the Finnish Arctic coast.

1800–1600 BC
The Central European "Boat Axe" culture arrives from the east. Trade with Sweden begins.

c. AD 100
The historian Tacitus describes the Fenni in his *Germania*, probably referring to the Sami.

c. 400
The "Baltic Finns", or Suomalaiset, cross the Baltic and settle in Finland. Sweden's influence over its "eastern province" begins.

SWEDISH RULE: 1157–1808

1157
King Erik of Sweden launches a crusade into Finland; further Swedish invasions subjugate large areas of the country.

1323
The Treaty of Pähkinäsaari establishes the border between Sweden and Russia; western and southern Finland become Swedish, while eastern Finland is now Russian.

1523
Gustav Vasa ascends the Swedish throne. Lutheranism introduced from Germany.

1595
The 25-year war with Russia is concluded by the Treaty of Täyssinä; the eastern border extends to the Arctic coast.

1640
Finland's first university is established in Turku.

1696
One-third of the Finnish population dies of famine. Sweden offers no assistance.

1710–21
The "Great Wrath". Russia attacks Sweden and occupies Finland. Under the Treaty of Nystad (present-day Uusikaupunki) in 1721, the tsar returns much of Finland but keeps eastern Karelia.

1741
The "Lesser Wrath". Following Sweden's declaration of war, Russia reoccupies Finland until the Treaty of Turku in 1743.

1773
Finnish attempts to gain independence fail. A peasant uprising results in several reforms.

THE RUSSIAN YEARS:
1808–1917

1808
Tsar Alexander I attacks and occupies Finland in an attempt to force Sweden to join Napoleon's economic blockade.

1809
The Treaty of Hamina cedes all of the country to Russia. Finland becomes an autonomous Russian Grand Duchy.

1812
Because of Turku's proximity to Sweden, Tsar Alexander shifts Finland's capital to Helsinki.

1863
Differences of opinion between the Swedish-speaking ruling class and the Finnish nationalists are resolved, giving Finnish-speakers equal status.

1899
Tsar Nicholas II draws up the "February Manifesto" as part of the Russification process. Jean Sibelius composes *Finlandia* but is forced to publish it as "Opus 26, No. 7". Russian suppression lasts until 1905.

1905
Russia is defeated by Japan and the general strike in Moscow spreads to Finland. Finland regains some autonomy.

1906
Finnish women are the first in Europe to get the vote.

1907–14
Tsar Nicholas II reinstates Russification and removes the new parliament's powers; any laws passed in Finland still have to be ratified by the tsar.

EARLY INDEPENDENCE: 1917–39

1917
The October Revolution in Russia. Finland declares its independence from the new Soviet Union.

1918
A Russian-style revolution plunges Finland into civil war. The "White Guard", right-wing government troops with German military support, finally defeat the "Red Guard".

1919
On 17 July 1919 the Republic of Finland comes into being, under its first president, K.J. Ståhlberg (1919–25).

PRECEDING PAGES: the Battle of Poltava ends Swedish domination. FAR LEFT TOP: woodcut showing reindeer being milked, 1555. LEFT: King Gustav Vasa of Sweden. ABOVE: a woman votes in 1906. RIGHT: Nobel-winner Martti Ahtisaari.

1922
The Åland Islands are ceded to Finland and granted autonomy.

FINLAND AT WAR: 1939–47

1939–40
Soviet territorial demands spark off the "Winter War" between Finland and the Soviet Union. Stalin is victorious and Finland is forced to surrender 11 percent of its territory to the Soviet Union.

1941
Finland clings to its neutrality, but in fear of Soviet invasion is drawn closer to Germany. Hitler begins his Russian campaign. The "Continuation War" breaks out between Finland and the Soviet Union. Britain, allied with Russia, declares war on Finland.

1944
Peace treaty signed between Finland and the Soviet Union. Finland is forced to give up the Petsamo region. The retreating German army destroys many towns in Lapland.

FINLAND IN EUROPE: 1948–2009

1948
The Treaty of Friendship, Co-operation and Mutual Assistance (FCMA) is signed, laying the foundations for good relations with the Soviet Union.

1952
Helsinki hosts the Olympic Summer Games.

1955
Finland joins in the formation of the Nordic Council and is admitted to the United Nations.

1972
The Strategic Arms Limitation Talks (SALT) are held in Helsinki.

1994
Finland joins the European Union.

2000
Helsinki celebrates its 450th anniversary and is one of nine European Cities of Culture. Tarja Halonen becomes the first female to be elected president of Finland. The country signs a new constitution.

2003
Anneli Jäätteenmäki becomes Finland's first female prime minister, only to resign in scandal two months later.

2006
Rovaniemi-based heavy metal band Lordi wins the Eurovision Song Contest, Finland's first ever victory in the competition.

2008
Former president Martti Ahtisaari is awarded the Nobel Peace Prize for his work in the resolution of global conflict.

2009
The Finnish government discontinues its interests in Lapland's Santapark, citing the global financial crisis as the cause.

Te igitur clementissime pater per ihesum xpm filiu tuu dnm nostru suplices rogamus ac petimus vti accepta habeas ✠ benedicas ✠ Hec dona ✠ Hec munera ✠ Hec sacta sacrificia illibata·In primis que tibi offerimus pro ecclesia tua sancta catholica quã pacificare·custodire·adunare et regere digneris toto orbe terraꝝ vna cũ famulo tuo papa nro·N. et antistite nostro·N·et rege nostro· et omnibꝛ orthodoxis·atꝗ catholice et apostolice fidei cultoribus·

Memento dñe famuloꝝ famula rũꝗ tuarũ·N·Memoria viuoꝛum et omniũ circũstantiũ quoꝝ tibi fide cognita est ✠ nota deuotio pro quib

THE FINNS ARRIVE

The life of the early Finns is one of the least understood of all European cultures, but by the 12th century Sweden had dominated its eastern neighbour

The study of race was an infant science in 1844 when M.A. Castrén pronounced: "I have decided to prove to the people of Finland that we are not a … nation isolated from the world and world history, but that we are related to at least one-seventh of the people of the globe." Castrén had persuaded himself that language equalled race and had concluded that the Finns were kith and kin with every single tribe which had originated in the Altai Mountains of Siberia and Outer Mongolia.

A race apart

That the Finnish tongue is a branch of the Finno-Ugric language tree is undeniable and, to those who maintain, like Castrén, that language kinship equals racial relationships, the matter ends there. "The Finns speak a Mongoloid tongue. Ipso facto they are a Mongoloid people." To a scientist-patriot such as Castrén, this Far Eastern theory had the added attraction of establishing a relationship between his own people and a large part of the global population.

The conjectures of Castrén and others arose because of the exceptional isolation of Finnish as a language. Hungarian was, and still is, often mentioned as a language akin to Finnish, but the connection is actually remote. Finnish and Hungarian are about as similar to one another as English and Persian, and only Estonian is close enough to be even remotely mutually intelligible with Finnish.

Castrén's followers – and many millions who may never have heard his name – adhered to his

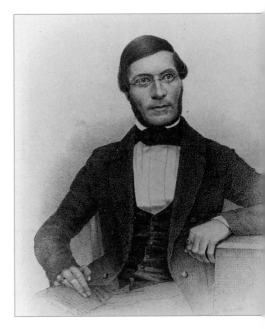

theory. This led to the long-held belief that the Finns were a race apart from the mainstream of Europe, their language firmly classifying them as being of Asiatic extraction.

Theory rejected

This rather neat little slot in the huge and ever complex question of the origins of peoples is still accepted by the world at large. Many Finns, however, have for some time rejected this theory – most notably those in academic circles.

Recent archaeological research points to a Baltic people moving gradually into Finland from around 1800 BC to about AD 400, but there are no empirical signs of a migration from

LEFT: a page from Finland's first Bible, now on display at Turku Castle.
RIGHT: M.A. Castrén, creator of race theories.

further east. All cultural contacts point to Western Europe and Scandinavia, even from the earliest times. Such theories lend credence to the

> While western Finns adopted Catholicism from Sweden, the Karelians followed the Orthodox faith, influenced by Russia to the east.

notion that Finns and Europeans are intimately related, and discredit ideas of the Great Siberian Migration. The anthropological verdict now accepted by all but Castrénite primitives is that

the Finns and their racial forebears are "purely European". In common with Swedes, Norwegians, Danes and Germans, Finns are tall and blond, although there are slight height differences and there is a variant type known as the East Baltic.

The migrants from the Baltic who took up residence in the land of lakes and forests to the north were destined to live an age-long existence isolated from the mainstream of Europe. The longships left from the lands just over the Gulf of Bothnia or the other side of the Danish Sounds, and the trading, raiding and general sea roving of the Vikings involved little, if any, Finnish participation. Instead, the Finns were hunters and gatherers, surviving largely on the abundance of fish in the country's lakes.

Secret past

Cut off in their sub-Arctic homeland from these early days, little light has been shed on the life and times of the early Finns. No single chronicler emerges from the forest mists to give later generations a glimpse of primeval life. There may well have been an oral tradition of poetry, song and story, a collection of folk memories passed down from generation to generation. The *Kalevala*, Finland's national epic, points in this direction, but it was compiled and published in the 19th century and cannot itself therefore claim immemorial antiquity.

When Finland finally emerged into the history books through the flickering candles of Roman Catholic crusading, around the year 1157, we find the Finns living in clans. They had apparently never developed statehood; the clans were descendants of common ancestors, often warring with one another and submitting to priests who led them in the worship of nature and natural forces.

Taming pagan warriors

Just as Finnish scholars had established a theory of race and language, a parallel movement in academic circles was arising on the subject of the arrival of Christianity. According to prevailing wisdom, the Finns had become a nuisance and a danger while raiding the Christian people of southern Sweden. Furthermore, they were pagans. In 1157, King Erik of Sweden lost patience and set off on a "crusade" to Finland. Taming the Finns was a vital key to trading routes to the east, particularly Russia. Sweden was to control Finland for almost the next 700 years.

Once subdued, the Finns were submitted to baptism by an English-born bishop, Henry of Uppsala. Swedish secular dominance and, with it, Roman Catholicism, were thus introduced into Finland.

Yet once again this theory, much like the language theory, has been discredited. Rome has no record of these events and Church documents make no reference to Erik or Henry. Many archaeologists have helped Finnish integrity with the assertion that the Finns practised Christianity years before 1157. The Swedes brought Romanism to Finland, but not a new faith. ❏

LEFT: an illustration from the epic poem *Kalevala*, which details ancient folk stories. **RIGHT:** the Russian Orthodox Uspenski Cathedral in Helsinki.

ANNO 1615.

BIRTH OF A NATION

Finland's relationship with Sweden was peaceful in the early days, but by the 16th century Russia wanted control of its western neighbour

The Finns lived under the reign of Sweden for nearly seven centuries (*c.* 1150–1800), but never once was there a Swedish "conquest" of Finland. Instead, a race had developed between Sweden and Russia – in those days known as Novgorod – to capture power over the land of the Finns. Sweden won the race – and did so without resorting to conquest or dynastic union or treaty. Remarkably, the future relationship between Sweden and Finland was largely free of the stresses and strains that normally accompany such often hostile takeovers.

A happy union

Although there is no official documentation, it is quite likely that Swedes had hunted, traded and settled in Finnish lands for centuries. On both sides of the Gulf of Bothnia the land had sparse resources and gave little cause for friction. In effect, Sweden and Finland merged as constituent parts of a larger whole. No distinctions in law or property were made, and the history of these two people under one crown has been described as "a seamless garment".

Finns took part in the election of the king, although they were not involved in the choice of candidates. In areas of mixed population language was the only real difference. Castles functioned as administrative centres, not as garrisons to subdue the people. The influences of the one people on the other were neutral largely because the cultures were identical. In one respect only did Sweden effect a dominating influence, and that was in the sphere of religion.

LEFT: a stained-glass window in Turku Cathedral shows Gustav II Adolf of Sweden.
RIGHT: Bishop Henrik in Hollola Church.

DANISH AMBITION

At the end of the 14th century there was an attempt to unite Denmark, Norway, Sweden and, by implication, Finland as a result of the Kalmar Union of 1397. All the devices which had not been employed between Sweden and Finland were invoked in this fated union, the dream of the Danish queen, Margrethe I.

In 1509, Finland became violently involved when the Danes burnt and sacked Turku (Åbo), the "capital" of the country. It was just one incident in more than 100 years of conflict over the treaty, which was finally broken in 1523 in a rebellion by Gustav Vasa, who became king of Sweden.

Spreading the faith

Various monastic orders launched a slow but steady penetration of Finland during the 14th and 15th centuries. Dominicans, Franciscans and the Order of St Bridget installed themselves alongside the clergy, greatly strengthening the power and influence of the Roman Catholic Church in the region. This activity gave impetus to church-building, worship, renovation and adornment. Life became more settled in the relatively densely populated areas of western Finland. Further east, people's lives were more mobile, less settled, and depended on hunting across the sub-Arctic tundra, a region rich in animals and game birds, but largely unsuitable for crop cultivation.

The most important centres from which the new influences spread were Turku (Åbo in Swedish, *see page 205*), with a bishop's seat and cathedral, and Vyborg (Viipuri in Finnish). Both towns had close links with Tallinn (Estonia), Danzig (now Gdansk, in Poland), Lübeck (Germany) and Stockholm.

In these Finnish towns, artisans and professions flourished alongside the clergy and a civilised urban culture was spawned, markedly different from the coarser, more basic ways of life further east.

Stirrings of nationhood

Sweden was now powerful and independent. The Middle Ages were over; the Reformation challenged Rome. Here was a mélange of influences, almost modern in their impact. Sweden and Finland were both slipping away from the old moorings. Slowly, the relationship was changing, and the first stirrings of nationhood date from this time.

Many more Swedes and Finns fell under the influence of Martin Luther in Wittenberg. The Reformation also attracted Gustav Vasa, because the Swedish crown needed more revenue and the Church could provide it. In fact, the Reformation was so irresistible that Sweden was the first state in Western Christendom to break with

Rome. The split took place in May 1527. All over Sweden and Finland the Church suddenly lost property, authority, ceremonies and rites. Holy water, customary baptism and extreme acts of

> Military service was compulsory except for the cavalry, in which volunteers enlisted eagerly in order to escape the harder life of an infantryman.

piety were banned, as were colourful processions and the worship of relics. But transforming Finns from a Catholic to a Protestant people was not

with both Poland and Russia raised taxes and took Finnish men away from the land – the burden of providing levies always fell heavily on the farmers. Finns were a vital part of the Swedish army, comprising a third of the foot soldiers and cavalry. In the wars with Russia, Finland bore the brunt of the suffering. City development became sluggish and many Finnish cities frequently went up in smoke. Turku (Åbo) suffered 15 major fires between 1524 and 1624; the worst reduced the city to ashes. Pori and Viipuri also suffered a similar fate several times, though fires were not the only dangers that beset the cities.

painless. The early Lutheran pastors were a motley rabble – "violaters of the laws of man and God". Yet Finns took a leading part in the transformation, and Pietari Särkilahti, Mikael Agricola and Paavali Juusten aided their Swedish brethren in severing links with Rome.

Peasant soldiers

During the three centuries before 1809, when Finland finally broke with Sweden, the Swedish crown was at war for more than 80 years. Involvement in the Thirty Years War and wars

LEFT: Mikael Agricola's 16th-century Bible translated into Finnish (Turku Cathedral).
ABOVE: building Häme Castle.

The Dutch influence

In Turku, Helsinki, Porvoo and Viipuri, as well as the other Baltic trading cities, many leading merchants who controlled much of the foreign trade were of German or Dutch descent. "The general area of our economic history during the 17th century and part of the 18th century bears a marked Dutch stamp," remarks V. Voionmaa, a prominent Finnish historian. The Dutch were well established, and foreign ways of doing business gained ground in Finland. Foreign as well as Finnish capital fuelled industry and trade.

Sweden no longer dominated the land and conflicts with the Russians kept recurring. The innumerable wars were destructive to Finland: 1554–7; a 25-year war (interrupted by truces)

which started in 1570; two wars in the 17th century and the great Northern War from 1710–21; war again 20 years later; and yet again from 1788–90. Sweden regained partial confidence and began to improve Finnish defences with the construction of fortresses such as Suomenlinna *(see page 179)*, but when Peter the Great in 1703 founded St Petersburg, Russian power was again in full force.

Carrot and stick

The Swedish crown demonstrated an inability to hold Finland against Russian assault. It lost Finland on two occasions (1710 and 1741),

separate state whose head, the Tsar-Grand Duke, was an absolute ruler; Tsar of all the Russias. Yet in Finland he agreed to rule in partnership with the Finnish Diet. This made the tsar a constitutional monarch in the newly acquired territory. It was an experiment in kingship, and one which was an unqualified success for 60 years.

The Grand Duchy was declared before the end of the 1808–9 war with Sweden at the Diet of Porvoo. As a Grand Duchy, Finland benefited from Russia's precedent of allowing the countries annexed into its empire to retain social systems such as the legislature. The Baltic states, and later Poland, were granted the same rights.

regaining it in 1721 and 1743, respectively. In 1808, Great Britain became a Swedish ally. The Russians now saw a dire threat to St Petersburg and to Russian naval access to the Baltic. Yet again Russia and Sweden fought. This time Russia held on to Finland and offered Finns a large say in the running of their land, while retaining Russian overall rule.

A nation is born

Sweden formally ceded Finland to Russia by the Treaty of Hamina on 17 September 1809. Along with Finland proper it gave up the Åland Islands, between Sweden and Finland, which had long been an administrative part of the Finnish half of the kingdom. Finland became a

The enlightened policies of Alexander I could be seen as a step towards wider, progressive changes planned in other parts of the empire.

For most ordinary Finns however, very little changed. No pressure was put on the people to switch from the Lutheran Church to the Orthodox, and Swedish continued as the language of government. Yet the formation of a Finnish Diet, as well as an administrative, senate-led body, allowed for the gradual rise in influence of the Finnish language and, over time, the general spread of the idea of Finnish nationalism and independence. ❑

ABOVE: the house of Johan Ludvig Runeberg (1804–77), Finland's patriotic poet *(see page 103)*.

A Winter Journey

The early adventurer Joseph Acerbi left an interesting account of his travels across the ice from Sweden to Finland.

At the end of the 18th century, Joseph Acerbi embarked on what was then the only practical way of crossing from Sweden to Finland in winter, by sledge across the frozen Gulf of Bothnia. The distance was 70km (43 miles) but, using the Åland Islands as stepping stones, that left 50km (30 miles) "which you travel on the ice without touching on land".

Acerbi was advised that his party of three, plus two servants, would need to double their number of horses and hire no fewer than eight sledges for the crossing. He suspected that he was being swindled by the Swedish peasants but, as things turned out, it was a sensible precaution.

Acerbi published the details of the difficult and at times terrifying journey in his work *Travels Through Sweden, Finland and Lapland to the North Cape, 1802*, as follows:

"I expected to travel 43 miles without sight of land over a vast and uniform plain, and that every successive mile would be in exact unison and monotonous correspondence with those I had already travelled; but my astonishment was greatly increased in proportion as we advanced from our starting-post. At length we met with masses of ice heaped one upon the other, and some of them seeming as if they were suspended in the air, while others were raised in the form of pyramids. On the whole they exhibited a picture of the wildest and most savage confusion... It was an immense chaos of icy ruins, presented to view under every possible form, and embellished by superb stalactites of a blue-green colour.

Hazards on the ice

"Amidst this chaos, it was not without difficulty and trouble that our horses and sledges were able to find and pursue their way. It was necessary to make frequent windings, in order to avoid a collection of icy mountains that lay before us. The inconvenience and the danger of our journey were still far-

---

RIGHT: Joseph Acerbi's travelogue details the trials, tribulations and triumphs of a winter's trip in Finland.

ther encreased *[sic]* by the following circumstance. Our horses were made wild and furious, both by the sight and the smell of our great pelices, manufactured of the skins of Russian wolves or bears. When any of the sledges was overturned, the horses belonging to it, or to that next to it, frighted at the sight of what they supposed to be a wolf or bear rolling on the ice, would set off at full gallop, to the terror of both passengers and driver. The peasant, apprehensive of losing his horse in the midst of this desert, kept firm hold of the bridle, and suffered the horse to drag his body through masses of ice, of which some sharp points threatened to cut him in pieces. The animal... continually

opposed to his flight, would stop; then we were enabled to get again into our sledges, but not till the driver had blindfolded the animal's eyes: but one time, one of the wildest and most spirited of all the horses in our train, having taken fright, completely made his escape...

"During the whole of this journey we did not meet with, on the ice, so much as one man, beast, bird, or any living creature. Those vast solitudes present a desert abandoned as it were by nature. The dead silence that reigns is interrupted only by the whistling of the winds against the prominent points of ice, and sometimes by the loud crackings occasioned by their being irresistibly torn from this frozen expanse; pieces thus forcibly broken off are frequently blown to a considerable distance." ❑

LIVING WITH RUSSIA

For 90 years Russia ruled Finland in relative peace but at the beginning of the 20th century the union dissolved into revolt and war

Annexation by Russia defied all gloomy prophecies, at least at the outset. Tsar Alexander I seemed open to suggestions, and a group of leading Finns suggested that Finland should hold elections. Alexander agreed, and the first Finnish Diet met at Porvoo in 1809. The tsar had styled himself "the Emperor and Autocrat of all the Russias and the Grand Duke of Finland." Invested with this new title, the prototype of future constitutional monarchs, Tsar Alexander formally opened the Diet. In return, he promised to respect and maintain the laws, religion and constitution of Finland.

A diplomatic success

The constitution's main pillar was a unique device in nation-building of those days: Finland was to be in personal union with the tsar. This meant that the Finns dealt direct with their head of state, bypassing the Russian government. Ultimately this became the cause of much jealousy, but the arrangement lasted for 90 years and was the basis of the relationship between Russia and Finland. When Nicholas I succeeded Alexander in 1825 a strong bond of mutual trust had developed. The change of overlord had brought advantages: the fear of attack from the east had gone; Finns could conduct their internal affairs but, if they felt cramped, opportunities existed in the armed forces and civil service of Russia. The Finnish army was disbanded, though its officers received generous pensions. Russian troops garrisoned Finland

but never in large numbers. Taxation was raised for domestic needs only.

Behind all this liberality lay firm policy: to pacify Finland and woo it away from Sweden. To keep Sweden sweet, Alexander signed an agreement, in 1812, in support of moves to unite Norway with Sweden. This became Sweden's new ambition.

The new capital

The Grand Duchy chose a small, rocky fishing port as its capital, and within two generations, Helsinki had become a city of major importance. One visitor in 1830 remarked that the Finns were "converting a heap of rocks into a

---

PRECEDING PAGES: Tsar Alexander I leads the Finnish Diet at Porvoo in 1809.
LEFT: Russia's Imperial throne in Finland.
RIGHT: Tsar Nicholas I.

beautiful city". The urban centre was conceived and planned on an imperial scale, with neo-classical buildings designed by German architect C.L. Engel. The University of Turku moved to Helsinki in 1828, one year after Turku suffered yet another disastrous fire, making its eclipse inevitable.

The university became a tug of war between languages. There was no discrimination against Finns as a separate linguistic group within the Russian Empire, and the idea of introducing Russian in schools was canvassed, but little was put into place. Finns wishing to serve the tsar abroad had to learn Russian, but to serve the Grand Duke of Finland the requirement, until 1870, was to speak and write Swedish.

Peasant power

The all-important vernacular being promoted by nationalist Henrik Porthan already resided in the countryside, on the farms and in the forests. But the farmers and peasants of the country were slow to awaken to the power they possessed. In part, the peasants distrusted notions of independence. The rural poor, workers, smallholders and the landless were on the periphery of political life and thought. In contrast to the elite, they were indifferent to ideas

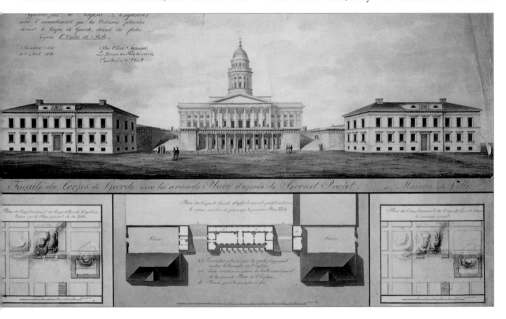

THE FATHER OF FINNISH HISTORY

Bold ideas of Finnish independence had been nurtured by educated Finns ever since the days when Sweden had started to lose its grip during the struggles with Russia through the 16th century. Henrik Porthan (1739–1804), known as the "father of Finnish history", awakened intellectual leaders. "We must pray", he said, "that Russia will succeed in situating its capital in Constantinople... But now that its capital city (St Petersburg) is located so near, I am afraid that Finland will... fall under the power of Russia."

Nevertheless, the Finnish people, he advocated, should use this as an opportunity, and not be despondent. They must think of themselves above all as Finns. History, language and tradition (according to Porthan) all suggested a Finland that was ultimately free. But barbarous, Byzantine and Eastern Russia – not Western, democratic Sweden – was the stepping stone to this end.

Porthan can be considered to have been ahead of his time, but his long-term, pragmatic philosophy took hold and became the prevailing wisdom of his own and succeeding generations of Finnish nationalists. Their patience was finally rewarded when, in 1906, the goal of nationhood was achieved. His disciples realised very quickly that if the Finnish language could replace Swedish, the battle for independence, at least in the hearts and minds of Finns themselves, would triumph.

of liberty and national independence. When autonomy was in jeopardy under a changed Russian attitude at the end of the 19th century, some pamphleteers got to work to raise national con-

> *Many of the signatures on the petitions to Tsar Alexander were collected by nationalistic students who skiied from remote farm to distant cottage across the country.*

sciousness. Grumpy peasants tossed back at them remarks such as, "Now the gentry are in a sweat," and, "These new laws don't concern us peasants, they're only taking the power off the gentry."

Yet, all the time, opportunities in higher education were increasing among the working class. Vernacular Finnish was introduced into secondary education, university and the new polytechnics, gradually supplanting Swedish. In spite of harvest failures and famine in 1862 and 1868, freehold peasant farmers with timber land grew richer as the demand for timber increased and prices rose. Their wives could now afford tables, sideboards and chairs in place of rustic benches and chests. Life for some was becoming more genteel and less rough-hewn. Since 1864 peasants had been able to buy land on the open market. Now their sons were taking advantage of higher education – reason for interest in the Finnish language to flourish.

Ruthless governor

Tsar Alexander III, who freed the Russian serfs, knew his Grand Duchy. His son, the ill-starred Nicholas II (1894–1917), did not. The conception of a docile and contented satellite country acting as a buffer on Russia's northwest flank, the cornerstone of policy for 90 years, was cast aside. A new governor, General Bobrikov, fresh from a ruthless administration in the Baltics, was installed in Helsinki.

Finland lost its autonomy. Laws, soldiering and taxation, those pivotal issues which previous Grand Dukes had treated so delicately, were henceforth to be Russian concerns. It was too much for the Finns: 522,931 signatures on a petition were collected in just two weeks.

LEFT: C.L. Engel's original drawing for the design of Senate Square in Helsinki. **RIGHT:** statue of Alexander II in front of Helsinki Cathedral.

Abroad, another petition was launched in support of the Finns, signed by many eminent people. They addressed Tsar Nicholas: "Having read and being deeply moved by the petition of 5 March of over half a million Finnish men and women in which they made a solemn appeal to Your Majesty in support of the maintenance of their full Rights and Privileges first confirmed by… Alexander I in 1809… and subsequently re-affirmed in the most solemn manner by all his illustrious successors, we venture to express our hope that Your Imperial Majesty will take into due consideration the prayer of the said Petition of Your Majesty's Finnish subjects."

The tsar was unmoved. *The Times* of London thundered a declaration that "the Finnish Diet can, legally, only be modified or restricted with its own consent". This too fell on deaf Russian ears. They imposed strict censorship on the Finnish press. Conscription into the Russian army was the last straw.

The Finns revolt

Resistance began to escalate. Half the conscripts ordered to report for military service in the spring of 1902 did not turn up. In 1904 the governor general was assassinated by a patriotic student, Eugen Schauman, who then turned the gun on himself. Schauman became a national hero and is buried at Porvoo.

The Russian Revolution of 1905 and the Russo-Japanese War brought a respite. The Finns took the opportunity to put forward a bold

> "We are no longer Swedes, we will not become Russians, so let us be Finns," had been the cry for some decades by nationalists.

measure. The franchise was outmoded; industrial workers had no representation; women no vote. This was par for the times in Europe, although New Zealand had just granted women

but the event was to be marred by a bitter civil war between the "Whites" and the "Reds".

The cause, in short, was the overspilling of the Russian October Revolution into Finland, where there remained contingents of Russian soldiers who sided with the Soviets. Thus Finland had a Red Army in its midst. Luckily, the Soviet government did not participate officially in the civil war in Finland, but Russian aid played a significant part in the Red revolt. Finnish Red Guards were supplied with arms by the Russians. Russian officers and NCOs provided leadership; in the case of the artillery, they provided the entire command.

the vote. Finland proposed no less than a universal franchise and a unicameral parliament. The tsar, doubtless distracted by the stirrings of revolt in Russia – a chain of events that would eventually bring him down – agreed to the changes. The Finns got their modern parliament. The electoral role was increased tenfold. The Social Democrats won the subsequent election.

Civil war

Now the country was united as never before in a determination to be free and Finnish. The decisive moment came during World War I, when the Russian army collapsed and Lenin seized power. The Bolsheviks allowed Finland to go free. Independence had finally arrived,

The civil war's major contributory cause was labour unrest. After the Bolsheviks seized power in Russia, radical Finnish socialists became determined to overcome their minority position in parliament by increasing their extra-parliamentary activity.

A strike was the first step, accompanied by widespread lawlessness on a grand scale. After a week the strike was called off, but events escalated and a Central Revolutionary Council formed the Red Guards. They struck at the end of January 1918, in the hope that Russian aid would be enough to secure a quick victory. The civil war saw atrocities committed by both sides, with Mannerheim, for example, being condemned by the international left as a war criminal. The psychological wounds of this period of Finnish history are only recently being brought out into the open.

Military genius

The government lacked adequate forces to meet this situation. It did, however, appoint a commander-in-chief to a non-existent army. General Carl Gustaf Emil Mannerheim was an inspired military leader on a par with Turkey's Kemal Ataturk and the British General Montgomery. Mannerheim had been persuaded by Premier Svinhufvud to organise a government force to uphold law and order. On 18 January, he went to Vaasa on the west coast of Finland, and northern Finland, and then turned them into bases from which government forces waged war against the enemy in the south. Tampere, Helsinki and Viipuri were retaken by the spring. After a last stand on the Karelian Isthmus, the Reds capitulated on 15 May. On 16 May Mannerheim's "people's army" held a victory parade in Helsinki to celebrate the end of the "Red" threat.

After a brief flirtation with the idea of a monarch, during which time both Svinhufvud and Mannerheim acted as regent, the Finns elected K.J. Ståhlberg, author of the form of government, as its first president.

he went to Vaasa on the west coast of Finland, to plan for and organise a "White" army. Vaasa became the seat of government when war broke out. Four cabinet members escaped there from Helsinki hours before the Reds seized control of the capital on 27 January.

Red defeat

The Reds, without full Russian support and up against the strategic ability of General Mannerheim, found their hopes short-lived. Mannerheim disarmed Russian garrisons in central

---

LEFT: Eugen Schauman assassinates General Bobrikov in 1904.

ABOVE: White and Red troops at war in 1918.

PREMIER LEADERSHIP

Although different in character from Mannerheim, the civilian leader Pehr Evind Svinhufvud was very much his equal. He was an experienced political leader and had been a member of the Turku Court of Appeal, which was dismissed early in the 20th century for indicting the Russian governor of Helsinki for his brutal suppression of a peaceful demonstration. In 1917, Svinhufvud travelled to St Petersburg to gain the recognition of the Council of People's Commissars for Finland's independence. When the Red Army seized Helsinki, Svinhufvud was still in the capital and was forced to hide, eventually escaping to Vaasa, via wartime Germany and many adventures.

An insecure start

In 1920 the conflicts between Finland and the Soviet Union were dealt with by the Treaty of Tartu, which recognised Finland as an independent republic and ceded it the Arctic port of Petsamo. Some small adjustments were made to the geography of the border, while Finland neutralised its islands close to Leningrad. However, the Soviets seemed unable to forgive the Finns for their bourgeois defeat of revolution; in turn, there arose an almost fanatical distrust of the Soviet Union in Finland. Fear of Russia, civil war and the political polarisation that had caused it deeply affected the national psyche.

ing votes to both men and women. But social and economic disparities were not mitigated by legalities. Two symptoms were manifest. One had been the upsurge of Red rebellion, which was ably put down but which caused a severe shock to the body politic. The second problem was emigration.

Land hunger

Once Russian overlordship had taken a nasty turn, the resulting insecurity had already started a trend towards emigration. But there were other causes, and land hunger was the foremost. "No land, no fatherland," was the

Sandwiched between Communist Russia and neutral Sweden, and with a militaristic Germany to the south, independent Finland was born, one historian has noted, "not with a silver spoon, but with a dagger in its mouth". Finland had to learn the trick of "sword-swallowing".

> Finland was the first European country to give women the vote and an equal political voice when it became independent in 1906.

One matter that needed no adjustment in the constitution of independence was the Parliament Act of 1906, far ahead of its time in grant-

cry. There was a landless proletariat of 200,000 in the 19th century, plus a host of peasants with meagre plots. These people looked to the New World for opportunities.

Before and after the civil war there had been times of famine in the countryside. "Nature seems to cry out to our people 'Emigrate or die'," one university lecturer told his students in 1867. By the 1920s, 380,000 Finns had left for other lands, the majority to the USA. The Great Depression hit Finland in 1929, and by 1930 the figure for emigration had reached 400,000.

Divided politics

In the 1920s the two branches of the labour movement (the bulk of the "Reds") grew further apart.

For election purposes, the outlawed Communist Party metamorphosed into the Socialist Workers' and Smallholders' Election Organisation, while

> *"The heart pleaded no, but the stomach commanded yes," ran a line in the novel* Amerikkaan, *referring to Finland's emigration.*

the Social Democrats began to co-operate with the bourgeois parties, culminating in a Social Democrat government in 1926, led by their moderate leader, Väinö Tanner.

left to Svinhufvud to persuade the rebels to disband peacefully. Despite these strains, Finland grew closer to the Scandinavian countries, where democracy was advancing, with a long period of cooperation between the Agrarian Party and the Social Democrats, the aptly named "red-green" coalition.

Cultural advances

Though the initial priority of the infant nation had to be survival and the strengthening of its democracy, life was not all gloom. In the 1920s, sport, travel and the cinema all came into their own, with a profound effect on social habits. It

Anti-Communist feeling continued, nevertheless, and led to the Lapua movement which resorted to violent methods, such as capturing and driving suspected Communist leaders over the Soviet border. Even the respected former president Ståhlberg did not escape one attempt and was driven close to the border. In 1930, the Lapua movement inspired a peasants' march to Helsinki, and led to armed rebellion in 1932.

The formidable duo of the Liberation period, Svinhufvud and Mannerheim, returned and, after anti-Communist laws were passed, it was

LEFT: King Gustav V of Sweden on a state visit to Finland in 1925, with President Lauri Kristian.
ABOVE: civil war bomb damage in Tampere, 1918.

was a time of strong cultural expression, particularly in architecture and design. Up until 1939, a degree of cultural and commercial harmony had existed between Russians and Finns. Communism kept a low profile, while Fascists failed to gather significant support. By the time of the war, Finland's agriculture had developed and the forest industry took the lead, supporting progress in other industries; forest product exports boosted national earnings. Optimism was rife. Still, despite a growing threat in Europe (particularly from Germany) and Mannerheim's warnings, little was done to build up the country's armaments. When parliament eventually approved 3 billion marks for military procurement in 1938, it was already too late. ❏

THE TWO WARS

The bravery and prowess of Finland's soldiers on their
treacherous, ice-bound terrain became legendary
during the Winter and Continuation wars

By the spring of 1938 Moscow was making demands on the Finnish government to give guarantees that, in the event of hostile acts by Germany, Finland would accept Soviet military aid. The railway line between Leningrad and Murmansk was vital to Soviet security: hence Moscow's fear of German invasion through the Gulf of Finland.

Perilous times

The Finnish government was reluctant to enter into discussions, fearing that doing so would compromise neutrality. The Munich Agreement of September 1938 prompted Finland to build up its defences, and Mannerheim advised the government to carry out partial mobilisation. The Soviet Union again made representations to Finland, this time suggesting that the Finns lease the islands of the Gulf of Finland to them for 30 years. Soviet pleas to Britain and France for collective security had fallen on deaf ears and Leningrad was vulnerable from the sea.

> By April 1939, Hitler had managed to drive a wedge through Finland's policy of joint Nordic security. Estonia, Latvia and Denmark accepted a German plan of non-aggression, while Sweden, Norway and Finland refused.

Unsurprisingly, Finland was still suspicious of Soviet ambitions. After Sweden withdrew, and Germany and the Soviet Union had signed a non-aggression pact (which included a secret protocol on spheres of influence), Finland, placed within Moscow's sphere, was in a very dangerous position. After the German invasion of Poland, the Soviet Union began to press the small countries within its sphere to make pacts of "mutual assistance". Delegates from Helsinki travelled to Moscow for discussions. Mannerheim now pressed for full mobilisation of Finnish forces, and the Soviet Union moved swiftly onto a war footing.

Winter warriors

The first Soviet demand was to move troops from the Karelian Isthmus. When Mannerheim

---

PRECEDING PAGES: Finnish Alpine troops on skis ("ghost troops"), 1939. **LEFT:** Field Marshal Mannerheim. **RIGHT:** war memorial to the dead of the 1939 war.

refused, the Kremlin broke off diplomatic relations and launched an attack on Finland on 30 November 1939. What became known as the Winter War had begun.

While Soviet forces had almost overwhelming superiority, they were untrained and ill-equipped to fight a war in severe winter conditions. Finnish soldiers, though they were short of heavy armaments, had already been training for just this sort of warfare. They were used to moving in dense forests through snow and ice, and the Finnish army's tactical mobility was at a high level. The Finns were also accustomed to the climate and dressed sensibly when winter set in and the temperature dropped several degrees below zero. Soldiers were issued with white "overalls" – now standard for winter warfare – to cover their uniforms so that they blended invisibly with the snow.

By copying the methods used by farmers and lumberjacks to haul logs from the forest, the Finnish army solved a second key problem: how to operate in the forests flanking the roads. They would open a trail in the woods using skis, avoiding gorges, cliffs and steep rises. When a few horses and sleighs had moved over this trail, a winter road would form along which a horse could pull up to a 1-tonne load.

SURVIVING THE LANDSCAPE

One of the most difficult problems for winter warfare had already been solved by Finland in the 1930s: how to camp and make shelter in a winter wilderness. Finland had developed a tent for the use of half a platoon (20 men), which could be folded into a small and easily handled bundle. A portable box-stove was enough to keep the tent warm even if the temperature fell to −40°C/F. It was also relatively easy to prepare coffee and other basic warm food on top of the stove. The Finns also had the valuable know-how to operate for several weeks in uninhabited regions without tents by building shelters out of snow and evergreens.

War preparations

Anticipating what might happen, the army had already perfected these techniques in its pre-war winter manoeuvres and, when war started in 1939, Finland had about half a million horses in the country. The army used around 20 percent of them and, as half the reservists called up to fight were farmers or lumberjacks, there were plenty of skilled horsemen. During the summer of 1939, the Finns had also built dams in the small rivers on the Karelian Isthmus and elsewhere, which raised the water level to form an obstruction against the enemy advance. When the Finnish army opened the gates in the Saimaa canal in March 1940, the Russians found operations in the flooded areas difficult.

Attempts to raise the water level were less successful during the coldest winter period; but equally, as the ice covered the uneven features of the terrain, the enemy had less shelter and was not concealed from air reconnaissance. Later, the Finns opened lanes by blowing up the ice and developed special ice mines which detonated when the Soviets approached.

Surprise tactics

Finns and Russians fought the Winter War during the darkest period of the year. In the area of Viipuri, daylight lasted from 8am to 5pm. On the level of Kajaani the day was a couple of

vented the enemy (with its command of the air) from noticing and disturbing operations. Furthermore, the troops carried out all their tactical movements in the forests, which offered even better protection.

As the Soviet army moved west, the Finns had insufficient forces and equipment for classic air, tank, artillery and similar operations, and their aim had to be to force the enemy to attack under the worst possible conditions. But the Finns, bred on the land, knew the terrain. The Soviet divisions, in contrast, had no choice but to stick to the roads, advancing in a tight column, strung out over some

> To compensate for the lack of anti-tank guns, the Finns used gasoline-filled bottles and TNT-charges and destroyed a large number of tanks in this way.

hours shorter while, at the turn of the year, Petsamo in the north had hardly any hours of daylight at all. Finnish soldiers made use of the darkness for the loading and unloading of trains, transports and supply traffic. This pre-

LEFT: a female cook working in a military field kitchen in 1939. ABOVE: Finnish refugees flee from advancing Soviet troops, 1939–40.

100km (60 miles). On either side lay a strip around 110–220km (70–140 miles) wide of uninhabited, forest-covered wilderness, with numerous lakes and marshes, where the Finnish troops had all the advantages of surprise and manoeuvrability.

For these attacks, the Finns either carried their ammunition, mines and explosives or pulled them along on sledges, which they also used to evacuate the wounded, often along the specially prepared winter roads through the wilderness. At night, for longer distances, they ploughed a road over ice to bring troops and equipment. In any attack, surprise was the essence. Strike force commanders and their troops, all on skis, moved stealthily forward to

block the road so that the sappers had time to destroy the bridges and lay mines to catch the tanks before any counter-attack.

> British leader Winston Churchill was unstinting in his praise of Finnish resistance during the Winter War. He wrote: "Finland – shows what free men can do."

The Finns fought against great odds during this Winter War (and partly during the Continuation War that followed). Their number of

Honourable peace

Though the resourcefulness of Marshal Mannerheim's troops had taken full advantage of territory and climate to achieve several victories, Finland could not last long against such an incredibly powerful enemy. The Finnish army was forced to surrender at Viipuri, and the Soviet Union set up and then abandoned a puppet government on the Karelian Isthmus. But the long front held out to the end. This guaranteed pre-conditions for an honourable peace and, in 1940, the two sides concluded an armistice. The Soviet Union's original aim – a base in Hanko, in the southwest, and the mov-

anti-tank guns was so limited that the troops could use them only against an armoured attack on an open road, and gasoline bottles and TNT-charges were more likely to destroy an enemy tank. Despite that, the advantages were not always on the side of the invading army. The ill-informed and often ill-clad Soviet troops could not move from or manoeuvre outside the roads, and they, too, often lacked supplies when insufficient air drops left them short of ammunition and food. Throughout the war's skirmishes and more formal encounters, the "ski troops" inflicted hard blows on this badly deployed Red Army. (It was partly this poor performance that persuaded Hitler later to launch an attack on Russia.)

ing of the border further from Leningrad – were its only gains.

Nevertheless, Finland had to surrender around a tenth of its territory, with a proportionate shift of population, and, in this respect, suffered a heavy defeat. On the other hand it was obvious that Stalin's real intention had been to annex the whole of Finland, and their defeat in the Winter War was mitigated for the Finns by the maintenance of national sovereignty.

The Winter War lasted exactly 100 days. But the European powers were still fighting and the inevitable result for Finland was to be swept up in yet another conflict. On 22 June 1941, Operation Barbarossa went ahead. Hitler attacked the Soviet Union, achieving complete surprise. Russian commanders signalled to Stalin: "We are being fired on – what shall we do?" Stalin didn't believe them and instead scolded them for sending unencrypted messages. There had been some collusion between the German and Finnish military authorities and the Finns had had to allow the west of Finland to be used for transit traffic. Partial Finnish mobilisation was ordered, and 60,000 civilians moved from front-line areas.

Alongside Germany

On the day preceding Barbarossa, Hitler had announced that "Finnish and German troops

Winter War. Even so, Marshal Voroshilov, who was in charge of the Russian Northwest Army Group, had a formidable number of troops under his command.

Many in Finland expected the army to make an advance towards Leningrad. The idea of capturing this city had at one time attracted Mannerheim, but now he informed the Finnish government that "under no circumstances will I lead an offensive against the great city on the Neva". He feared that the Russians, faced with an advance on Leningrad, might summon insurmountable forces and inflict a heavy defeat on the Finnish army.

stand side by side on the Arctic coast for the defence of Finnish soil." Marshal Mannerheim was convinced that his statement was intended as an announcement of a *fait accompli*. "This will lead to a Russian attack," he said, "though, on the other hand, I am convinced that in any case such an attack would have occurred." The Russian High Command retaliated against the Finns. Russian bombs fell on Finland even before any were dropped on German targets.

The Finnish army was larger, war-hardened and better equipped than at the start of the

LEFT: Danish volunteers fighting for Finland, on the march with skis and white camouflage, January 1940.
ABOVE: aerial view of Tampere in winter.

The campaign aimed to reconquer Ladoga-Karelia, followed by the Isthmus, and finally penetrate Karelia. All these objectives were

> During the Winter War, some units had been short of potatoes. This led to a few veterans reporting for duty in World War II carrying a sack or two of potatoes as well as their kit.

achieved. Mannerheim had some German units placed at his disposal, but he kept them at arm's length. The Finns were co-belligerents, not allies of the Germans. When the Finns had regained all of their old frontiers, Mannerheim commented: "Here we could have stood as neutral neighbours instead of as bitter enemies."

Admiring allies

The fact that Great Britain and Russia were allies led to a tricky diplomatic situation between Mannerheim and Churchill, as is illustrated in the following exchange of letters. At this point, the outcome of the war was far from clear.

Churchill wrote asking Mannerheim to halt the advance of his troops. "It would be most painful to the many friends of your country in England if Finland found herself in the dock with the guilty and defeated Nazis. My recollec-

tions of our pleasant talks… about the last war lead me to send you this purely personal and private message for your consideration before it is too late."

Winston Churchill wrote to Mannerheim on 29 November 1941: "I am deeply grieved at what I see coming, namely, that we shall be forced within a few days, out of loyalty to our ally Russia, to declare war upon Finland."

Following this request, Field Marshal Mannerheim replied to Prime Minister Churchill: "I am sure you will realise it is impossible for me to halt the military operations at present being carried out before the troops have reached the positions which in my opinion will provide us with necessary security.

"It would be deplorable if these measures, undertaken for the security of Finland, should bring my country into conflict with England, and it would deeply sadden me if England felt herself forced to declare war on Finland. It was very good of you to send me a… message in these critical days, and I appreciate it fully." Nevertheless, a few days later, in order to satisfy his ally Josef Stalin, Churchill did declare war on the Finns.

Payment in full

The 1941–4 war is known in Finland as the "Continuation War" because it was understood as an extension of the Winter War and as an attempt to compensate for losses suffered in that war. In the Continuation War Finland's number of dead was 65,000 and wounded 158,000. Homes had to be found for more than 423,000 Karelians. After 1945 the Soviets insisted on staging show trials in Finland of the politicians who had given the orders to fight. These men received prison sentences, but served less than a full term and, in some cases, returned to public life with little or no damage to their reputation.

Finland also had to pay reparations to the Soviet Union, mostly in the form of metal products. The Soviets insisted on calculating their value according to the exchange rates of 1938, thus Finland paid almost exactly twice the price stated in the agreement. The reparations to the Soviet Union were paid in full. This was a point of honour to the Finns.

The years of struggle and of suffering were over at long last, and a war-weary Finland set about the difficult and lengthy business of national reconstruction. More poignantly, the dead soldiers, who had been removed from the battlefields to their home parishes, were buried with full honours in cemeteries alongside memorials attesting to their courage and sacrifice. Unassuming, dignified and patriotic, the spirit of these graveyards and memorials is a fitting tribute to the memory of a people who had persevered and conquered. ❏

LEFT: Field Marshal Mannerheim with officers near Helsinki in 1939 prior to the Russian invasion.

The Great General

Commander-in-Chief of the Finnish army, Mannerheim was one of the country's most influential figures from the civil war to World War II.

Carl Gustaf Emil Mannerheim was born at his family's country house at Louhisaari on 4 June 1867. The Mannerheim estate was in Swedish Villnäs, in the Turku district. The family was Swedish-speaking and of Dutch origin.

Furthermore, this great son of Finland, to whom the modern nation state probably owes its very existence, was a Russian officer for 28 years before he ever served Finland's cause. Yet Gustaf (he used his second Christian name) was not following any family tradition when he enlisted as a cavalry officer cadet in 1882. He was even expelled from the cadet school, and considered for a brief moment becoming a sailor. Fortunately for Finland he was given a second chance and went to St Petersburg for cavalry training; in 1889 he was commissioned into the tsarist army, passing out in the top six out of a total of 100.

International experience

While waiting for a Guard's commission he was posted to Poland as a subaltern in the 15th Alexandriski Dragoons. The Poles were far more restive under Russian rule than the Finns and had nothing like the same freedoms as the Grand Duchy. But Mannerheim later recalled: "The better I got to know the Poles, the more I liked them and felt at home with them." Transferred to the Chevalier Guards, he returned to St Petersburg to train recruits, and in 1892 married Anastasia Arapov, a relative of Pushkin. They had two daughters, and a son who died at birth. The marriage lasted seven years, although they did not divorce until 1919.

Mannerheim served as a colonel in the Russo-Japanese War, journeyed for two years through Siberia, Mongolia, China and Japan, and then came back to Poland to command a cavalry regiment in 1909. In World War I, he served in the Eastern European theatre, fighting against the Germans and Austrians. By 1917 he was a lieutenant-general.

RIGHT: Mannerheim, standing, gives an after-dinner speech during Hitler's visit to Finland in June 1942.

The Russian Revolution cut short his career in the Emperor's Army, and after the tsar was murdered and Russia seething with revolutionary activity, Mannerheim considered himself released from his Oath of Allegiance.

After Finnish independence, the senate named Mannerheim commander-in-chief of the armed forces in Finland. Quickly, he had to raise and mobilise an army against the Red Guards and Russian troops. When the war was over and won, the senate appointed Mannerheim regent of Finland but he lost the presidential election.

His finest military hour came during the Winter War in 1940, when Finland fought against Soviet

Russia for three-and-a-half months under ferocious winter conditions. It came through the war with its independence intact, due largely to the deployment of mobile "ski troops".

Mannerheim was briefly president of Finland after the war, but retired due to ill health in March 1946. His final years were spent quietly, mainly in Switzerland, where he died in 1951, aged 83. His home in Helsinki is now a museum, and holds trophies and mementoes from the five wars in which he fought. On the library wall is a painting of military personnel on skis and in white overalls. Urgency in the human figures contrasts with the peace of the Finnish forest. Most curiously, the painting is dated 1890 – the year the oppressive Russian rule began in Finland. ❏

A SHIFT IN BALANCE

In breaking free from Russia and moving towards a higher profile in Europe, Finland has endured economic hardship. But its efforts have clearly borne fruit

innish statesman Max Jacobson once stated that, "until the disintegration of the USSR, [Finns] were subjected to a kind of character assassination through use of the term 'Finlandisation' to denote supine submission to Soviet domination". Although in the past, Finland has often been strongly associated with a backward, Cold War Russia – a fact clearly due to its tangled and tumultuous political history with the country – this conflation has all but disappeared over the past two decades since the opening of the Iron Curtain. Finland has discarded its dual identity, in which it was seen on the one hand as an enlightened, peace-loving Nordic nation, clean and unspoilt and heroic and healthy, and on the other hand as dictated by its position – both physical and political – in relation to Russia.

> By committing itself to active membership of the EU, which it joined in 1994, and by participating in the euro single-currency system, Finland has made it clear that it is a long way away from the Russian sphere of influence.

Baltic attitudes

In 1991, President Mauno Koivisto referred to the crisis in the Baltics as "an internal Soviet affair", causing dismay to some Western and Baltic leaders. Most betrayed of all, perhaps, were the Finns themselves, among whom pro-independence

sentiment for the Baltics, especially Finland's ethnic cousin Estonia, ran high. One newspaper editorial remarked: "Public opinion is finding it difficult to accept the realism of this country's foreign policy leadership and its appeal to Finland's own national interest."

Defenders of the government line explained their belief that interference from the outside would only increase tensions. (A week after the Koivisto statement, Russian Interior Ministry troops attacked the Lithuanian TV station and more than a dozen ended up dead.) Some also reasoned that other countries could take stronger stances because they did not share a border with the Russians, and that this border

---

PRECEDING PAGES: President Urho Kekkonen meets Soviet leader Nikita Khrushchev in 1960.
LEFT: Parliament Building, Helsinki.
RIGHT: night view of the capital.

has always made things different for Finland.

As well, Finnish Communists played a big role in organising the labour force that powered early post-war industry. At one stage they held 50 out of 200 seats in the *Eduskunta* (parliament or national assembly). The Russians used them as a vessel through which to channel influence. This method was most effective when the Communists were most powerful. Twice, the Russians were able to wield enough influence to lead the government to resign.

There was a flip side as well. Until 1947, Finland was observed by the Allied Control Commission, which included many Russian officers.

blue" coalition with the leading rightist party, the conservative Kokoomus.

Moving right

The Social Democrats' gradual move towards the centre was emblematic of the political picture as a whole. Since the war, the sympathies of the majority have moved steadily towards more traditional, "bourgeois" European values. After the 1991 parliamentary vote, Finland was ruled by a centre-right alliance that was the most politically conservative in the republic's history.

The move right kept step with the economic growth of Finland, a phenomenon of rapid

(The Commission among other tasks observed war crimes trials; the longest sentence given was 10 years, served on ex-president Risto Ryti for his dealings with the Germans.) The officers' presence was often frightening to the anti-Communist Finns. The fear that Finland would go the way of Czechoslovakia in 1948 so rattled even the brave Marshal Mannerheim (who was regent briefly after the war; *see page 57*) that he made personal provisions to flee the country, just in case.

The Communist left eventually lost its grip on the country, and in time the Social Democrats (SDP) became the dominant political party in Finland and held that position until 1991. The SDP found itself in a so-called "red-

change. Divested in 1917 of the lucrative 19th-century trade links it had enjoyed as a trading post of Imperial Russia, Finland had to start from scratch. Until World War II, Finland had a stagnant subsistence agricultural economy. Post-war industrialisation pulled it out of this quagmire, and Finland became, eventually, relatively wealthy, even if some of the richest individual Finns often lived abroad in order to avoid the otherwise unavoidable massive tax bills. This accomplishment was of crucial importance to Finns, and also somewhat calmed Western worries that the country was too close to the USSR.

But long before the current economic miracle, Finland had to carve out its political place in the post-war world, a world that rapidly began to militarise along East–West lines. Finland chose neutrality. Fathered by J.K. Paasikivi, as prime minister (1944–6), then president

In 1955 Finland was admitted into the United Nations; in 1994 it became a member of the NATO Partnership for Peace programme.

(1946–6) of the Finnish republic, and Urho Kekkonen, president from 1956–81, the doctrine of neutrality was one that shunned commitment in favour of "peace-oriented policy".

Neutrality has meant many different things in many different situations. In post-war Finland, the neutral Paasikivi-Kekkonen line seemed to reassure Finns that their country would not become a battleground for the Soviet Union and its considerable enemies. To gain such reassurance, Finland had to walk a narrow line. The tense mistrust that ruled East–West relations during the Cold War caused a foreign policy challenge that would have been formidable even to a nation far older and more powerful than this one.

Finland, which was not even three decades independent by the war's end, resolved that it

Non-alignment remains the official government foreign policy line, and was confirmed as such in security and defence reports in 1997 and in 2004.

But newspapers no longer temper their criticisms of their eastern neighbour, as was the case under Kekkonen's code of "self-censorship". Finland also allows itself the option of participation in United Nations or NATO crisis management, a policy that saw Finnish forces in Lebanon and Kosovo.

FAR LEFT: logs awaiting transport to a paper mill in Finland. **LEFT:** Finland was among the first to adopt the euro in 2002. **ABOVE:** Finnish parliament, with one of the world's highest quota of women, in session.

wanted "out" of the conflict, and bargained for post-war agreements along this line. The Soviet Union pushed hard for certain concessions, and a much-depleted Finland had little bargaining power. Compromises were inevitable.

Soviet lease

The most controversial compromise was in the 1944 peace treaty with Moscow. In it, the Finns agreed to lease the Porkkala Peninsula (near Helsinki) to the Soviets for 50 years for use as a military base *(see page 190)*. The situation was defused in 1955 when the two parties agreed to the lease's cancellation. Porkkala's return seemed to signal good things to the West, as Finland joined the United Nations; in the

1950s, the country also joined the International Monetary Fund.

When Paasikivi began formulating his foreign policy line he stressed "correct and irreproachable neighbourly relations" with the Soviet Union. The phrase may have sounded like grovelling to Western ears but made sense to the majority of Finns, who needed to believe that the Soviet Union could be moulded into a benign neighbour.

In 1948, Finland and the Soviet Union signed the Treaty of Friendship, Cooperation and Mutual Assistance (FCMA), which was originally to have expired in 2003. This complex

agreement was not a military alliance per se. Drawn up in clear reference to the Germans' having used Finland to attack the Russians, it demanded mutual protection; both pledged to prevent outside forces from using their territory to attack the other; and Finland promised not to join any alliances hostile to the Soviet Union.

This last measure was perceived by the Finns to be in line with the neutral policy they had already decided on. Other Western nations, however, beginning to labour under sharp Cold War polarities, felt that if Finland was not for them, it could easily be against them. In this way began the declamations that Finland was teetering on the edge of becoming part of the Eastern Bloc.

The NATO question

All the other nations liberated by the Western Allies in World War II eventually became NATO members. It was only Finland, the one country with a border with the Soviet Union to emerge outside the Eastern Bloc after World War II, and Yugoslavia who did not become allies of either East or West.

When Finland joined in the formation of the Nordic Council in 1952, the Soviet editorials became hysterical: "Surely this means Finland will be joining NATO?" read one Russian headline. The fact that the Summer Olympics were set to be held in Helsinki also in 1952 added fuel to the fire. The Soviets interpreted preparations for the event, such as the building of a south coast highway, as proof of more plans to include Finland in a general military threat – perhaps even war – against the USSR.

SUPPORT FOR THE UNITED NATIONS

In addition to economic success, another Finnish accomplishment has been its deep commitment to the United Nations since joining in 1955.

Finland strongly supports UN peacekeeping functions, in which thousands (some 30,000 military personnel in 1990) of Finns have participated. This has declined in recent years (to 700 troops in 2009) on account of the fact that many countries, Finland included, have become more active in the field of crisis management as opposed to on-the-ground military action. Finland has also contributed a high number of UN military observers and specialists.

Involvement began during the Suez Canal crisis in 1956. There has since been a strong Finnish presence in peace-

keeping operations in Lebanon, Golan, Gaza and the Sinai. But the most outstanding efforts were made on behalf of Namibia. On a Finnish initiative, in 1970 the UN set up a Namibia Fund, and Finland also pursued the 1971 International Court of Justice ruling that South Africa's presence in Namibia was illegal. When Namibia gained independence in 1990, it was Martti Ahtisaari who directed the transition.

Finland contributes generously to refugee aid programmes; the total Nordic contribution equals 25 percent of the UN High Committtee on Refugees fund. As a result of all these efforts over the past few decades, Ahtisaari was awarded the Nobel Prize for Peace in 2008 to acknowledge his long-lasting contribution to global peace.

Whatever else is true of the immediate post-war period, the fact that Finland decided not to enter into the Western fold but rather chose to go it alone did not endear it to the non-Communist world: a lone wolf is always suspect. Finland even refused to join the Marshall Plan.

Economic progress

Nonetheless, economic progress began in earnest. The Finnish-Soviet 1944 peace agreement had included demands for war reparations of over US$600 million. Ironically, this demand for money helped build the new economy. Post-war Finland was low on cash but met payments by negotiating the payment of some of its debt in manufactured engineering products such as farming and forestry machinery, and ships.

These items became staple sources of export income in Finland's post-war years as a growth economy. Before that economy got off the ground, however, most Finns lived in poverty. To this day, older Finns enthusiastically buy chocolate when they travel abroad because of post-war memories of chocolate being impossible to obtain.

Finland had to stretch its meagre resources yet further to deal with one of the largest resettlements of a civilian population in the world. Nearly 400,000 dispossessed Karelians (and a handful of Skolt Sami) were given free land and donations of whatever the others could afford to give, which was not very much. Most Karelians, already poor in their homeland, arrived only with what they and their horses could carry.

In 1950, a barter agreement was signed between the Finns and the Soviets. It was in force until 1990, when the Soviets abruptly announced they would not sign the next five-year extension. The reason given was that continuing it would hinder Soviet pursuit of survival on a free market economy basis. The true Soviet aim was to sell its oil for hard cash. While in force, the barter agreement was worth a fortune. It provided Finland with a completely protected market for tonnes of consumer goods each year. The heavy equipment and cheap clothes and shoes sent over were

traded for Soviet oil, enough to cover as much as 90 percent of Finnish needs.

The Finnish trade balance suffered for the treaty's cancellation by a disputed but significant amount as the USSR was Finland's fifth-largest trading partner. Soviet-orientated Finnish producers foundered or went bankrupt. The Finns had to pay cash for oil and wait for the Soviets to pay them a US$2 billion debt.

Continuing crisis

While Finland was quickly able to shine in the United Nations arena, crises at home went on. In 1961, the USSR sent Finland a note suggest-

ing "military consultations" regarding the 1948 FCMA. That note was probably sent because of Soviet fear of escalating (West) German militarism in the Baltic. The harm the note caused to Finland derived from the term "military consultations". Both sides had maintained the Treaty of Friendship, Cooperation and Mutual Assistance, which was not a military alliance, but an emblem of cooperation between two neighbours who were not allied.

Nikita Khrushchev and Urho Kekkonen conferred privately and the consultations were announced "deferred". What the Soviets had been worried about, though, was clear: that Finland was not equipped to stop the West from using it as an attack flank. The Kekkonen-

LEFT: floating logs down lakes and rivers to Finland's wood and paper factories.
RIGHT: President Kekkonen arriving in Moscow, 1961.

Khrushchev exchange was never made wholly public, but after the "Note Crisis", Finland began shoring up its military forces. Finland sought, and got, from the British a reinterpretation of the Paris Peace Treaty of 1947, allowing it to purchase missiles, forbidden by the original treaty.

The Soviets throughout the 1970s tried to make life difficult for the Finns several more times. When one Soviet ambassador decided to meddle in an internal wrangle of the Finnish Communist Party, President Kekkonen swiftly demanded his deportation back to the USSR. With the fibre of Finnish society now more firmly established, such left-wing elements were mere ragged ends.

A more prosperous Finland was much harder to strong-arm, and this time West Germany, Sweden and the United Kingdom had become Finland's major trading partners – no longer the USSR. Trees had become the country's "green gold", and it looked as though the pulp and paper industry's economic success meant no end to prosperity.

High living

In the 1970s and 1980s, Finland enjoyed one of the highest gross national products in the world

and pulled up its standard of living and social services to be in line with those of Sweden. It is now one of the most expensive countries in the world – even outstripping Japan. Fantastically high agricultural subsidies and industrial cartels that set artificially high prices have been the main culprits and often carried difficult consequences.

A lot of Finns, however, made a lot of money and spent it with abandon. Finnish shops purveyed either high fashion or tatty, raggedy clothes, but there was little in between. By the end of the 1980s, the gap was closing, but prices were still wildly high, especially on imports. It was not until EU membership in the latter half of the 1990s that prices levelled and began to resemble those in other Western European countries. Although it was once the world's most expensive city, it has since been overtaken by European rivals such as Oslo and London. It also has the honour of being in the top five cities in the world in terms of lifestyle.

Economic agony
Beginning in the late 1980s, Finland entered economic recession. At the same time, the challenges of the "new" Europe were growing. While the rest of Europe was drawing together like a large mutual aid society, Finland seemed to repel the trend, being committed to the

domestic product and unemployment soared from 3 percent to around 20 percent. Pragmatists saw the need to shift from a commodity-based economy looking towards Russia to a manufacturing and service economy looking towards the West. Nokia, the country's leading electronics company, paved the way when its sales of mobile phones doubled its profits, and by the end of the 1990s the company had established itself as the world leader in the communications sector. The changed circumstances also convinced many people that it would be worth seeking safety within the parameters of the European Union, and 57 per-

European Free Trade Association but strongly opposed to joining the European Community. Under such circumstances, however, the Finnish economy was not very likely to make rapid improvements.

Those attitudes changed rapidly in the 1990s. The collapse of the former Soviet Union, which had accounted for a fifth of Finland's trade, combined with the world slide into recession to produce the worst slump suffered by any European state since the 1930s. Between 1991 and 1993, the economy lost 14 percent of its gross

LEFT: industry plays a key role in modern Finland...
ABOVE: ...as does increased leisure time and the incessant chatter of mobile phone users.

cent of the country's 4 million voters opted in a consultative referendum in October 1994 to become part of the EU from January 1995.

Reluctant members
Objections to EU membership were still vociferous. Many argued that joining the European Union would not improve things since the EU had an unproven agricultural policy. However, in the first year of membership, food prices fell by 8 percent, and the feeling of being part of a massive trading group created a sense of security that promised well for the future. The five-party "Rainbow Coalition" that came to power in 1995 promised little except austerity, but the new mood of realism enabled them to

peg pay rises to 1.7 percent and 2 percent over two years, helping to keep inflation very low at around 1.5 percent.

Deeply rooted agrarian loyalties were also hard to shake in Finland, even if full-time farmers were a dying breed. Finally, Finns had an instinctive wish to keep foreigners from buying a slice of their wealth-producing forests. The idea of foreigners buying up forests brought fears of loss of privacy, something sacred to the national character. The forest industrialists had more pragmatic fears: namely, that introduction of foreign buyers would mean the break-up of the cartel-style domestic price-fixing mecha-nisms which helped shield the industry from real competition. Prices in this and other industries were thus artificially high, and in some sectors competition was virtually impossible.

The objection to EU membership had always been the risk of compromising Finnish neutrality, although neutral countries like Ireland had flourished in the EU and neutral Sweden was keen to join (which it did, also in 1995). Not only was Sweden one of Finland's most important trade partners, it was also a beacon of political and socio-economic policy for Finland.

Ten years prior, the country could never have contemplated a move such as joining the EU

BUSINESS IN FINLAND

With a population of just over 5.2 million, Finland maintains one of the wealthiest and healthiest economies in the world, boasting a 2006 GDP of 180 billion – a record growth of some 4.5 percent on the previous year. Furthermore, according to the most recent Global Competitiveness Report, the Finnish economy is the most competitive in the world. Helsinki, home to a quarter of the country's population, generates a third of the country's revenue production, serving as headquarters to thousands of businesses, the largest of which trade in paper manufacturing, shipbuilding (every fourth cruise-line ship in the world sails out of a Finnish port on its maiden voyage) and information technology (make a phone call from Dublin to Delhi and you're likely to ring through Finnish networks, hubs and routers).

With its high proportion of specialists in the science and technology industries, Helsinki is well placed to ride the current economic downturn. High levels of expertise, training and savvy are supported by a strong tradition of cooperation in research between technology companies and Finnish universities. And thanks to government assistance available to small- and medium-sized firms, many foreign entities doing business in Helsinki often grow at a quicker rate than native Finnish companies. This all means that there are tremendous opportunities for business and trade in Finland, and every year many foreign investors discover Finland to be an economic goldmine for their trade.

without first seeking permission from Russia. But Finns were now beginning to enjoy the freedom of making their own decisions – even if Russia would eventually regain its economic strength. There was some immediate benefit, too: because of poor storage and transport facilities at Russian ports, Western exporters began shipping bulk goods to Finnish harbours and transporting them on by road to Russia.

Pruning the welfare state

Until the recession that hit Finland in the early 1990s, the welfare state was one of the great sacrosanct untouchables of Finnish life. Using

the late 1950s, along with the introduction of the private pensions option. The 1960s and 1970s also saw the establishment of laws that made provision for sickness insurance and health care.

Unemployment was in any case insignificant in European terms, and poverty was all but eradicated. Then came the economic turmoil of the early 1990s: suddenly, the percentage of unemployed was soaring into double figures and reaching unprecedented post-war peaks of about 20 percent, and Finnish banks found themselves in a crisis which had to be solved with the backing of state funds. Pressure

the model provided by its neighbour Sweden, Finland launched a programme to extend its state welfare facilities in the years following World War II.

Before the war these facilities had been relatively modest, with the first measure affecting the whole (still largely rural) population taking the form of a Pensions Act in 1937. A Child Allowance Act followed in 1948, giving state recognition to the need for child protection, and the Pensions Act was brought up to date in

LEFT: the Kiasma art complex, one reason Helsinki was named as European City of Culture in 2000.
ABOVE: a Nokia mobile phone factory in Salo, west of Helsinki.

mounted on the availability of funds for welfare state provision, and the agreements between business, government and then influential trade unions no longer seemed written in stone.

> For decades, Finns were prepared to endure massive income tax rates in return for generous and comprehensive welfare benefits.

Charges for health care increased and taxation on pensions was introduced, at the same time as workers were encouraged by tax breaks to contribute to private pension schemes to supplement their less generous state pensions.

Finland's social structure has withstood considerable pressure from the increased poverty and unemployment that followed the recession. Still, the welfare state has held firm and continues to provide a sound, basic safety net. Finns have been prepared to see it trimmed and pruned, but most would baulk at the idea of removing it completely.

Electing a new future

The last decade has seen an element of stability in Finnish political life, with successive Social Democrat-led coalition governments under Paavo Lipponen ruling from 1995–2003, and

Social Democrat presidents gaining victory in 1994 (Ahtisaari) and 2000 (Halonen).

In recent years, however, Finns have voted for change, and in the March 2003 election the Centre Party was returned as the largest group in parliament. The former Rainbow Coalition has been replaced by a Rainbow Opposition – the Conservatives lost heavily in 2003, while the Left Alliance had their participation in government vetoed by the Centre Party.

The most notable change was the election in 2003 of Finland's first female prime minister – Anneli Jäätteenmäki. However, she was forced to resign two months later amid accusations of using leaked secret information regarding the weapons inspection and subse-

quent war in Iraq to secure her victory. She was replaced by Matti Vanhanen.

A modern European state

At the end of the day, it must be said that Finland has evolved into a more outward-looking and cosmopolitan country. Finns, especially the younger, urbanised generations, have looked to Europe as their centre of political reference. And with the benefits and advantages of Europe come the responsibilities of a modern nation.

Finland had its chance to prove such responsibility in the second half of 1999 when it took on the EU presidency, hosting over 70 special European meetings, including two major summits. Helsinki's European City of Culture role, shared with eight other European cities in 2000, and the celebration in the same year of the capital's 450th anniversary, gave the whole country a confident platform upon which to enter the new millennium.

Of course, with the good must come the bad – or rather, the real. The country's brushes with corruption have brought it closer, paradoxically, to a "real world" from which it had always felt protected by the cocoon of its neutrality. The 1999 shareholding scandal surrounding the resignation of the minister of transport and his role in the Sonera telecom company was a reminder that accountability is still an operative word in the public – and political – sphere.

Nor has the global economic crisis spared Finland. In early 2009, Nokia planned to cut 1,700 jobs. While this makes up a mere 1 percent of its workforce, the fact that the world's biggest supplier of mobile phones has taken a sizeable hit has not inspired much confidence in other Finnish business entities. Finland will survive, but Finns must be reminded that their high standard of living and cradle-to-grave care is not impervious to the ways of the world at large.

The Finnish capital of Helsinki has developed to such a point that it is now a city where many languages – English, Russian, German, Swedish, French and Italian, among others – are routinely heard *(see page 111)*, yet where the local language remains as strong as ever. It is the capital of a country that is newly certain of its place in the world and which is learning to relish and rear that self-confidence. ❏

LEFT: a ship unloads its cargo at Helsinki's busy harbour, an economic success story for Finland.

Ladies First

When it comes to gender equality and provision of childcare, Finland is streets ahead of most European countries.

Compared to other European countries, Finnish women maintain some of the strongest advantages around. They claim a pioneering pedigree in equal rights, since in 1906 their country was the third in the world, after Australia and New Zealand, to enshrine in its law universal suffrage and rights for women. It has been progressive in most areas of gender equality too, making it possible for Finnish women to join the clergy of the country's biggest Church and stipulating a 40 percent quota of women in leadership in national and local government.

Finland narrowly missed out on electing its first female president in 1994, when Martti Ahtisaari pipped Elisabeth Rehn, but only just. It rebounded in 2000, when the Social Democrat Tarja Halonen beat the Centre Party's Esko Aho. Halonen had a long past in radical and social politics, and in spite of the reduced powers of the president, has enjoyed very high approval ratings over her several terms in office.

"Power to the women" has spread through all levels of government too, with Eva-Riitta Siitanen, Helsinki's mayor at the end of the 1990s, and Anneli Jäätteenmäki, prime minister for a brief

ABOVE: Sirkka Hämäläinen, the first female governor of the Bank of Finland. **RIGHT**: President Tarja Halonen.

period in 2003, two conspicuous examples. Sirkka Hämäläinen was the first female governor of the Bank of Finland in the early 1990s, and even before her election as president in 2000, Tarja Halonen had excelled as foreign minister. The male–female ratio of parliament members is 60 percent to 40 percent, one of the highest in the world for women,

and eight of the 17 Council of State members (ie government ministers) were women. Even the first Finnish parliament had 19 women representatives, an unprecedented number at the time.

Still, while the picture is quite rosy in government, it may not be everywhere in the public sector. Even if female lawyers, editors-in-chief, doctors and other professionals abound, women have yet to make a significant breakthrough into the higher echelons of business. Sari Baldauf, former president of Nokia Telecommunications, was a rare exception to this boardroom gender rule.

But legislative support for women at work is very strong and very effective. The Finnish woman who does not work full-time has become a rarity and time off to raise a family is not a hindrance. Since 1996, all children up to the age of seven are guaranteed a day-care place. Both parents are entitled to childcare leave until their child turns three, during which time their jobs are secured and an allowance is granted. Standard parental leave of 158 days after the birth of a child, usually taken by the mother, is subsidised by an allowance equivalent to two-thirds of the parent's normal income. Clearly, Finland trumps scores of other countries in how it provides for the rearing, education and professional success of its men, women and children. ❏

THE FINNISH SOUL

Blond, reserved, rustic – some of these stereotypes are not far off, but Finns are moving with the times, embracing a more international approach to modern living

Are Finns manic-depressive by nature? What else can one be when the climate changes so abruptly from freezing winter (with almost total darkness 24 hours a day) to balmy summer with 24 hours of daylight?

It is perhaps because such seminal change is so deep-rooted in the Finnish soul that the nation accepts most innovation – technology, cuisine, transport – with little resistance. "The only constant is change," many Finns will tell you. Still, long-standing national traditions are never completely forgotten.

Change is most visible in nature – no new day is similar to yesterday. After the springtime thaw, everything grows rapidly until its time arrives for a slow death before the onset of winter. For only a few weeks around the winter solstice, nature stops, deep-frozen, for a pause – but then Finns prepare for the busy Christmas time and their New Year's resolutions.

Pacifist nation

Finns have entered the 21st century with style and class. But what a difference to the way the century began. A hundred years earlier, this small nation struggled to defend its language against the Russian tsarist regime. Having been dominated by both Swedes and Russians, Finns harbour some amount of ill will against both nations today, and small details such as success in sports or international trade are scrutinised carefully. Finnish Nokia mobile phones, for example, sell more than their Swedish competitors, and, in ice hockey, Finns often defeat both Swedish and Russian teams. These things matter to Finns. But while they may not forget, they are willing to forgive.

By nature, in fact, Finns are peacemakers. In the recent past, Finland has helped broker monumentous peace deals in the Balkans and Northern Ireland, and its enthusiasm for UN humanitarianism contrasts with a scepticism about NATO operations.

Ghosts from the past

To what extent can a land be judged by its ancient heroes? In the case of many countries, only an enemy would wish to invoke the memory of certain inglorious characters. With

---

PRECEDING PAGES: Tampere's funfair; skidoos have become popular. **LEFT:** husky rides provide an entertaining way to travel. **RIGHT:** fun in the snow.

Finland, however, the idea is appealing. The main characters in the Finnish epic the *Kalevala* are patriotic, with the heroes painted as noble warriors *(see page 103)*. Yet these strong men are troubled hair-tearers in private, and experience great difficulty in waxing poetic when setting out to woo and win the girl. The women, in contrast, are strong-headed, matriarchal, and very family-orientated.

The land itself is filled with nature and wood spirits. No one in the *Kalevala* would deny that the woods have sanctity, and that the lakes and rivers are a pieces of heaven on earth. When one of the female heroes wants to escape her fate,

Yet some national stereotypes are universally recognised as being more valid than others – the importance of the forest to the Finns, for

> "We are forest people," says Jarl Kohler, managing director of the Finnish Forest Industries Federation. "The forests are our security and our livelihood."

example: more than 400,000 Finns own a plot of forest and by law every citizen has the right of access to the land *(see page 130)*.

for example, she simply turns into a nimble, stream-swimming fish.

One can only take the analogy so far, of course, but it's far better to start with a nation's self-made heroes, where at least some roots are tied to reality, than the stereotypical characters other nations, often invading armies in the case of Finland, have created for them.

There are so many paradoxes in the Finnish character that it would be hard to convince the sceptical foreigner that there isn't more than a dash of schizophrenia in the national psyche. For every ranting drunk, there's a raving teeto-taller. For every patriotic Finn who is as attached to Finland as to his own soul, there's one who leaves to make it big abroad, seldom to return.

Nordic links

The "typical Finn" is the result of a genetic combination that is 75 percent identical to that of Swedes or other Scandinavians, but 25 percent descended from tribes that wandered to Finland from east of the Ural Mountains – even though some academics now dispute this *(see page 29)*. This Western Asian strain accounts for certain physical traits that set Finns apart from their Nordic neighbours – finely pronounced cheekbones and comparatively small eyes, often blue or slate-grey.

Karelians, meanwhile (Finns from the very east of the country) are stockier and often have more sallow complexions than other Finns. They are slightly smaller in stature than people from the west coast, whose ancestors mingled with the gargantuan Vikings. Until the end of World War II, the Karelians' diet was extremely poor and they experienced one of the highest incidences of heart disease in the West, which may in part account for their occasionally less healthy looks.

The remaining Finns are taller, usually fair-haired (though, overall, Finns are the "darkest" of the Nords) and, much like any other nationality, vary greatly in most other ways.

Some of the most famous Finns are sportsmen and women, taking advantage of their generally strong and healthy physiques. As a nation,

ing change. Finns are on a pendulum swinging out towards the rest of the world, but they are far better equipped than they think they are to meet the challenges with equanimity.

For a traditionally rural country, Finland has become much more urbanised in recent years. Some 80 percent of Finns now live on 2 percent of the land. Domestic emigration is accelerating – Finns are moving from small towns to bigger centres such as Greater Helsinki, Tampere, Turku and Oulu. While many Finns are early adopters of *etätyö* (telecommuting), just as many people still try to escape to cities. This shift is often a result of unemployment

Finns are great lovers of the outdoors and of sport, and some young Finns seem to live for little else *(see page 119)*.

The Finnish personality is harder to pin down. Often considered the most reserved people in Europe, this trait actually applies as much to other Nordic peoples as it does to Finns.

City versus country

The ideas of those who would totally subjugate Finnish culture are no more appealing than those of the super-patriot who would have noth-

---

LEFT: cooking over a campfire in Ruunaa, eastern Finland. **ABOVE:** enjoying a drink at a pavement café in Helsinki.

A RESERVED NATION

If Finns are known for anything, it is being quiet, laconic and reserved. It's a stereotype, but one that you'll find much proof of. Finns, like their other Nordic brethren, put great value on privacy. Something as seemingly simple as the very placement of the summer cabin *(kesämökki)*, for example, can communicate the fundamental tenet of Finnish privacy. These are usually set back from the lakeshore among the trees, and as far from other dwellings as possible. The idea of time spent here is to enjoy your own space on your own time. Even if you meet a well-travelled and cosmopolitan Finn, you'll still find much of this reserved nature to hold true.

and a reduction of services as post offices, shops and bus services close in villages.

But rural life has its attractions. People tend to live in large houses surrounded by gardens. Farmers are fewer but receive enough subsidies to continue a comfortable lifestyle. Farm holidays are common, although some wonder whether parts of rural Finland may be turning into a tourist reserve.

Society and culture

Although Finns fought a bloody class war in 1918, modern Finland is less class-conscious than it has ever been. The distinction between town and country is more relevant as the Rainbow Coalition (*see page 67*) includes both left- and right-wing parties, and the "rural" Keskusta Party remains outside the government.

But the traditional welfare society is losing its grip, with the rich getting richer and poor remaining poor. Unemployment was cut from over 20 percent to around 10 percent during the second half of the 1990s, and by 2009 it was hovering between 6 and 7 percent. Still, poverty does haunt certain suburbs in Helsinki and entire regions in the northern half of Finland.

Popular culture has exploded, along with commercial media (there are now four national TV channels, two financed commercially, and many local TV stations) embracing young and old. The Kouvala Karaoke Club entered the *Guinness Book of World Records* in 2007 when it sung the longest karaoke session, slogging through 214 continu-

> *Honesty is another Finnish stereotype, and Finns regularly are considered to have the world's most honest business practices. In spite of high taxes, evasion is no higher than in any other European country.*

ous hours of songs. Even the Swedish-speaking minority is persuaded to consume mainstream culture, especially in big towns. Many younger Finns, shedding their parents' unease, have gone on to study, work and travel abroad, and now eagerly welcome all things foreign to Finland. While some older Finns may not have abandoned the dreary, grey outfits that once dominated the clothing racks, their grandchildren adopt the latest fashions as quickly as anyone in New York, Milan and Paris.

The home is still highly venerated, and Finns spend a considerable amount of time and money on their properties. In contrast to many southern countries where people may dress well but live poorly, Finns live like royalty but can often dress somewhat crudely. One female minister raised eyebrows in an international meeting by wearing a violet jeans jacket. Despite the move towards international lifestyles, you might find that sartorial style remains somewhat low on the Finnish agenda. ❑

GYPSY ROOTS

One of the oldest groups in Finland who are not ethnic Finns are the Romany gypsies, whose womenfolk are instantly recognisable by their elaborate embroidered lace blouses and voluminous skirts. Although today most speak only Finnish, few have intermarried, so their swarthy, Southern European looks stand out against fairer-skinned Finns.

Most gypsies are no longer nomadic and live fairly modern lives in one place, but some families do still wander, especially in autumn, from one harvest festival to another. Little horse-trading is done these days, however, and the gypsies' appearance at these fairs is merely continuing an age-old tradition.

LEFT: Finns are brought up with a deep appreciation of their countryside.

Finnish Youth

Finland may seem a long way from the heart of Europe, but young Finns are as tuned in to the next big thing as their fellow Europeans.

Be it roller-skating or bungee-jumping, young Finns eagerly jump on the tails of modern trends faster than many of their European counterparts. And Finland itself creates new trends: mobile phones, for example, are more common here than anywhere else in the world, with Finnish company Nokia a world leader; innovative mobile technology, from buying a tram ticket to paying a parking ticket, often originates in Finland. As in many other countries, the internet is a defining daily ritual of Finnish youth. Internet service is available at most schools and public libraries for free, and home usage is increasing exponentially.

Subcultures are strong, from religious networks within the Lutheran or other Churches to pagan cults that occasionally feature in national headlines through their attacks on graveyards. Indeed, Finland is no longer a land of innocents – if it ever was: almost any phenomenon can be found, from punk hairdos to perpetually drunken teenage girls.

Young Finns are very much like other European youngsters; they watch a Scandinavian version of MTV, as well as American TV series and reality shows: they compete in *Idols*, *Popstar* and *Top Model*, while many more dream of fame.

Young Finns, of course, are no strangers to hedonism, least of all in the warmer months. During the summer in Helsinki, you find them sitting on the lawn in front of Kiasma chatting and gawking at

ABOVE: snowboarding is popular in winter.
RIGHT: ice creams in the sun.

the skateboarders who also gather there. It is a sign of spring when you hear the rattle of skateboards on the pavement. Many young people change their skateboards to snowboards when the snow falls. For some, snowboarding is not just a hobby – Finnish snowboarders have been very successful in international competitions.

More commercial attractions are available: multiplex-style cinemas in the larger cities, a number of which screen locally produced films – Finnish film production has been booming since 1998. Local and amateur radio stations and podcasts have mushroomed, and popular music sung in Finnish is growing all the time – despite the obvious economic potential of recording in English.

Young rock bands may be homegrown, but success has to be sought internationally. Finnish group Lordi won the 2006 Eurovision Song Competition. Another group, Hybrid Children, a heavy rock band that has been playing since 1991, has done extremely well in Japan, but in Finland it sells only a few thousand records. "It's not a way to get rich – we earn about the same as being on the dole," says one band member. However, numerous summer festivals all around the country mean that new and innovative Finnish groups are able to find a soapbox and fans to listen to them.

Many of the youthful IT-millionaires of the late 1990s lost their money as quickly as they had made it, but Finnish youth culture continued to make an impact. While drug use tends to be lower than in much of the rest of Europe, it is on the increase, along with under-age sex and drinking, causing parents to worry about where the new generation is headed.

Some people think that the current global crisis is to blame, as many parents are unemployed and youth culture is reacting. Others argue that it is merely one aspect of the new, liberal Finland. ❑

ART, ARCHITECTURE AND DESIGN

Finland's struggle for national identity has led to an
artistic heritage that spans ancient rural traditions
all the way up to sparkling Modernism

When Diaghilev, founder of the Russian Ballet, divided the Finnish painters of the 1890s into two camps – "those with a nationalistic outlook and those who follow the West" – he described a tension which has been present in Finnish art ever since.

The art world of Western Europe and the artistic expression of Finnish nationalism have been persistently seen as opposing forces: artists either belonged to Europe or to Finland. Paradoxically, those who have achieved world renown were able, by creating something essentially Finnish and therefore unique, to leap over national boundaries. Today, Finnish design and architecture are among Finland's best-known products, partly because they combine a universal Modernism with something inherently Finnish.

Because Finland is still relatively young as an independent country, much of the art produced during the past 100 years has dealt with the creation of a national cultural identity. Until the 1880s, the nascent Finnish cultural scene was influenced by the country's political masters – first Sweden, then tsarist Russia. The few practising Finnish artists who were able to make a living from their work either trained or lived in Stockholm or St Petersburg.

Searching for identity

The seeds of a specifically Finnish culture were sown when organised, professional art training began in Turku in 1830. In 1845, Finland held its first art exhibition, then, in 1846, the Finn-

ish Art Society was founded. But it wasn't until the 1880s and 1890s that a truly Finnish artistic idiom began to emerge, and Finnish artists were at long last granted some recognition at home and, by the end of the 19th century, internationally as well.

European artistic influences were strong as painters such as Albert Edelfelt (1854–1905) utilised the style of French Naturalism. Yet, while his style was initially imported from abroad, the specific subjects of Edelfelt's paintings became increasingly Finnish in character.

In the 1880s, a motley group of painters took up the struggle for cultural identity, which paralleled the growth of Finnish nationalism and

PRECEDING PAGES: Karelian women, painted by Albert Edelfelt in 1887. **LEFT:** Mariehamn, Åland Islands. **RIGHT:** Akseli Gallén-Kallela, Finland's "national" artist.

the desire for independence. Among those artists were Akseli Gallén-Kallela (1865–1931), Pekka Halonen (1865–1933), Eero Järnefelt (1862–1937), Juho Rissanen (1873–1950) and Helena Schjerfbeck (1862–1946). They looked to the Finnish landscape and to ordinary Finns for subjects that were quintessentially Finnish. Within that framework, artistic styles varied from powerful realism to mythology, and sentimental bourgeois or fey Naturalism.

National Romanticism

While some painters, like Hugo Simberg (1873–1917), followed idiosyncratic, transcendental and Europe-based modes of Symbolism, a body of artists came to represent what was to be called Finnish National Romanticism. Their focus on Finnish-ness – a subject dear to the heart of every Finn – meant that these artists enjoyed, and continue to enjoy, considerable popular appeal in Finland. Several artists chose deliberately to move among people whose mother tongue was Finnish (at that time many urban intellectuals spoke Swedish) and whose traditional folk culture and rural living had, the artists believed, remained largely uncorrupted by either Swedish or Russian influences. They maintained that the Finnish peasant was the

KARELIAN INFLUENCE

Still in hot pursuit of the essence of Finnishness, several painters began to go on forays to Karelia. Gallén-Kallela, often acclaimed as one of the most original talents in Nordic art, ventured to Karelia in 1890 and began the "Karelia" movement which sent 19th-century artists and writers to the area in droves, and drew upon the travels of the author Elias Lönnrot *(see page 103)*. *Aino, The Defence of the Sampo (Sammon puolustus)* and *Joukahainen's Revenge (Joukahaisen kosto)* show his use of a stylised, allegorical idiom. A seminal figure in Finnish culture, Gallén-Kallela's enormous contribution laid the foundations for contemporary Finnish design.

true Finn, and that a rural landscape was the only credible Finnish landscape – the country's cities had been planned and designed under the sway of foreign rulers.

Breaking free from nature

In a general sense, the legacy of National Romanticism is large, often restricting later artists who wished to look at urban Finland, to follow European movements, or to pursue abstract styles. Finnish popular taste in art continues to be dominated by both a nationalistic and a naturalistic preference.

Groups like the October Group, whose motto was "in defence of Modernism, against isolationist nationalism", pushed hard against what is sometimes forbiddingly described as the "Golden Age" of Finnish art. Sculptor Sakari Tohka (1911–58) was a founding member of the October Group. Overthrowing the classicism of his Finnish forebears, he cast his sculptures in cement.

The October Group was not alone. Townscapes and urban Finland were the chosen subjects of another artistic backlash group, the Torch Bearers, which consisted of Väinö Kunnas (1896–1929), Sulho Sipilä (1895–1949) and Ragnar Ekelund (1892–1960).

Today, contemporary art in Finland is well supported by state and private grants, and the

National architecture

The pattern of Finnish fine art – ranging from nationalism to Modernism – is mimicked in other art forms, especially crafts, architecture and design. Firmly turning their backs on the neoclassical designs of their predecessor C.L. Engel (1778–1840), whose buildings include Helsinki's Senate Square and the Cathedral, the architectural leaders of National Romanticism – the partnership of Herman Gesellius (1874–1916), Armas Lindgren (1874–1929) and Eliel Saarinen (1873–1950) – used peasant timber and granite architecture as their sources.

Another leading exponent of the movement

work on show in the permanent and temporary exhibitions at Kiasma, the city's Museum of Contemporary Art in Helsinki, would hardly be recognised as art by the National Romantics. "There are more opportunities to be experimental in Finland because of the support for the arts," says Minna Heikinaho. Her three-screen video installation *Mun koti on katu ja se on näytelma (My Home is the Street and it's a Performance)* was one of Kiasma's early shows, and her work epitomises the bolder attitude of Finnish artists born in the early 1960s.

LEFT: Kiasma, the striking Museum of Contemporary Art in Helsinki, designed by Stephen Holl.
ABOVE: inside the Alvar Aalto Museum in Jyväskylä.

was Lars Sonck (1870–1956). Decidedly Gothic in outline, and uneasy on the eye because of the clash of smooth timber or symmetrical roof tiles with rough-hewn granite, National Romantic buildings like Helsinki's National Museum (designed 1901) and Tampere's Cathedral (designed 1899) maintain something of a gawky ugliness. The partnership trio of architects did, however, begin to draw on more soothing, elongated Art Nouveau influences too. The plans for Helsinki Railway Station, originally designed by all three, were amended by Saarinen. The fetching building as it now stands is far more Art Nouveau than National Romantic.

After independence in 1917, the driving need for a national identity diminished in the face of the need to rebuild the country. Beyond the capital, there are abundant instances of original and well-considered municipal architecture: the public library in Tampere, for instance, completed in 1986, is named *Metso*, Finnish for wood grouse, the forest bird whose shape its plan resembles and one that cropped up in seminal works of Finnish painting. The forest reference is deliberate, but the attractive combination of copper and granite, both indigenous Finnish raw materials, transcends the gimmick. The library's design was the result of an architectural competition and was the work of the husband-and-wife team of Reima and Raili Pietilä.

Struggling with Modernism

This relatively new nation whose cities were also deeply scarred in World War II has bravely embraced Modernism and tried to make a virtue of it. Not all efforts have been successful, however. The Merihaka estate of apartment blocks near Helsinki's Hakaniemi Square is bleak and heartless, while many individual buildings in the Sörnäinen district make one wonder quite how Finland earned its reputation for fine architecture.

Nor is there a universal consensus about the virtues of various showpieces which shot up in central Helsinki towards the end of the 1990s.

ALVAR AALTO

One designer who became a household name in Finnish architecture was Alvar Aalto (1898–1976), who managed to fuse something Finnish with Modernism and revolutionised 20th-century architecture in the process. Aalto was the foundational mover in the struggle to get the principles of modern architecture, and Modernism as a whole, accepted in Finland. Once that was achieved, he then turned his attention to the rest of the world at the Paris Exhibition of 1937 and the New York World Fair of 1939. This was primarily to prove that Finland could contribute internationally to the world of architecture and design.

Aalto practised "organic" architecture, designing buildings to suit their environment as well as their purpose. Some of his designs (such as the Enso Gutzeit building in Helsinki) appear to be of the archetypal "concrete block" variety – but, aesthetics aside, they are respected by most people because they were the first to employ nakedly modern materials. More highly regarded is Aalto's Finlandia Hall, the capital's concert and congress complex. Its crisp white profile seems to complement the contours of the park overlooking Töölö Bay, and it's hard to imagine Helsinki without it.

Kiasma, the extraordinary Museum of Contemporary Art designed by American Stephen Holl and opened in 1998 *(see page 175)*, sprawls in metallic asymmetrical splendour behind the statue of the national hero, Field Marshal Mannerheim, and it was this bold contrast –

The new glass and steel music hall, Musikkitalo, currently under construction just behind Kiasma, will meld well with the neighbourhood and bring new architectural pizzazz and panache to Helsinki's expanding centre.

Superb designs

There is boldness in the field of design too. Whatever the object – a tap, a telephone, a bowl, a chair – if its lines are smooth, if it employs modern materials like chrome or plastic with confidence or reinvents glass or wood, and if it fits its purpose perfectly, it is likely to be Finnish. Encouraged, like architecture, by the financial and prestigious carrot of open competitions, everyday items are ceaselessly redesigned and reinvented.

It's an environment that has given rise to the creative spirit of the spiky inventions of internal and industrial designer Stefan Lindfors (born

and the choice of an American architect – that was condemned by older Finns. It does, however, provide an ingenious, striking counterpoint to the stolid, humourless Parliament House across the road.

The adjacent glass cube of the Sanoma-WSOY media group head office is regarded as cold and transparent by some, while the stately new Finnish National Opera House (Karhunen-Hyvämäki-Parkkinen, 1993), another landmark near Töölö Bay, is sometimes described as a characterless block *(see page 172)*.

1962) on the one hand, and the gentle paper jewellery of Janna Syvänoja (born 1960) on the other. Finland's giant names in the plastics (Neste), ceramics (Arabia), textiles (Finlayson, Marimekko), jewellery (Kalevala Koru, Lapponia) and glass (Iittala, Nuutajärvi) industries periodically introduce pieces by new designers as well as those with established reputations such as Yrjö Kukkapuro, whose contemporary furniture is now displayed in New York's Museum of Modern Art.

Marimekko, specifically, is one of the country's most recognisable names, offering modern interpretations of kitschy, polka-dot styles that are some of the trendiest-looking items in the world today.

LEFT: Alvar Aalto Museum in Jyväskylä, Lakeland.
ABOVE: a selection of ceramics by Pentic; Finland is well known for its glassware and ceramics.

A legacy of Alvar Aalto is the Artek design and furniture company set up with his wife Aino, critic Nils-Gustav Hahl and arts patron Maire Gullichsen in the 1930s, which still has a showroom in central Helsinki. The company's designers, working with bold colours and geometric shapes, have created products which are as identifiably Finnish as the traditional handicrafts – woodcarving, rag-rug weaving and tapestry-making. The distinctive and popular Fiskars scissors (Fiskars being a small village in southern Finland and a once-thriving foundry) is one more example of how Finnish design has invaded international consciousness.

A talent for invention

Just to the west of Helsinki, in the neighbouring city of Espoo close to the Helsinki University of Technology, is the Innopoli Building, housing the Foundation for Finnish Inventions. Started in 1971 with backing from the Finnish Ministry of Trade and Industry, the Foundation epitomises Finland's encouragement of the inventive spirit. But this is not a case of inventiveness for its own sake. The Foundation's function is to serve "as a link between inventors, innovators, consumers, businesses and industry in Finland or other parts of the world". The Foundation's activities are also a sign of how Finns have recognised the need to diversify their industry. The staples of pulp and paper

and related metals and engineering remain strong, but there is a need to look elsewhere.

Finland's most conspicuous and commercially successful inventions are those being placed on the market with dizzying regularity by Nokia. The company, often mistakenly believed to be of Japanese origin, takes its name from the small and uneventful town in central Finland where it was founded. It has stayed ahead of the field in mobile phone technology by virtue of its slim and stylish cellphone designs and innovative gadgetry and applications. While Swedish rivals Ericsson have floundered, Nokia has managed to keep ahead in this cut-throat business.

Nokia has given Finnish information technology a powerful boost: evidence of this is provided by the work, for example, of Risto Linturi, one of whose missions as head researcher with the Helsinki Telephone Corporation was to supervise the Helsinki Arena 2000 project, placing every aspect of Helsinki daily life and services on to its own internet "mini-web". Elsewhere, California-based Finn Linus Torvalds was the inspiration behind the wildly successful and geek-friendly Linux operating system in the late 1990s.

A better margarine

But Finnish innovation is not confined to communications technology. It spreads to Benecol, for instance, a birch extract margarine proven to decrease blood cholesterol levels by as much as 14 percent. The only problem for the manufacturing company, Raisio, is how to bring the price of this product, a headline-grabber in the fanatically health-conscious USA, down to a level near that of other margarines. Birch is also the source of the sweetener Xylitol, pioneered in Finland in the late 1970s, used to flavour chewing gum and confectionery, and clinically proven to prevent tooth decay.

Finns have exploited their maritime heritage to good effect as well: shipbuilding innovations include the Azipod propulsion unit. The Azipod was developed and installed in vessels made at the Kvaerner-Masa shipbuilders, whose yards in Helsinki and Turku have turned out the most advanced icebreakers and the biggest passenger ships in the world. ❏

LEFT: Finnish linens incorporate ancient traditions of textile production.

Glass and Wood

Finland has long been at the cutting edge of modern design, and today's artists sculpting in glass and wood are no exception.

I n view of the prominence of its modern glass design, it is surprising that Finland's glassmaking industry dates back only to the late 17th century, when the first glass factory, at Uusikaupunki on the west coast, enjoyed a brief life. Glassmaking was the first design industry to make attempts at breaking away from copies of standard European prototype designs. A turning point was a competition staged by the Riihimäki glass company (named after the southern Finnish town of the same name, today the home of the Finnish Glass Museum) for the design of cocktail glasses. Individual glass designers began to make names for themselves, not least Aino Aalto, who was upstaged by her husband Alvar in 1936 when he contributed his celebrated Savoy vase to the Milan Triennale.

Gunnel Nyman became well known in the following decade for his designs for Iittala, Riihimäki and Nuutajärvi, setting standards which were then equalled and later surpassed by designers such as Tapio Wirkkala (thanks to him the frosty surface of the Finlandia vodka bottle), Kaj Franck and Timo Sarpaneva. Eero Aarnio and Yrjö Kukkapuro were other notable design innovators of the period.

Young designers

Their traditions of style and a distinctively Finnish grace have been maintained more recently by the likes of Brita Flander, Vesa Varrela and Heikki Orvola. Nathalie Lahdenmäki, one young designer, was awarded the prize for best young Finnish designer in 2008 for her sophisticated and sensitive melding of old and new materials in glassware

and ceramics. Harri Koskinen, who won the same prize in 2005, has done extensive work for Iittala, producing lamps, glass and industrial design work that has garnered international acclaim – one of his items is already in the permanent collection at New York's MoMA. Items from Iittala, Pentik and Nuutajärvi's frequently updated glassware ranges have become iconic items in Finnish design and are popular and desirable gift items.

Art from the forests

Finland has also been exceptionally good at taking its natural resources and utilising them for design purposes. Finland's forests have always been (and hopefully will continue to be) the country's most plentiful and ubiquitous natural resource, and the traditions of woodcraft were crucial to every aspect of Finnish agrarian life right into the early 20th century, providing shelter, tools and even clothing. Old wooden quarters of the earliest urban milieus were vulnerable to, and were frequently ravaged by, fire, but the old parts of Porvoo, 50km (30 miles) to the east of Helsinki *(see page 198)* and Rauma on the west coast, preserved since the 17th century *(see page 240)* contain charming remnants of wooden house-building skills.

These basic timber patterns used in rural buildings around the country are today preserved in the structure of the country's lakeside log cabins and saunas *(see page 250)*. But wood has also been adapted with characteristic Finnish innovation to everyday functions, most notably with Alvar Aalto's "bentwood" technique that skilfully moulds birch into laminated fluid curls and curves.

The Aarikka gift shops are some of the best places to buy glass and wooden Finnish souvenirs, utensils and jewellery. *See page 318 for more information.* ❑

ABOVE: traditional Finnish birch cups called *kuksa*.
RIGHT: the ultimate in stylish glassware.

MUSIC AND FILM

On the international stage, Finland's artistic heritage
has long been associated with Sibelius, but modern
classical musicians, rock bands and film directors
are keeping the country's arts alive

When people think of Finnish music,
they still think of Jean Sibelius. The
great Finnish composer, after all, sprang
from a little-known country to become one of
the most famous composers of all time – and
Finland's most famous export. But there is
much more to modern Finnish music than simply Sibelius, and audiences everywhere are starting to recognise this.

*Bearing in mind the country's population of
just 5 million, a startling number of Finnish
musicians and orchestras have won both
domestic and international acclaim.*

Classical music

The Association of Finnish Composers today
numbers over 100 members. All have had works
performed professionally, and many possess distinguished discographies. Playing their works
in Finland are 14 professional orchestras, over
two dozen semi-professional and other orchestras and numerous ensembles. Helsinki is
home to two symphony orchestras: the Finnish
Radio Symphony and the Helsinki Philharmonic, the first permanent orchestra anywhere
in the Nordic countries.

Finland takes its music seriously and has
proved it through a generous policy of funding
for musicians and musical institutes; there are
around 100 such institutes, with a student body
of 60,000, offering free instruction; talented

graduates can audition for one of the seven free
conservatories or the celebrated Sibelius Academy in Helsinki. Finland also sponsors scores of
annual music festivals *(see page 100)* attracting
both native and foreign artists.

Finnish instrumentalists have also been winning global attention. Cellists, of whom Finland
has an especially strong tradition, have done
particularly well. Arto Noras, second prize winner at the 1966 Tchaikovsky Competition, and
Erkki Rautio are renowned virtuosi, as are Anssi
Karttunen and Martti Roussi. Cellists aren't the
only ones. The brothers Pekka and Jaakko Kuusisto, still in their early twenties, are regularly
featured violinists in many concerts. Classical

PRECEDING PAGES: the Sibelius Monument in Helsinki.
LEFT: Finnish composer Esa-Pekka Salonen.
RIGHT: Karita Mattila, Finnish operatic soprano.

guitarist Timo Korhonen may be less known, but he is often compared to Andrés Segovia. Pianist Ralf Gothoni commands a confirmed place in Europe and further afield, as does pianist and composer Olli Mustonen – "Finland's Mozart" – who performed his own concerto with the Radio Symphony Orchestra at the age of 12. Esa-Pekka Salonen is the most notable achiever, a principal conductor with an international reputation second only to Sibelius.

After Sibelius and Salonen, however, it is Finland's singers who have gained the most fame. Foreign audiences adore Finnish basses: Matti Lehtinen in the 1950s, Martti Talvela before his premature death in 1989, and Matti Salminen and Jaakko Ryhänen. Baritones Jorma Hynninen, Tom Krause, Walton Grönroos and tenor Peter Lindroos grace houses like London's Covent Garden and Berlin's Deutsche Opera. Nor have sopranos missed out; Ritva Auvinen, Anita Välkki, Taru Valjakka and Karita Mattila have attained stardom, and Soile Isokoski, winner of the Elly Ameling contest, is joining their ranks.

Although its sopranos have sought fame overseas, the Finnish National Opera has always punched above its weight. It made operatic history in 1983 as the first foreign company to be invited to perform at New York's Met.

WANDERING MAESTROS

Talented Finns are often lured abroad, thereby spreading the musical word. Finnish conductors are particularly in demand. Every Nordic capital has had a symphony orchestra with a Finn as principal conductor. The country has many world-class maestros, including Paavo Berglund, Okko Kamu and Salonen. Prolonging the fine tradition are the likes of Sakari Oramo, who became conductor-in-chief of the City of Birmingham Symphony Orchestra in 1998, and is now chief conductor of the Royal Stockholm Philharmonic Orchestra. The well-loved Leif Segerstam has been extremely prolific, both as a conductor and as composer of about 20 symphonies.

Vocal works have always been the backbone of the Finnish musical tradition, which may, perhaps, explain why about three new Finnish operas are published every year. These operas offer additional proof that Finnish composition, too, lives on beyond Sibelius. Joonas Kokkonen might be called the country's preeminent living composer, but excellence is also to be found in the works of Erik Bergman and Einojuhani Rautavaara, two other acclaimed senior composers. Among younger composers, Magnus Lindberg, Kaija Saariaho, Aulis Sallinen and Einojuhani Rautavaara are of special note. Lindberg's *KRAFT* (1985) won the Nordic Council's music award and the Koussevitzky disc award. *Le Monde de la Musique* has called him "one of the best composers in the world of his age". One of his modern orchestral works, *Fresco*, made its world première with the LA

> Even the most recalcitrant sopranos come home for the annual Savonlinna Opera Festival. Held in a 500-year-old castle in July, it is one of the most delightful opera festivals in the world.

Philharmonic, conducted by Esa-Pekka Salonen. Saariaho, an electro-acoustic innovator, has also received much acclaim.

to compete with Sweden's pop success, from ABBA to The Cardigans, Finns have recently felt quiet pride at the international success of Darude, the pop and rap ensemble Bomfunk MCs, indie players The Rasmus and heavy rockers HIM.

The best-loved bands, such as the veteran Eppu Normaali outfit and the bluesy J.J. Karjalainen, can all play as well as any rock group in Europe, and are affected by the same fashions. But their style is still sufficiently Finnish to restrict them largely to an exclusively Finnish audience – language being the other barrier.

Some groups, such as the sophisticated, harmonic folk-pop of Värttinä, a group of female

Popular music

One of the refreshing aspects of Finnish art generally is its lack of elitism. Still, the lines are as well drawn between classical and rock music here as in most places. One notable exception is the internationally recognised band Nightwish, which combines heavy rock music with classical singing. Finnish rock thrives but on its own terms. The best-known Finnish band was probably Hanoi Rocks, a kitschy, hard rocking band founded in 1985 that in 2009 came together for a reunion tour. While Finland has not been able

singers who have adapted the traditional motifs of ancient styles to a modern swing, have risen to the top of the charts outside the country.

One other aspect of the Finnish music scene which is a true regional phenomenon is the passion for the tango. It may sound unlikely, but Argentine melodrama converts convincingly to the melancholy of the Finnish crooner. The Tango Festival at Seinäjoki is Finland's best-attended summer gathering, with dancing that continues through the night.

Generally, the further north you travel, the louder the music gets. Windy and cold Oulu in northern Finland has the most intense core of rock fans, as well as the only male choir in the world that doesn't even try to sing: Huutajat

LEFT: outdoor classical concert in Esplanade Park, Helsinki. **ABOVE:** tango festival in Seinäjoki, one of the biggest summer festivals in Finland.

(literally The Shouters). Dozens of long-haired men in suits and gum ties shout their hearts out in perfect order – Arctic hysteria at its best.

Finns on film

It is the Kaurismäki brothers, Aki and Mika, who are largely to thank for wrenching the Finnish cinema industry to worldwide attention with their rough-edged individuality and prolific output. Contemporary Finnish cinema received little exposure until the advent of the brothers, most notably Aki, who was the youngest director ever to receive a retrospective at the Museum of Modern Art in New York.

Born in Helsinki in 1957, Aki toiled as a postman and film critic before working as a scriptwriter, assistant and actor on his elder brother's 1980 film *Valehtelija (The Liar)*. The following year, the two men formed a production company. They also own a distribution company, a cinema in downtown Helsinki and were among the founders of the Midnight Sun Festival held each June in Sodankylä, Lapland.

Aki, the better known of the siblings, worked with Mika on the 1983 rock documentary *Saimaa-Ilmiö (The Saimaa Gesture)* before striking out with a freewheeling adaptation of *Crime and Punishment* (1983). A lugubrious figure of laconic manner and dismissive attitudes to his work, Aki has a self-proclaimed reputation as

"the biggest drinker in the world". His films revel in the deadpan humour of morose outsiders desperate to escape the confines of a gloom-ridden country. *Calamari Union* (1985) is an

> *Film directors Mika and Aki Kaurismäki have created a body of work that has been seen in 65 countries, won prizes at international festivals and brought the two widespread acclaim, veneration and fame.*

unscripted comedy in which the 17 characters are all called Frank, while *Hamlet Liikemaailmassa (Hamlet Goes Business)* (1987) is a modern-day version of Shakespeare set in a rubber duck factory. Aki then moved his settings from his native land with the Ealing-style comedy *I Hired a Contract Killer* (1990), filmed in London, and, more recently, *Drifting Clouds*, *The Man Without a Past* and, in 2006, *Lights in the Dusk*.

Mika, two years older, studied film in Munich and has lived in Brazil since 1992, working in a variety of genres from the road movie *Helsinki Napoli* (1987) to the comedy *Cha Cha Cha* (1988) and *Amazon* (1990).

Flying the Finnish flag in quite a different way is Hollywood action specialist Renny Harlin, director of special-effects blockbusters like *Cliffhanger* and *Deep Blue Sea*, whose latest project is a biopic of Mannerheim. Closer to home is *History is Made at Night* (1999) by Ilkka Järvi-Laituri, with Hollywood star Bill Pullman. Finns have rediscovered their own environment as a setting, and in the late 1990s, Finnish films attracted half the cinema audiences. Meanwhile, the new millennium has seen a number of cinematic successes, including A.J. Annilaśs *Sauna*, Kaisa Rastimośs *Myrsky (Stormheart)* and Dome Karukoski's *Tummien perhosten koti (The Home of Dark Butterflies)*, all of which won international awards in 2009.

Still, one of the most beloved depictions of Finland in any film – foreign or domestic – is Jim Jarmusch's 1991 *Night on Earth*, in which famed actor Matti Pellonpää brings a winter Helsinki to life through his role as poker-faced, late-night taxi driver Mika. ❑

LEFT: Finnish actress Anna Falchi at the Cannes Film Festival for the premiere of *Les Chansons d'Amour*.

Jean Sibelius

Finland's most famous artist is Jean Sibelius, whose music played a significant role in the formation of the Finnish identity.

I t cannot be easy for a man to find himself a figurehead in his country's search for an identity, yet it was this label rather than the simple genius of his music that many Finns tied to their most famous composer, Jean Sibelius (1865–1957), during the years before Finnish independence. His tone poem *Finlandia* in particular became an emblem of everything Finnish, and this aura of reverence must have, at times, irked the composer.

Yet Sibelius did embody many things Finnish; even his ancestry took in areas of Finland as far apart as the coastal town of Loviisa, towards the Russian border, the Swedish influence of Turku, the northwest Gulf of Bothnia and, nearer at hand, Häme province where he was born.

Sibelius's background

Though Sibelius's family in Loviisa was wealthy, his father, a well-known doctor, was better known for his medical care than his skills in financial management. When his father died looking after his patients in the typhus epidemic that raged during Finland's last great famine, young Jean's mother, Maria, had little choice but to file for bankruptcy. The family remained in Hämeenlinna. All three children showed musical talent, displaying their concert skills on family visits to Loviisa.

Although it is simplistic to think of Sibelius as being solely influenced by the Finnish landscape, he was undoubtedly part of the late 19th-century movement of artists, writers and intellectuals who turned for inspiration to Finland's land, people and past. Yet, after the first performance of his early *Kullervo* symphony, based on Finnish folklore at the height of the National Romantic movement *(see page 86)*, Sibelius withdrew the work and it was not played again until after his death.

The great Sibelius scholar Erik Tawaststjerna insists that Sibelius moved in the mainstream of European music and was heavily influenced by Beethoven, as well as by Bruckner and Tchaikovsky.

RIGHT: Sibelius wrote seven symphonies and many other compositions, including *Finlandia*.

His relationship to Wagner's music could best be described as love-hate.

Sibelius travelled to Bayreuth and Munich in the 1890s and planned an opera, something he did not achieve, though some of its proposed music went into *The Swan of Tuonela*. He wrote his *First Symphony* just before the turn of the 20th century and followed it with the popular *Second* in 1902, at which time he began planning his *Violin Concerto*, now regarded by many as his greatest work. Its first performance in 1904, arranged hurriedly because Sibelius had financial problems, was not a success and it was revised.

Not long after, the family moved to Ainola *(see page 226)*, close to the retreat of his friend the artist Pekka Halonen. The site for Ainola (named after his wife Aino) was located by the painter Eero Järnefelt, Aino's brother. Another friend, architect Lars Sonck, designed the house, and Sibelius wrote some 150 works there, including the remaining symphonies. Sibelius lived for 53 years at Ainola until his death in 1957, and the small artistic colony spent much time in one another's houses. To compose, Sibelius needed silence: his children were sent away to friends, while the servants would creep around the house on tiptoe.

Sibelius wrote no music in his final years. Until his death, there were constant rumours of one more symphony, but nothing can have satisfied him. The *Seventh Symphony* was his last. ❏

FINLAND'S SUMMER FESTIVALS

In common with other Nordic countries, Finland has a long tradition of festivals, which make the most of summer nights in music, song and dance

The soprano Aino Acte founded Savonlinna in 1912, and it remains the most dramatic setting for any music festival the world over. After this came Jyväskylä, opened in 1955 by the composer Seppo Nummi. The tradition for music festivals continues today, many in rural areas and many which now draw international audiences. One of the most remote is the Kuhmo Chamber Music Festival close to the Russian border, founded in 1970 by cellist Seppo Kimanen. It now draws 150 international musicians to more than 60 concerts, attended by around 35,000 people.

Other arts festivals include Tampere (theatre), Kuopio (dance), Pori (jazz), Imatra (big bands), Lieksa (brass bands) and Sodankylä (film).

Folk Festivals
One source of traditional festivals was the old-time fire brigades, who got together to play music and dance at annual festivals. Some festivals have their roots in a more sinister past: in 1643, the Ruovesi Witch Trials condemned Antti Lieronen as "a witch most obvious and potent" and burnt her at the stake. Today's "trials" include drama and concerts, but no one is burnt.

In 1968 the organisation Finland Festivals was formed, to monitor festivals, propose new ideas and guarantee high artistic levels. As a result, new festivals are born every year.

ABOVE: a folk dance in national costume, performed on the Åland Islands, where traditions are strong.

RIGHT: performing on the Espa Stage in Esplanade Park, Helsinki; this is also where folk and jazz festivals are held on summer evenings.

LEFT: Finland's festivals are not just local events – international artistes bring their own shows and traditional national costumes.

ROCK, JAZZ AND BLUES FESTIVALS

Finland has a broad rock scene, highlighted by a number of summer rock festivals. Provinssirock, held in Seinäjoki in early June, traditionally marks the opening of the rock festival season. A four-hour train ride north of Helsinki, Seinäjoki turns into a rock heaven for one weekend. As well as the best of the Finns, Provinssirock attracts big names from abroad, such as Nick Cave and David Byrne. As elsewhere, there are beer tents selling brew. (Drugs are remarkably low-profile in Finland and you are unlikely to see any.)

The other important summer rock festival is Ruisrock in Turku. The oldest rock festival in Finland, Ruisrock faded for a few years but has now been revived and hosts some of the biggest names; recent guests have included Bob Dylan and Billy Idol. For jazz, the best festival in all the Nordic countries is the huge Pori Jazz Festival *(picture above)*. Another festival with a family atmosphere is Puisto Blues in Järvenpää, north of Helsinki, at the end of June.

ABOVE: Savonlinna provides a fabulous setting for its opera festival; in all, the fortress has seen the world premières of no fewer than five operas by Finnish composers.

ABOVE: a samba dancer outside Helsinki Cathedral. Samba may not traditionally be associated with Finland, but a popular samba festival is held in June each year.

RIGHT: huge bonfires, built up on lakesides and by the sea, are common as part of the midsummer celebrations, observed on the nearest Saturday to Midsummer Day, between 20–26 June.

BELOW: founded in 1970, Ruisrock is the oldest rock festival in Finland, and some of the ageing rockers may have been coming here since its inception.

THE WRITER'S DILEMMA

Finnish literature emerged in the 19th century as an embodiment of national character. Today, Finnish writers continue to use writing to understand their world

Eino Leino, poet, novelist and playwright, wrote of Finnish literature in 1910: "Literature is the country's interpreter. Literature is the nation's mirror. Without literature the nation is like a blind man, like a deaf mute."

The story of the past two centuries of Finnish literature is the story of a country struggling to find its voice and its identity. Mimicking Finland's political development, there have been peaks and troughs, high expectations and disappointments. Writers have expressed the fortunes of their country by veering from romanticism to cynicism and realism. The written portrait of the Finn has covered the spectrum from noble hero to drunken buffoon.

A blank canvas

Until the 19th century, Finland's literary tradition had been primarily an oral one. Because there was no written precedent, writers had a free hand to invent the Finn on paper, and many made him a hero.

Finland's epic poem from the 19th century, the Kalevala, *is based on four pairs of syllables on each line, with two or more lines having a synonymous meaning – making it particularly easy to remember and recite.*

Johan Ludvig Runeberg (1804–77), Finland's national poet, offered just such a romantic vision of his countrymen. In his three collections of

LEFT: Elias Lönnrot, creator of Finland's national epic poem, the *Kalevala*.
RIGHT: Gallén-Kallela's illustrations of the *Kalevala*.

Swedish-language poems, *Dikter I–III (Poems)*, and in his patriotic ballad series, *Fänrik Ståhl Sägner (The Tales of Ensign Ståhl)*, he created loyal, gracious and noble Finns., and they were readily embraced.

In the 1820s, Elias Lönnrot (1802–84) began a project which was to generate yet more national pride. Lönnrot travelled through Finland recording folk poetry. The result was the *Kalevala* of 1835 (now commonly called the "Old Kalevala"). A new, longer version was published in 1849.

The *Kalevala* itself is a heroic epic on the scale of the *Odyssey* or the *Iliad*. But it is also a ragbag of narratives and light interludes, existing to preserve old customs and songs. The narrative is interrupted by poetic "charms", some of which belong to the realms of Shakespearean comedy. Lönnrot's Finn is a participator in the creation of the world, a classical figure with a Finnish twist.

The *Kalevala* managed to include in its poetry a national fiction-cum-history which stretched back to the beginning of time, and which did not include the humiliating details of real life – never-ending domination by foreign rulers. In Lönnrot's mythical Finland, power lay with the good and the just, with prose that reads like literature as old as Greek classics or Norse sagas.

At the same time as Lönnrot was compiling the *Kalevala*, other Finnish-language writers such as Aleksis Kivi (1834–72) were celebrating rural life, casting the ordinary people in the role of heroes: true Finns leading virtuous lives among the forests, harmonious with nature.

Twentieth-century works

By the early 20th century, real events began to cast doubts on this unimpeachable national character. Political achievements were quickly soured by subsequent crises. It became the job of writers to make sense of events such as the civil war, which lay heavy on the nation's conscience. Mainstream Finnish writing concerned itself with events in the world at large.

Notable exceptions include Mika Waltari (1908–79), an escapist writer. His main work, *The Egyptian*, has been translated into more than 25 languages. F.E. Sillanpää, too, wrote about the mystical rural life and won the Nobel Prize for literature in 1939 – his books include *Meek Heritage* and *The Maid Silja*.

During this time, Swedish-language writers drifted away from the main pulse of Finnish writing, becoming more isolated, and occasionally more daring. Some, like the poet Edith Södergran (1892–1923), nonetheless enjoyed considerable popularity. Christer Kihlman, author of *Den Blå Modern (The Blue Mother)* and *Dyre Prins (Sweet Prince)*, and Tove Jansson's Moomintroll books, show just how idiosyncratic Swedish-Finnish writing has become.

Contemporary voices

Today, Finnish heroes no longer have to act as vessels for the nation's pride. They are as troubled and beset by worries as the heroes of other literatures. Modern writers like Leena Krohn and Pentti Saarikoski reflect Finnish humanity. Veijo Meri is seen as a reformer of Finnish prose with his *Manilla Rope*.

As modern Finnish writers become more international, the *Kalevala* may still be reflected in popular Finnish literature. The bestselling authors Kalle Päätalo, Laila Hietamies, Arno Paasilinna and Veikko Huovinen place their stories in the same regions where the *Kalevala* was collected. Päätalo's nostalgic rural landscape and Hietamies's lost Karelia both evoke the eternal yearning for youth. Paasilinna and Huovinen both meld reality and imagination in a Karelian-style setting and use onomatopoeic words – the backbone of both the *Kalevala* and modern Finnish short stories.

Other authors, meanwhile, draw on the new diversity of Finland and its people for inspiration. Prominent recent authors include Johanna Sinisalo, Kjell Westö, Kari Hotakainen, Leena Lehtolainen, Hannu Raittila, Asko Sahlberg, as well as Ranya El Ramly, Johan Bargum, Margaretha Hupa and Rakel Liehu. While their interpretations may have diverged from the "classic" notion of what it means to be Finnish, they are serving to make the cultural heritage of Finland richer and more complex. ❏

LEFT: Viejo Meri, one of Finland's most respected modern writers.

The Moomins

Tove Jansson's eccentric Moomin family – with its quirky bohemian characters – struck a chord with readers all over the world.

At first sight Tove Jansson's Moomin books seem like storybooks to buy children as gifts. But the mystical fairytale world of mighty nature and ever-changing seasons inspires even diehard realists.

Tove Jansson (1914–2001) was born to an artistic family – both brothers were artists and writers. A diminutive Swedish-speaking woman, meek to the point of humility, Jansson lived much of her life in seclusion with her female partner on a small island off Finland's southern coast. Here Jansson created another world, just as C.S. Lewis and J.R.R. Tolkien did in their books.

And like the works of Lewis and Tolkien, Moomin books appeal to both children and adults. Younger readers may be more attracted to the books' imaginary worlds and colourful illustrations, while older readers enjoy Jansson's basic philosophy of acceptance, a quest for space and solitude.

Moomin characters

The books are all led by the Moomin family characters. The bohemian Moominmamma takes care of everything, while Moominpappa is a philosopher, who writes his memoirs and becomes active only when it's time to explore the unknown. The Moomin house is always open to adopted children and strange creatures that seem to appear from the valley. Love and tolerance reign; difference is always accepted. There are no wars, and nothing threatens the idyll except natural phenomena.

Each character is a sensitively illustrated personality, so every reader will identify with at least one of them. Children fear the monstrous Groke who only appears in winter. He is cold as winter and no one wants to be near him. But even he has human qualities – poor lonely Groke suffers greatly while missing contact with just about anyone. Little My is an adventurous girl, who, along with Moomintroll, is perhaps Tove Jansson's own alter ego. Snufkin is a world traveller who prefers wandering alone. Snitt

RIGHT: the Moominworld theme park near Turku recreates favourite Moomin characters.

is a coward; the Fillyjonk is a neurotic pedant. Hemulen is an absent-minded botanist and Snork an engineer who does little else than design a light aeroplane. The Snork Maiden, Snork's sister, is extremely feminine. The strange, worm-like electric creatures Hattifatteners represent foreigners, with whom communication is possible if not easy. All these characters lend themselves to fine psychological drama.

The Moomin life pauses for hibernation when the winter comes, and is reborn at the thaw when Snufkin returns from his world travels, except when the magical winter is brought to life in *Moominland Midwinter*.

These unpretentious little books have conquered the world, having been translated into over 30 languages. In Finland, there is Moomin-world in Naantali, the Moomin Museum in Tampere and yet another theme park being planned in – of all places – Hawaii. The Japanese love the Moomin figures; Finnair has had Moomin figures painted on planes flying to Japan, and Finnair's flight attendants sell enormous quantities of Moomin paraphernalia to travellers. (Be aware that the commercialised Moomins are not always entirely faithful to the originals.)

Though Jansson's world was based around the village at Pellinki, south of Porvoo, a modern Moominworld theme park (www.muumimaailma.fi) recreates the stories at Naantali, near Turku. ❑

FINNS WHO SPEAK SWEDISH

Finland is officially bilingual, using both Finnish
and Swedish, a tradition that goes back centuries
between these two neighbouring countries

W hy do so many Finns speak Swedish is
a question that is often asked by visitors. The main reason is that for 600
years, Finland was a part of Sweden. In that
time it is not so surprising that Swedish became
the language for administration, and many
Finns adopted the language to survive in society. The great-grandchildren of some of these
early Finns still use Swedish, the language having been passed down the generations. But the
answer isn't quite as simple as that – politics
and education have also played their part.

Early settlers

The earliest inhabitants on the Åland Islands
and many other coastal communities were
Scandinavian settlers, adventurers and fishermen, who brought their language with them.
Many who still live on these islands speak a
unique Swedish dialect which may be difficult
to understand, even by Swedish tourists.

As Finland was a lucrative territory, many
Swedes also emigrated, mostly to Nyland ("New
Land") and Osterbotten. Some came as industrialists and founded factories and sawmills. Many
of these ancient communities remain, including
the cardboard factory in Verla, now a Unesco
World Heritage site.

The military also played a major role in the
Swedish "takeover". In many cases, successful
soldiers in the Royal Swedish Army were
granted privileges in Finland, such as territory
and tax-free status, which brought with them a
Swedish upper class to many previously remote
regions of Finland.

LEFT: Åland Islanders feel more Swedish than Finnish.
RIGHT: a typical Swedish area near Turku.

As Swedish soon became the *lingua franca* in
large towns such as Turku, Helsinki and Vyborg,
many German, Jewish or Russian burghers living in these areas adopted Swedish, and this
usage remains today.

A bilingual nation

Swedish-speaking Finns, or Finland-Swedes as
they are described by the government, are not
immigrants, nor are they Swedes. They may not
even have any family connections with Sweden.

When Finland is described as a "bilingual"
nation, it means that the two languages are
given an official status, very much the same as
English and French in Canada – one may

assume the right to use either Swedish or Finnish at offices or even in shops in "bilingual" towns. However, this is not always successful – in some cases Finns have to resort to English in order to understand each other.

Linguistic roots

Swedish-speakers are a reminder of the 600 years when Finland was the eastern part of the Kingdom of Sweden. At that time, and even during the time when Finland was a Grand Duchy of Russia, from 1809 to independence in 1917, Swedish was the official language, the language of the civil service, of the law, of higher education, at the University of Turku (Åbo in Swedish), and of the monied classes.

Fed by students from Turku University, Finnish cultural life was dominated by Swedish-speakers too. It was not until 1828 that the university established a Finnish language lectureship, and not until 1850 that a professorship of Finnish was introduced.

Because the Swedish language held sway in this way, it was the principal language of the nascent Finnish mid-19th-century cultural and political life. Early political activists like the Fennomen, who supported the Finnish language and campaigned for its recognition as an

SWEDISH-SPEAKING WRITERS

The compiler of the epic poem the *Kalevala*, Elias Lönnrot (1802–84), was born in Nyland in southwest Finland and has a Swedish name. Yet he was a great champion of the Finnish language and folklore and went on to become Professor of Finnish at Helsinki University. He also produced a Swedish–Finnish dictionary, which is credited with establishing a Finnish literary language. Johan Ludvig Runeberg (1804–77) taught at the Porvoo University for 20 years. The opening words of his Swedish-language *Fänrik Ståhl Sägner (Tales of Ensign Ståhl)* became Finland's national anthem (*Vårt Land*, or *Maamme* in Finnish).

official language, often faced the paradox that they were Swedish-speakers whose love of their country was paramount. A number of 19th-century cultural ambassadors, painters and writers, who searched determinedly for an artistic expression of Finnish nationalism, were also Swedish-speakers.

It was not surprising, therefore, that when Finland gained its independence, the 1919 Constitution decreed that Finland should have two official national languages: Finnish and Swedish. At that time, Swedish-speakers accounted for 12 percent of the Finnish population. Today, the figure has shrunk to around 6 percent.

Swedish-speakers are very much spread out around the country. About half of them live in purely Swedish regions in Nyland, around Turku, on Åland and on the west coast. Regional centres, such as Ekenäs (Tammisaari in Finnish), Borgå (Porvoo) and Jakobstad (Pietarsaari) have their indigenous Swedish culture, and larger towns such as Åbo (Turku), Vasa (Vaasa) or the capital Helsinki (which Swedish-speakers call Helsingfors, actually the city's original name) are home to about half of the Swedish-speakers.

With encouragement from individuals like Tsar Alexander II, who made it official in 1863, Finnish gradually overtook Swedish to become the dominant language and the language of

Highs and lows

Sadly, the population of Finland-Swedes is decreasing; as of 2007 it was just under 290,000, or 5.5 percent of the country's total population. In 1960, there were 21 Swedish-language newspapers (182 Finnish); in 1988, the figure was 14 (with 374 Finnish publications), and by 2007, the number had decreased to 11. Finland-Swedes have a choice of papers from either Sweden or Finland. Daily papers from large publishers in Stockholm are always available in Finland's Swedish-speaking centres, and Sweden's culture, politics and daily gossip is popular among Finland-Swedes.

power. But political disputes over the two languages and their relative prominence have flared up from time to time, especially in the 1920s and 1930s, when it became a central political issue. Common comparisons with the Republic of Ireland are not far-fetched – the difference is that, in fact, English has been more dominant than Swedish. Accusations that Finland-Swedes were more wealthy or disproportionately powerful have rumbled on over the decades.

LEFT: the League of Nations meets to decide the fate of the Åland Islands' status in 1921.
ABOVE: Swedish Ålanders enjoying a summer's picnic lunch.

In fact, Finland has been dubbed a model for minority policy. The government spends much more money per capita on Swedish radio and

> *Swedish spoken in Finland is not identical to that of Sweden. Many local dialect words which have their roots in Finnish are included in Finland's Swedish, and the language maintains a very distinct accent.*

TV programmes, and the largest Swedish daily in Finland, *Hufvudstadsbladet*, manages a circulation of 51,000, which means one paper for every five Swedish-speakers. As a comparison,

Wales has no daily newspaper in the Welsh language – a language that is spoken by approximately 20 percent of its population.

As Finland and Sweden entered the European Union in 1994, Swedish became an official language once again, which boosted its significance all over Europe. The language is also a gateway for Finns to live, study and work in Sweden, Denmark, Norway and Iceland. Finnish-speaking Finns, therefore, readily understand the usefulness of Swedish in many aspects of their lives – foreign and domestic.

The growing number of "mixed marriages" between Finnish- and Swedish-speakers has

doubled the number of bilingual Finns – many families choose to use both languages at home, and Swedish schools are becoming popular once again, even among purely Finnish-speaking families.

A unique situation

The case of the Åland Islands, which lie off the southwest of Finland almost halfway to Sweden, is unique. Though this is Finnish territory, the roles are reversed. When Finland became independent in 1917, the Ålanders' background and culture were (and are) more clearly Swedish and they voted overwhelmingly in a referendum to become part of Sweden. After much wrangling, the matter went to the infant League

of Nations in the early 1920s, complicating what could then have been a relatively simple settlement by deciding that the Åland Islands remain Finnish but that the islanders' use of the Swedish language would be safeguarded.

The official, legal language, therefore, is Swedish. However, the 25,000 residents consider themselves to be autonomous from the government of Finland, with their own flag and postage stamps. The Ålanders have their own parliament and government to run their internal affairs out of a proportion of the Finnish budget. They also send a member to the main parliament in Helsinki *(see page 231)*.

As part of Sweden, Ålanders would be "normal" citizens; as part of Finland, however, they may retain their "special" status. Åland became even more of a special case on 1 July 1999, when tax-free sales were banned within inter-EU travel. Åland is "outside" the Union, however, and some ferries between Finland and Sweden stop briefly at the Långnäs pier to take advantage of the popular tax-free sales.

Political representation

The main political party representing mainland Finland-Swedes, the Swedish People's Party (SFP), was founded in 1906. The SFP got 4.6 percent of the vote in the 2003 elections and their seats in parliament fell from 11 to 8. However, in spite of this, it could be argued that they were one of the big winners – the nature of Finnish politics (post-vote negotiations as to who should enter government) meant that the SFP not only remained in government, but actually secured two ministerial posts.

Frequent coalition governments have resulted in some cabinet prominence for SFP Members of Parliament. Elisabeth Rehn was the first female Minister of Defence in the early 1990s, and was a candidate for Finland's president *(see page 71)*.

Talk to Finland-Swedes about the problems of being a linguistic minority and you may end up in a fascinating conversation lasting several hours – both on the complications of being able to express oneself fully in two languages and on the advantages of hailing from a cultural background comprising three different societies: Sweden, Finnish Finland and Swedish Finland.   ❏

LEFT: although strictly speaking part of Finland, the official language in the Åland Islands is Swedish.

Immigrants

In Finland, immigration is not the political hot potato it is in other countries, and more and more migrants are attracted here.

Finland's transformation over the past 50 years from a primarily agriculture-based society into a competitive, technologically advanced information society makes it an attractive option for both economic and forced migrants.

These days Helsinki is international, with over 5 percent of the population speaking a foreign language (other than Swedish). It doesn't compare with Stockholm, where 18 percent are foreigners, but the figure is growing. The densely inhabited Kallio suburb in Helsinki is home to many immigrant families.

Although immigrants are not always welcomed, many Finns now realise that labour from outside is required both to keep the service sector ticking over, and to pay taxes into the treasury. Finland is the only major European country which has not generated a far-right, anti-immigration political party.

Ethnic makeup

The biggest influx of foreigners occurred soon after the Soviet downfall, when Russia's borders opened up, allowing freer movement in this region. Russians and Estonians now constitute the largest ethnic groups in Finland and many have taken Finnish citizenship.

Among Asians, the Chinese are the largest ethnic group, while more than 3,000 Vietnamese also live in Finland, most of them originally having arrived as refugees. The arrival of the Vietnamese was a media event, many of them hand-picked at refugee camps by Finnish government officials. At the same time Finland gave developmental aid to the Vietnamese government. This was, and still is to some extent, the official refugee policy – a few hundred "quota" refugees who were given full financial support. Other nationals who arrived as refugees came mainly from Chile, or the Kurdish regions in Turkey and Iran.

When the Somalis came, however, the situation changed. Somalis represent Finland's largest non-European immigrant population; the Somali diaspora

in Finland numbers around 10,000, half of whom have taken Finnish nationality. Gang wars against Somalis occurred, especially during the harsh recession years in the early 1990s when Finland's unemployment figures hovered above 20 percent. The small town of Joensuu became notorious for a "skinhead" gang who terrorised foreigners. While unemployment among Somalis remains high, racism seems to have cooled for the time being, with organisations like the Finnish Somali Association helping to forge understanding.

Restaurants – most especially the ubiquitous kebab shop – are typical employers for many immigrants to Finland. Most employers demand full

knowledge of Finnish, and many foreigners will take low-paid jobs that Finns refuse to accept.

Loneliness or isolation is one of the biggest social problems among foreigners. Some refugees are settled in tiny towns where contact with locals is practically non-existent. And small talk, as every Finn knows, is hardly the most accepted of pastimes.

All these issues notwithstanding, many immigrants still choose to live in Finland over warmer, southern countries: some may fall in love with a Finn, some appreciate its generous social security schemes and very high standard of living, while others – perhaps most importantly – find comfort in the increasing number of fellow foreigners – there are now approximately 145,000 immigrants in Finland. ❑

RIGHT: Finnish Somali Abdirizak Hassan Mohamed, president of the Finnish Somali Association.

THE SAMI AND THEIR LAND

The Sami of north Finland have a distinct culture that
remains an emblematic example of the struggle of
traditional peoples as they move towards modernisation

For the Sami (Lapps), who, generally speaking, prefer to mind their own business and hope other people will mind theirs, the second half of the 20th century brought mixed blessings, putting pressure on a fragile ecosystem of society and nature already under threat. With this tenuous relationship in relief, the many recent changes in the Sami world have also triggered a much greater awareness of their own identity.

Early development

Most academics agree that the Sami descend from a people who, following the retreating edge of the continental ice, reached Finland and East Karelia from the Ural Mountains in the last millennia BC. They thus share a common linguistic and ethnic heritage with the Finns themselves.

The cornerstone of early Sami society was the *siida*, a community of several families and the territories in which they cooperatively hunted, trapped and fished. Place names in southern and central Finland suggest that Sami communities thrived here until the Middle Ages. But as the Finnish settlers moved in, so the Sami – those who were not assimilated – moved on, ever northwards. In Finland today there are about 8,000 Finnish Sami, concentrated in northern Lapland around Utsjoki, Karasjoki, Inari and Enontekiö *(see page 292)*; this is roughly one-third of the number of Sami living in Norway or Sweden.

PRECEDING PAGES: Sami midday meal during a reindeer drive. **LEFT:** Skolte Sami woman in Nellim Church. **RIGHT:** a Sami woman in traditional dress lights a candle of prayer.

Land of the midnight sun

The Sami home in Lapland (Lappi) is Finland's northernmost province and covers nearly a third of the country's total area, most of it north of the Arctic Circle. Away from the few towns and scattered communities, its extraordinary beauty is still predominantly primeval wilderness. Extensive swamps and forests of conifer and birch rise in the far north to bareheaded fells, the highest topping 1,300 metres (4,270ft); all this is laced by swift rivers and streams and punctuated by lakes and pools.

You may think of it as the land of the midnight sun, which, depending on latitude (and cloud cover), is visible for up to 70 summer days. In winter there is an almost equivalent sunless period, tempered at times by the flickering veils of the Northern Lights or, around midday, by the lingering dawn effects from the invisible sun or the inescapable, all-pervading whiteness of the snow. Spring is a swift green renaissance in the wake of the big thaw. And autumn flares in colours so spectacular the Finns have a special term for it: *ruska*.

You may also think of it as the land of the Lapps. They, however, prefer their own name for themselves: Sami (pronounced "Sah-mi"), a preference which is now respected, revered and very much protected. Today the Sami's territory extends across northern Scandinavia and into the northwest corner of Russia.

Society and spirit

The nomadism associated with the Sami people of Norway and Sweden has never been so widely practised among the predominantly Forest Sami of Finland's Lapland and, gradually, an economy based on hunting and fishing evolved into one dominated by reindeer husbandry as the wild herds once vigorously hunted were semi-domesticated. Early on, many Sami adopted the more settled life of the Finns, keeping a few cattle and tilling scraps of soil to grow

SAMI WORDS AND MUSIC

The religious missions that came to Lapland to convert the Sami not only brought the influence of God, they also brought education. However, the Sami already had a rich oral tradition that ensured a wealth of tales and legends as well as centuries of acquired wisdom passed from one generation to the next. There was also their simple brand of pictorial art. Very special to Sami culture – and surviving still – is the *yoik*, a kind of yodelling chant, each a unique improvised tribute to an event, a landscape, an emotion or a person. The *yoik* has recently begun to make interesting alliances with modern music forms. Mari Boine Persen, a Sami based in Norway, is famous for having brought the *yoik* to the masses in a series of genre-breaking albums.

Sami culture has always lacked early written sources, and the first books in Sami were exclusively of a religious nature. Later, with education, came grammar books and dictionaries and, finally, though not until well into the 20th century, the beginnings of a Sami literature. One Finnish Sami writer, Nils Aslak Välkeapää, was one of the most fervent spokespersons for Sami art and culture through his successful career as a poet, composer and painter. In 1991 he was awarded the Nordic Council prize for literature and he performed at the opening ceremony of the 1994 Winter Olympic Games in Lillehammer.

Finland's Sami today have their own publication, *Sápme-lias*, as well as theatre, and arts and crafts organisations.

oats and potato, the only viable crops in these latitudes. In reverse, many Finns have opted for the reindeer economy.

Integral to early Sami culture were the shamanist beliefs rooted in the power of nature. Everything, it was believed, living or inanimate, had a soul and the spiritual world was as real as the material one. The wise man (*noaide*) was skilled in crossing one world to the other, achieving a state of ecstasy with his magic drum and entering the spirit world.

Religious missions made every effort to discourage such goings-on. Shamanism survived well into the 19th century, but drum-burning and many other deterrents led to the old gods giving way to Christian worship. Today many of the brightest events on the Lapland calendar are associated with Church festivals – notably Lady Day and Easter: popular times for Sami weddings, lasso competitions, reindeer races, and get-togethers for dispersed families.

Into the 20th century

The rebuilding programme following the devastation of World War II marked the beginning of changes that have altered Lapland for ever. Since 1945, Lapland's population has soared to 205,000 (predominantly Finns), though in an area of nearly 100,000 sq km (38,600 sq miles) this is hardly overcrowded: the population density is just 2.2 persons per square kilometre.

The administrative capital of Rovaniemi has been virtually rebuilt and expanded to take in a satellite sprawl of light industry. A network of new and improved roads penetrates regions only accessible a few decades ago by foot or ski. Rivers, notably the Kemi, have been tamed for their hydroelectric power. And a trickle of visitors has grown into a steady stream, spawning a whole range of facilities. Perhaps most importantly, the introduction of snowmobiles and motorbikes into Sami culture has for ever altered Sami patterns of settlement and nomadism, as well as the day-to-day lives of families and individual herders.

Organisations dedicated to Sami interests go back to the turn of the 20th century, but their efforts were only officially coordinated in 1956, when the Nordic Sami Council was founded to "promote cooperation on Sami issues between

Finland, Norway and Sweden". In 1973 Finland's Sami population acquired a parliamentary assembly, elected by them from among themselves. It has no legislative mandate, but it does provide a forum for promoting Sami concerns. Paramount are their rights to territory and its traditional usage in northern Lapland – age-old rights which have been gradually eroded (though never legally removed).

One may regret the adulteration of a culture under pressure, but people outside Finland have already begun to see the enriching potential emerging from the melding of the Sami's ancient culture with innovative modern ways of life. ❑

A VERSATILE BEAST

The docile reindeer has always represented much more to the Sami than a meal on four legs, its skin contributing to bedding and winter clothing, antlers and bones raw materials for tools and utensils. It has also provided a major means of transport, sledge-hauling across the winter snows, only recently ousted by the noisy, motorised skidoo. Even now, the annual cycle of the reindeer – rutting, herding, separating, slaughtering, calving, marking – moulds the north Lapland calendar. The winter round-ups are among Europe's most colourful events, resembling scenes from a Wild West film transposed to an Arctic setting.

LEFT: reindeer round-up at Vuotso, Lapland.
RIGHT: a man wearing traditional Sami dress.

FROM FLYING FINNS TO FORMULA ONE

A strong physique and a determined nature have combined to make Finns a force to be reckoned with in the world of national and international sports

Later on in his life, when asked about the relationship between Finnish independence and the performance of Finnish athletes in the early part of the 20th century, the great Finnish runner Paavo Nurmi commented: "The higher the standard of living in a country, the weaker the results often are in the events which call for work and effort. I would like to warn this new generation: do not let the comfortable life make you lazy!"

Despite their prosperity, Finns have managed to perform remarkably well in sport and achieve international reputations since Nurmi. Football players such as Jari Litmanen, now back at Ajax via Barcelona and Liverpool, and Liverpool's ex-captain Sami Hyypiä, have been among Europe's best-known players. Dozens of Finns play ice hockey in America, and Janne Holmén, a marathon runner from the Åland Islands, won gold in the 2002 European Championships, reviving Finland's long-distance traditions.

Start them young

The Finnish sporting tradition is ingrained in every child from the moment he or she is put on skis at the age of two. In the centuries before motorised vehicles, Finns often invented athletic ways to get across their great distances and traverse their vast forests and lakes. The best known was the church boat race, a rowing competition between villagers to see who would arrive at church first.

Sport was associated with religion at other times of the year, too. At Easter, there were competitions in tug-of-war and high and long jumping, while Christmas was the time for shows of strength by weightlifters and plough-pullers. Finland has, by virtue of its landscape, always produced a healthy crop of cross-country skiers. Even now, cross-country skiing is as much a form of transport as it is an enjoyable winter pastime. Visit Finland and you will be both amazed and impressed by the number of skiers practising on roller skis throughout summer and windsurfers converted to ice surfers in the winter.

A snow tunnel in Vuokatti sports centre, not far from Kajaani, enables skiers to practise in a realistic environment while ordinary people enjoy the few hot summer days.

LEFT: the great long-distance runner Paavo Nurmi lights the Olympic flame at the 1952 Helsinki Games.
RIGHT: Finn Andre Myhrer in the Slalom World Cup.

Formula One racing

Finns won eight World Rally Championships between 1991 and 2002, with Tommi Mäkinen, Juha Kankkunen and Marcus Grönholm dominating the sport to an even greater degree than Hannu Mikkola, Ari Vatanen and Timo Salonen did in the 1980s. Formula One racing has seen continued success, with Mika Häkkinen crowned World Champion in 1998 and 1999, and his place in the McLaren team being taken by prodigious compatriot Kimi Räikkönen. Räikkönen has since excelled at the sport and, after switching to Ferrari in 2007, became the highest-paid driver in motor sport – with an esti-

mated salary of US$51 million per year; he also secured his first Formula One World Drivers' Championship, beating McLaren drivers Lewis Hamilton and Fernando Alonso by one point.

No one has satisfactorily explained why Finns should excel in this particular field, but the answers perhaps apply to all successful Finnish athletes: the fact that Finns come from a quiet northerly country that feels a need to make its mark on the world must have something to do with it. Another reason is, of course, the landscape: anyone who can orientate himself or herself in the Finnish wilderness already has a strong, built-in sense of navigation (which comes in use-

FINLAND IN THE OLYMPICS

Outstanding performance in sport is a point of national pride which dates at least as far back as the Stockholm Olympics of 1912 (the last to be held before World War I), when Finland was still part of Russia. During those games, the Finnish medal winners far outstripped the Russian winners, gaining 23 medals against the Russians' three, although officially Finland and Russia were competing under the same flag.

At the 1912 Games, the Finnish competitors dared to raise a Finnish flag at the medal ceremonies, the first sign that the yearning for Finnish independence was not to be taken lightly. Five years later, Finland had become an independent republic.

At the 2000 Olympics in Sydney, Finns took two golds – with Arsi Harju (shot put) and Thomas Johansson and Jyrki Järvi (49er-class sailing) being propelled into the national spotlight. The 2004 Athens Olympics were anticipated enthusiastically, but Finland received only two silver medals (from skeet shooting and wrestling) and was left out of medals in traditional strongholds such as the javelin. In Beijing in 2008, Satu Mäkelä-Nummela took home the gold in women's trap – Finland's first ever gold medal in shotgun in the Olympics. Finns also took home medals in rowing, air rifle and javelin at Beijing, though they were disappointed not to win a single gold in the 2006 Winter Games in Turin.

ful in the more circuitous rally routes) and may, so the theory goes, have an advantage over someone who comes from a less rugged country.

Take any group of rally drivers – men and women who drive their cars into a pulp through forest, desert and farm tracks – and among them you are likely to find a puzzlingly high number of Finns.

Finally, one must look beyond the physical features of the country and examine the Finnish

pursuit: independence itself. From the republic's very early days – in fact, even before Finnish independence – sport and freedom were inseparably intertwined.

Long-distance runners

As proof of his durability, Jalmari Kivenheimo was still running every day even after his 100th birthday in 1989 (he died five years later). His more famous running mate, Hannes Kolehmainen, won gold in the 1912 Olympics.

But the Finnish runner whose name has been famous for most of the 20th century was just under competition age in 1912: Paavo Nurmi

personality. There is one feature of the Finnish character which the Finns themselves call *sisu*, a quality so central to their being as to make a dictionary definition nearly impossible. Roughly speaking, the word conjures up an enigmatically tough, independent personality. Hand in hand with the toughness is a determined staying power, even under the most adverse conditions.

Sisu has played its role not only in sporting achievement but in Finland's most important

FAR LEFT: champion driver Mika Häkkinen.
LEFT: Finnish football fans. **ABOVE:** Finland's Hannes Kolehmainen crosses the finish line to win the 5000 metres in the 1912 Stockholm Olympic Games.

(1897–1973). A multiple world record-breaker and medal-winner (with four gold medals), Nurmi first competed in the 1920 Olympics. Variously known as the Flying Finn, the Phantom Finn and the Phenomenal Finn, he is still remembered for his extraordinary running style, speed and tough character.

Nurmi had running in his blood from an early age. Although his father, a religious man, did not approve of running, believing it to be a frivolous pastime, Nurmi exerted his independence and spent every spare moment running with boys in his neighbourhood. He ran in competitions at school, and also alone in the woods. It's been suggested that sports competition between Finnish-speaking Finns and

Swedish-speaking Finns was particularly keen in Turku, Nurmi's home town in southwest and heavily Swedish-speaking Finland (*see page 205*),

> Finland's vast network of lakes frozen into ice for much of the winter means that virtually all Finnish children grow up as comfortable on ice skates as in shoes.

which may have further fired his ambition. If indeed some of Nurmi's determination was spurred on by local ethnic competition, it is

which the nation excels. Ice hockey is also one of the most important team sports in Finland. Almost all males participate at school, and the elite are filtered through and chosen for the best teams. Many Finns play in the North American NHL and many foreigners play in Finnish teams as well.

Ice hockey is also highly commercialised: one of the leading teams, Jokerit (the Jokers, referring to a deck of cards rather than humour), is run like a large company. Teams in Helsinki, Tampere, Turku and Oulu are usually the best, and spectators can number well over 10,000 per game. The World Cup was held in Finland in

interesting to note that later, according to his biographer, "no ambassador could have been more effective than Nurmi" in attracting positive international attention and even investment to the fledgling Finnish republic while it struggled to build a cohesive identity.

Snow and ice

Not surprisingly, skiing is one of the top sports in Finland, and the sport most readily associated with this snow-covered nation. Along with its Scandinavian neighbours, Finland has produced champion cross-country and downhill skiiers, who benefit from an extended winter season in which to perfect their skills.

But skiing is not the only winter sport in

2003 and the Finns were hoping to take gold for the first time since they beat the Swedes in Sweden in 1995. However, after some dramatic events, Finland was defeated 5–6 in the quarterfinals – by the Swedes. In 2009, a huge upset saw the Jyväskylä team JYP, which hadn't won a pennant in decades, becoming national champions after winning the final series 4-0 against the Oulu's Kärpät.

Track and field

The game of *pesäpallo* is a Finnish version of American baseball, first developed by Tahko Pihkala. *Pesäpallo* soon became a "national" hobby, especially in rural Finland. The best teams now participate in the national Super

Pesis League, which is well organised and has become increasingly commercial.

Finns also consider athletics as one of the most "Finnish" of all sports. "The Flying Finn" was a common nickname given to Finnish middle- and long-distance runners in the previous century. In addition to Paavo Nurmi's legendary performances, there are now several male long-distance runners, including Janne Sven-Åke Holmén, Samuli Vasala and Jukka Keskisalo, to keep up Finnish hopes, and javelin-throwing is constantly well represented. The current javelin world champion, Tero Kristian Pitkämäki, is Finnish.

Sports fields are available for schoolchildren and individuals in every town and village. Local governments finance these facilities and the use of equipment is free. Local championships start from elementary school, and reach their peak in the national level at the annual Kaleva Games.

Although summer sports are not generally associated with Finland, the golf scene has boomed in the last decade. For such a large country, 128 golf clubs may not seem a great number nationwide, but the wealthy Greater Helsinki area has 12 courses alone. But while the summer golf season is relatively short, the smart Rovaniemi enthusiasts will even play golf on ice in winter.

In February 2003, Mikko Ilonen became the first Finn ever to shoot a best round on golf's European Tour. Tennis has also enjoyed a boom in Finland in recent years, reflecting the success of Jarkko Nieminen in climbing up the ATP world ranking.

Sport and scandals

Joy turned to national shame during the World Skiing Championships in Lahti in 2001, when many of the Finnish medallists in the cross-country disciplines, including stars such as Mika Myllylä and Harri Kirvesniemi, failed doping tests. Both the men's and women's teams were affected, and the national mood afterwards was unbelievably sombre. The fact that cross-country skiing plays such a central part in the national psyche, and that Finland is one of the world leaders in the battle against drug cheats, made the shame even greater. The

scandal reached all levels of society, and overshadowed the 1998–9 *pesäpallo* match-fixing fiasco, which saw players winning large sums from betting on pre-arranged results.

Yet sport continues to dominate even the top level of Finnish society: former presidents Kekkonen, Koivisto and Ahtisaari enjoyed cross-country skiing, volleyball and golf respectively, former prime minister Paavo Lipponen was an exceptional water polo player in his youth, and former rally champion Ari Vatanen has been a member of the European Parliament since 1999. Who said Finns don't take their sports seriously? ❏

LEFT: all-weather skiing practice tunnel.
RIGHT: a game of *pesäpallo*, similar to baseball and considered to be Finland's national sport.

FOOD AND DRINK

Traditional Finnish cuisine makes fine use of its native ingredients, such as fish and game, washed down by locally brewed beer or strong coffee

Finland is a land of forests and lakes with abundant possibilities for fine dining. Take the trees – Finns have finally found edible substances in each variety: birch gives Xylitol, a sweetener very kind to teeth; spruce spring shoots are used to make sweet jam, a delicacy served with desserts; pine is a good source of tar, an aromatic substance, not oil but extracted from pine in traditional tar-burning pits. The light tar has a soothing aroma, used in Finnish sweets and ice cream. Pine is also raw material for the Finnish-invented Benecol margarine-style spread that has been found to have cholesterol-lowering qualities.

Unusual varieties

Finnish food is as innovative as Xylitol or Benecol demonstrate – the years of agricultural conformity are over. Be it ostrich farms, strawberry wineries or herb producers, Finnish food is becoming more varied by the day – Finnish restaurants are reinventing the cuisine they serve

The changing seasons, endless daylight in summer, deep forests, thousands of lakes and unpolluted environment all help Finland to produce interesting culinary delights.

all across the country – especially in the capital – and rarities such as bear meat or unusual fungi can be found more regularly on menus. Herbs are pleasant surprises, and often the least

PRECEDING PAGES: crayfish are an integral part of a Finnish summer. **LEFT:** the best way to smoke salmon. **RIGHT:** preparing traditional Finnish pies.

likely choices yield the best sensations – try the tiny vendace (*muikku*) with garlic and cream, an unpretentious fish that has more taste than all tropical varieties combined.

This is a country that also produces "non-vegetables" – varieties that are too small to be "accepted" by EU directives, but that is often the whole point: the "new" potatoes (the first in the season) are tiny but full of aroma. Small strawberries, blueberries or handpicked mushrooms from the forests all taste better than their fertilised varieties produced in bulk in warmer countries.

Finnish food as we know it today has a short history. Traditionally Finnish food comprised largely of fat, and was always homemade. Ham-burgers, kebabs and pizzas can satisfy most of the fast-food requirements in modern Finland, but tourists should now have no trouble find-ing genuine Finnish delicacies.

Finnish fish

Take fish, for example. Finland has lakes, rivers and the sea, brimming with local species, and what isn't available locally can be readily imported from neighbouring countries – Nor-way, for example. Fish has always been an important diet for Finns, and it is part of a long culinary tradition. Smoked fish is the speciality,

fish, typical in Finnish restaurants, but lamprey is not a "true" fish at all, and is found only in the

Rapujuhla *(crayfish parties) are by invitation only, although all fine restaurants serve crayfish during July and August. Much of the red delicacy is imported, with each small creature costing several euros.*

rivers of western Finland. Charcoal-grilled and eaten whole, it's another fine experience of Finn-ish haute cuisine.

although it may also be grilled, glow-fired, steamed, or basted in the oven. Fried fish is rela-tively rare in Finnish restaurants.

Salmon soup is another subtle delicacy: only a pinch of salt is added to the liquid, but the main taste comes from the fish. Each way of cooking salmon in Finland gives a distinctive experience, but *graavi lohi* (raw salmon marinated for a day in salt and herbs) is delicious. *Graavi* is the Finn-ish version of *sushi* – but instead of rice and sea-weed, small potatoes and dill are used.

While Finnish salmon should not be missed, don't forget to try *siika* as well. This white fish has a more subtle taste, and is also best in the *graavi* variety, with potatoes and dill. *Silakka* (Baltic herring) and *muikku* (vendace) are small

Hunting nation

Much of Finland's tasty elk meat disappears into private deep-freezes during the hunting season, but semi-domesticated reindeer is more common. The Lapland speciality is *poronkäristys* (reindeer casserole), served with mashed pota-toes and cranberry (lingonberry). It's an excel-lent way to fill oneself up after a week-long trek in Lapland's wilderness *(see page 287)*. The best part of reindeer is fillet steak, usually worth its price, though a real delicacy is smoked reindeer heart, with a cedar aroma and a subtle taste. This latter dish you can find at Juuri in Hel-sinki (Korkeavuorenkatu 27).

The best restaurants in Finland will also serve rare game birds during the season. Wild duck is most common. Its hunting season only runs from late summer to autumn, and it is worth trying when available. In Helsinki, both Suomi Lautasella (Lönnrotinkatu 13) and Sea Horse (Kapteeninkatu 11) prepare a number of traditional Finnish game dishes.

Sausage (*makkara*) is also very popular in summer – best grilled with local mustard. Typically, Finnish sausage has more flour than meat, but quality varies. In Tampere, *mustamakkara* ("black sausage") contains spices, barley and blood in real gut. Blood may also be added to the Åland Islands' *svartbröd* ("black bread"), a distinctively sweet brown bread.

delicacy, consisting of vendace fish inside a baked rye bread – although it is an acquired taste to some. The northwest coast is renowned for salmon soup and *leipäjuusto*, a bread-like cheese, often eaten with yellow cloudberries (a sour berry that grows on marshlands).

Potato and barley

Potato is the staple food, available all year round, but some restaurants have introduced more traditional barley to replace rice and pasta (which are common in Finland too). Barley is softer, bigger and, some believe, tastier than rice, but sadly quite rare in restaurants. Barley,

Regional dishes

Regional differences are notable around Finland. Salted fish, pies and pastries are typical in Karelia (you should avoid the pre-packed Karelian pies at supermarkets, which bear no resemblance to their originals). Rye dough is filled with barley or potato and then turned inwards to create the distinctive Karelian pie, baked in the oven and eaten with mashed four-minute eggs and some butter.

The Lakeland provides plenty of fish, as one would expect, and *muikkukukko* is a typical Savo

LEFT: stall at the Baltic herring market (*silakkamarkkinat*) in Helsinki. **ABOVE:** a spread of traditional Finnish food.

WHERE TO FIND SPECIALITIES

Helsinki and other big towns are the best places to look for fresh or smoked fish in supermarkets or markets, as small towns rarely serve culinary delights even for locals – there simply isn't enough demand. An exception is a *smörgåsbord*, or *seisova pöytä* in Finnish, which can be outstandingly good or simply bad. Many theme restaurants, such as Karelian houses along the eastern border, serve an excellent variety of marinated and smoked fish, pickled herring or *graavi* salmon, salads and other vegetables. The larger hotels invariably prepare a great breakfast buffet, and there are also innovative Finnish versions of international buffets.

oats, rye and rice are all used for porridges, which are typical breakfast items in Finnish homes. Barley dishes can be found, for example, at Restaurant Aino in Helsinki (Pohjoisesplanadi 21), which serves old-style beef and barley-filled cabbage rolls with mashed potatoes and lingonberry jam. Although traditional edible beets such as swede or turnip are seldom considered "gourmet food" in Finland, try one that has been on low heat for a day – fully softened swede requires no spices. Finns, in fact, seldom use spices. Many raw, locally farmed ingredients have a naturally strong flavour that may simply be lured out by the right cooking technique.

Bread

Rye bread is unique to Finland – Russians and Swedes produce similar but use different recipes, and Finnish rye bread is usually less sweet than its counterparts. It is healthy bread, available as crispbread (rougher and again less sweet that the Swedish variety), soft and fresh or slightly stickier and harder (*jälkiuunileipä*). The latter variety keeps edible longer and is good with cheese and cold milk.

Food from the forest

One special element in Finnish cuisine is the abundance of ingredients that are available free

on the forested landscape, including a wide range of berries, fungi and herbs. No one owns these foods, and Finnish law allows free access to the forests. However, berry- and mushroom-picking is hard work and time-consuming, and there is always a small price tag attached, unless you do it yourself. Blueberries are readily available in July, the native sour cranberries (lingonberries) by September. Numerous varieties of mushrooms show up on restaurant menus by the autumn.

What to drink

The Finnish *ravintola* may be a restaurant, bar or pub, and most often people go there to drink. Beer is ubiquitous, and one of the "big five" is most usually served: Koff, Lapin Kulta, Karhu, Karjala or Olvi (this last is in fact the only major brewery still Finnish-owned). But there

> Typically, Finns partake of kahvi *(coffee)* and pulla *(wheat buns)* after their meals. Cakes are also abundant; cream cakes topped with strawberries are typical.

are many more, as microbreweries are popping up with more frequency across the country. The same goes for wineries, which for the time

Where to eat

Whether it's culinary delights, fast food, coffee or a pint of lager, you will find it: there is a restaurant or a simple kiosk on practically every corner. The kiosk is another Finnish institution, selling chocolate and groceries when other shops are closed.

Helsinki is the best place to savour Finnish delicacies. Havis (Unioninkatu 23) specialises in fish and seafood, whereas G.W. Sundmans (Eteläranta 16) offers modern Finnish cuisine. Sundmans was chosen by the professionals as the second-best restaurant in Finland (after Chez Dominique). And Helsinki's restaurants

being seem unique for Scandinavia; Finland gave up part of the restricting alcohol policy, and private wineries number at least 20. Strawberries, blackcurrants and redcurrants, among others, are used to produce a distinctive red wine – not exactly Burgundy, but it is a well-balanced berry drink with 12 percent strength. In the same way, local producers are experimenting by adding other berries to stronger alcohol. Try Kasakka (Meritullinkatu 13), a hearty Russian restaurant that prepares an excellent cranberry vodka cocktail.

FAR LEFT: traditional Finnish Christmas dinner. **LEFT:** Finnish sweet pastries. **ABOVE:** Havis in Helsinki, a classic seafood restaurant.

are innovating as well: Demo (Uudenmaankatu 11), Olo (Kasarmikatu 44) and Carma (Ludviginkatu 3) are three haute fusion places that prepare some excellent modern cuisine. However, Chez Dominique (Rikhardinkatu 4), with two Michelin stars, is hailed as one of the top 25 restaurants in the world.

Saaga (Bulevardi 34) is a truly Lappish experience, with a rich menu of Arctic specialities, including reindeer and bear. The other end is represented by Zetor (Kaivopiha), with a rural 1950s decor that includes an actual tractor and plenty of typically Finnish meals on the menu. The trendy Bali-Hai (Iso Roobertinkatu 35) prepares a menu of excellent burgers and salads – with a slight Finnish touch. ❏

IN DEFENCE OF GREENNESS

Despite the familiar images of Finland's lakes and forests,
the country is striving alongside the rest of the world
towards finding solutions to environmental problems

Finns have long looked to their country's natural environment for a sense of identity. The national anthem celebrates the country's summer landscape; its blue-and-white flag is said to represent the white snow of winter and the blue lakes of summer; and literature, fine art, design and architecture have all drawn on the environment for a Finnish idiom.

As the environmental campaigner Martti Arkko put it in 1990: "We depend on nature and the environment for everything. If we allow our forests and lakes to become polluted, our Finnishness will disappear too. The hearts of the Finnish people lie in the lakes and forests. They are our identity, our capital and riches."

The defence of Finland's lakes is high on the political agenda, looked on as a battle to preserve nationhood and to save the country's greatest assets, and, as a race, Finns really care. One of the arguments against joining NATO is a fear that American army bases will spoil the beauty of Lapland, and an erosion of the principle of *jokamiehenoikeus* – the right of anyone to roam at will, and pick berries, wild fruits or mushrooms in the Finnish countryside.

Enter the politicians

The environment erupted as a political issue in the 1980s, and in 1987, the Green League won four parliamentary seats (4 percent of the votes). In the 1991 general election, this figure rose to 10 seats (nearly 7 percent of the votes), and in 1995 and again in 1999 they joined the five-party "Rainbow Coalition" government. In the

1999 EU Parliament election, they won two seats. A "green" Finland was on the agenda. In 2002, however, the Greens resigned from government in protest at the decision to build a new nuclear power plant in their country and continued in opposition after the 2003 elections.

Public concern for the environment is nothing new in Finland. As in other Nordic countries, civic organisations have been committed to protecting the countryside for years. The Finnish State Environmental Administration *(Ympäristöhallinto)* is a state department overseeing nature reserves, protection of wild plants and animals, and even sustainable housing in urban and rural areas.

PRECEDING PAGES: a sunny summer meadow.
LEFT: Pyhähäkki National Park.
RIGHT: Heidi Hautala, Finnish Green MEP.

Alarming incidents

Since the early days of national independence, the young republic introduced legal protection for the forests and threatened species, and the Forestry Act of 1886, which was intended to curb wasteful uses of the forests, predated the republic by 30 years. Later laws prohibited the devastation of forests and defended threatened forest areas. Still, when the owners of the private Lake Koijärvi decided to drain it, those who protested were prosecuted for civil disobedience.

The Ministry of the Environment was set up in 1983, after which the government surveyed, theorised and fomulated policies and assess-

The biggest issue concerns emissions and a long-term solution for suitable non-polluting energy sources. In 2005, for the first time since

> *Finland is currently constructing its fifth nuclear reactor, Olkiluoto 3, which will be the most powerful ever built. It is meant to be operational by 2012.*

the early 1990s, Finland's carbon dioxide emissions were below the targets of the Kyoto Protocol. But in 2007, they rose again – an increase

ments. Their conclusions identified many problems and put forward suggestions for controls, concluding: "General environmental protection goals have been comparatively little considered in Finland, especially from a long-term perspective."

Finland's problems are effectively those shared by industrial nations all over the world: air and water pollution, energy conservation, the despoliation of the natural landscape, endangered species and waste management. Finland has generated more solid municipal waste per capita than any other European country, but recycling schemes in municipalities around the country have only recently been properly implemented.

of about 30 percent – making the country again one of the largest emitters per capita in the EU. The main argument in the energy debate has been over a fifth nuclear power plant. After a series of protests and legal hurdles, parliament finally accepted the controversial plan to construct a new power plant on an island off the coast of Rauma, which already has two nuclear reactors.

Apocalyptic as this may sound, one should remember that, in comparison with extremely polluted areas of Europe, Finland is a model of purity. Where the country does suffer – perhaps more acutely than others – is from the atmospheric and water pollution of its neighbours. Russia is the principal offender, but Poland and the area comprising the former GDR have also contributed to the pollution of the Baltic Sea.

Since the 1987 report, the government has acted on some of its suggestions. There has been more talk – conferences and summits on the state of the Baltic, on the Arctic and on acidification ("acid rain") – and Finland has put its clean-air and clean-water industrial technology at the disposal of Russia and Eastern Europe.

Forest threats

Driving through Finland, you might feel there is little cause for concern about its endless green forests and lakes, but the Finns nevertheless large proportion of the country's income. It is indeed unfortunate, then, that forestry, timber processes and mining often cause the most damage to the environment.

Planting, bog-draining for plantations, fertilising and felling all have severe consequences, changing natural habitats and the balance of Finland's watercourses, and exploiting the soil. Responsible forest management has been one government solution but, as the state owns only 27 percent of the forests, it has had to offer incentives for private owners to subscribe to the national plan. In 1998 a forestry certificate system was initiated and forestry has since undergone

brought a Wilderness Act into force in February 1991 to defend areas which remain in their natural state. The Act designated as wilderness a dozen-odd areas in Lapland, each roadless and some 150,000 hectares (380,000 acres) in size. Protected zones – no extensive felling or clearing allowed – now account for nearly one-third of Lapland's area.

Forest accounts for 78 percent of the total land area, some 230,000 sq km (90,000 sq miles). It is Finland's largest resource and a source for a major export: forestry and mining provide a

LEFT: the image of summer that every Finn wants to preserve. **ABOVE:** wind farms are sprouting up as Finland finds alternative forms of energy.

HUMAN THREATS

The green sanctuaries that are Finland's forests are also the country's recreational playgrounds. The right of common access permits free access to all forests and allows such activities as the picking of berries and mushrooms, and fishing in the lakes, which are national summer pastimes. Of course, there is a trade-off in that the greater use of the forests for recreational purposes also, inevitably, brings problems – litter and other forms of pollution, such as the noise and exhaust emissions of too many vehicles, not to mention selfish drivers who thoughtlessly plough their cars at high speeds through uncharted territory.

extensive reforms to conform to EU and global requirements for better management.

Finnish lakes are in a better state than they were some 20 years ago, but fertilising residues from farmland and industrial run-off still pose a substantial threat to the environment.

While exploitation of the forests has spoilt some habitats, the trees are threatened by air pollution or acidification. Like other countries, Finland has legal limits designed to control industrial emissions. Policing of these emissions and the question of whether the limits are pitched at an acceptable level are the nub of the issue. Environmentalists push for tighter controls; industry argues for economically "realistic" targets.

Making improvements

"Green" policies have been part of everyday Finnish life for some time. Recycling schemes and attempts to improve house insulation continue, and the government has repeated its commitment to public transport. The merits of nuclear power over fossil fuels are still hotly debated. New worries, such as the damage salt on winter roads may do to the watercourses or Baltic pollution, also spring up regularly.

Small-scale Finnish projects, which might well solve some of the Western world's ecological problems, hit the headlines from time to time. The pioneering idea of constructing a road out of bits of rubber car tyres was intended to have a dual "green" purpose. Firstly, it gave a use for tyres, which are notoriously difficult to dispose of. Secondly, the experiment was an attempt to find a durable road surface able to resist the strains of the fierce winter ice, which calls for frequent road maintenance and endless resurfacing. Other experiments have involved research into biodegradable plastic – especially carrier bags – as a by-product of Finland's oil refineries.

In the world of design, too, specialists have been applying their minds to ecological considerations, with the maximum use of recycled and recyclable materials, the minimum use of energy during the manufacturing process, and the longest possible life for the product.

From a visitor's point of view, Finland may already represent a supremely unspoilt environment. The most successful marketing lines of the Finnish Tourist Board have invoked the country's landscape, supported by photographs of summer in Finland's green forests, its blue waters and its leafy towns. Human habitation appears in its proper context, a tiny sprinkling of buildings in a vast forested terrain.

This is a true picture of Finland. In a country which is the seventh-largest in Europe, its more than 5 million inhabitants are just a blip on the map: highly influential but outnumbered several thousand to one by trees. For this reason, if for no other, it is in Finland's best interest to secure and protect its natural domain. ❑

RAISING REINDEER

Lapland offers its own share of difficulties and paradoxes. The cultural traditions and the livelihood of the Sami, or Lapps, can both contribute to environmental damage and are threatened by it. Reindeer herds are fundamental to the lives of the Sami, but the strong winds during the Chernobyl meltdown in 1986, for example, meant that hundreds of reindeer had to be killed. Yet, in that same summer, the Sami reindeer herds exceeded quotas (introduced to prevent overgrazing) by almost 100,000. Another contradictory factor is the predators – wolves, lynxes, eagles, wolverines – protected by the government but seen by the Sami as an increasing threat to their reindeer.

LEFT: Finland recycles a high percentage of its waste.
RIGHT: unpolluted water is essential.

LAPLAND: THE HOME OF SANTA CLAUS

Everyone knows that Santa Claus comes from Lapland, and he is now one of the biggest tourist attractions in Finland

Since the beginning of the tourist boom in the 1950s that played on the legend of Santa Claus and Lapland, well over half a million children from nearly every country in the world write to Finland's Santa every year. Sweden's Jultomten is the biggest competitor to the Finnish Santa, but more than 32,000 letters arrive daily in Lapland in the run-up to Christmas, most often from the United Kingdom, Poland and Japan, all expressing their Christmas wishes for that year.

Santa Claus and the Arctic Circle bring nearly half a million visitors annually, and there may be 30 nationalities represented on any day. Fortunately, Santa speaks several European languages – including the essential phrases in Chinese and Japanese.

Protecting a Legend

Sinikka Salokorpi is a Santa Claus expert in Finland and has written the official Santa "thesis" for the Ministry of Trade and Industries. It is literally an official publication and includes photos of authentic Santa Claus garments. Although written with a tongue-in-cheek attitude, the booklet defines more than the dress code. It tells us, among other things, that while there is harmony with foreign Santas, the "real" Santa lives in Finland. "It's a commercial battleground – Santa is big business," says Salokorpi.

ABOVE: a magical grotto in Santa Park, inside Syväsenvaara Hill at Rovaniemi, the unofficial capital of Finnish Lapland, where it's Christmas all year round.

BELOW: Santa Claus officially lives in a small hut at the Korvatunturi, a 480-metre (1,580-ft) hill way up north on the Finnish-Russian border.

LEFT: there are many working Santas in Finland – it's too much work for one man. A special training academy opened in 1998, and its graduates can be hired via the Santa Claus Office.

SANTA CLAUS THEME PARKS

The Arctic Circle was never an entity until German soldiers marked the spot during World War II, but no one took much notice before Eleanor Roosevelt paid a visit in 1950; a simple shack was built for the occasion. Mrs Roosevelt became an unofficial sponsor for the growing Santa Claus village, which now includes shops, a Santa Claus Office and, of course, Santa's post office.

Santa Park, opened in 1998, is one of the biggest Santa-related tourist traps in Finland. Just 2km (1 mile) from the main Arctic Circle area, the "park" found an ingenious location inside an artificial cave. You walk 200 metres/yards inside Syväsenvaara hill and find the Magic Sleigh Ride and other attractions. A digitally produced photo with Santa is available in two minutes – a popular souvenir – but other companies want their share: Christmas paraphernalia and Finnish design is also for sale. In 2009, the Finnish government sold off its shares in Santa Park as a means of raising funds to aid the fiscally ailing state.

BELOW: hundreds of thousands of letters are sent to Santa every year; even those addressed to "Santa, North Pole" or "Reindeer Street" still find their way to the Arctic Circle, Finland.

ᴠᴇ: although Santa Claus sometimes travels by opter these days, he prefers to use his reindeer, cially Rudolph, to help him get around.

ᴛ: the giving of presents at Christmas may stem the story of the Magi, or Three Wise Men, jing gifts to the infant Jesus, but Christmas gift-g was not widespread until the late 19th century, n many of the customs we now think of as tional were initiated.

PLACES

A detailed guide to the entire country,
with principal sites clearly cross-referenced
by number to the maps

Nobody has managed to count how many lakes and islands there are in Finland – enough, it seems, for every Finnish family to have an island or lake of its own, with space for visitors too. No wonder an ideal Finnish summer is based on a wooden cabin at the edge of lake or sea and a wooden steam sauna house nearby. With good fishing, swimming and a small boat tied up alongside, this is Finnish perfection.

There are seemingly endless expanses of untouched landscape, criss-crossed by endless straight roads running between tall trees. As the road extends ever further north, the rolling farmland of the south becomes dense tracts of forests and, gradually, the dark green gives way to the peat and tundra of Lapland, where the midnight sun gives the landscape a red glow in the late evening. This is the territory of reindeer, and the animals of the wilderness areas – bear, wolf and lynx – though their numbers have declined in recent years. In the northwest the ground rises to more than 1,000 metres (3,000ft) as it reaches towards the fells and fjords of coastal Norway. Along the west coast of the Gulf of Bothnia, the beaches and surprisingly warm waters are ripe for exploration.

For a country of 5 million, Finland has produced an astonishing number of architects, artists, sculptors and designers – and it shows. In Helsinki, in particular, almost every nook and cranny of the city reveals an intriguing detail: an elegantly carved facade on a block of flats, a statue, a curved window, or a tiny figurine full of humour that you nearly miss but laugh out loud when you spot it. Older cities such as Turku or Porvoo, where the Swedish influence was strongest, hold some of the oldest buildings in the country.

Even the seasons seem more distinct. In winter, it is time for snow and skiing and also for the great reindeer round-ups in Lapland. In summer, sea and lake are full of sails and swimmers. Between the two are the bursts of spring when everything turns green within a few days, and autumn, full of reds and browns as the leaves fall onto the city squares. Finland is emphatically a land for all seasons. ❑

PRECEDING PAGES: remote cabin, Lakeland; setting for the Olavinlinna Opera Festival, Savonlinna; skiing at Saariselkä in Lapland. **LEFT:** Lakeland dawn. **ABOVE:** a design school in the Arabianranta district; attention to detail, both in Helsinki.

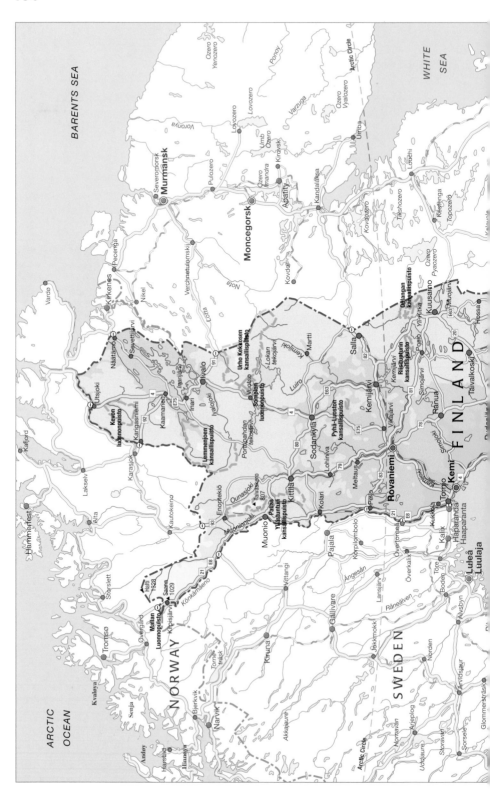

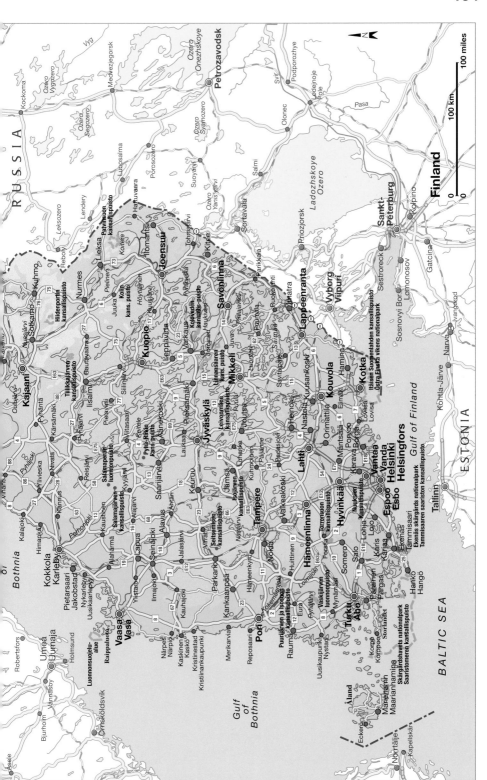

Finland

RUSSIA

ESTONIA

BALTIC SEA

Gulf of Finland

Gulf of Bothnia

Gulf of Bothnia

Petrozavodsk

Sankt-Peterburg

Vyborg
Vipuri

Kotka

Kouvola

Hamina

Lappeenranta

Helsinki
Helsingfors

Espoo
Esbo

Vantaa
Vanda

Lahti

Hyvinkää

Hämeenlinna

Tampere

Mikkeli

Savonlinna

Joensuu

Kuopio

Jyväskylä

Kajaani

Kuhmo

Nurmes

Lieksa

Iisalmi

Vaasa
Vasa

Pori

Turku
Åbo

Kokkola
Karleby

Pietarsaari
Jakobstad

Seinäjoki

Maarianhamina
Mariehamn

Åland

0   100 km
0   100 miles

N

HELSINKI

With its intriguing cultural mix of Russians and Scandinavians, the diminutive Finnish capital has a charm as fresh as the breeze that blows across its harbour from the Baltic Sea

PRECEDING PAGES: Helsinki at night. **LEFT:** produce on sale at the harbour. **BELOW:** festival, Esplanade Park.

Surrounding the city, the sea appears in Helsinki when you least expect it, its salty tongue lapping at the edges of metropolitan bridges and boulevards, pressing its way into residential areas, forming natural harbours and bays.

In summer, the sea glistens under a tireless sun, driving the light-starved locals wild with its rays and heat. Autumn arrives and, as darkness encroaches and the rains begin to fall, it begins its churn, spawning a world of wet and grey where the borders between sea and land are no longer distinct. Only during the long, cold winter does the sea finally rest, freezing into an endless expanse on which weekend promenaders can walk dogs or try out their cross-country skis.

Long referred to as the "Daughter of the Baltic", it is to the sea that Helsinki owes its fortunes, its climate and perhaps even the massive, undulating nature of its architecture. It is also to the Baltic that the city owes much of its relatively short but turbulent history.

Helsinki's history

Helsinki was founded in 1550 by King Gustav Vasa of Sweden-Finland to compete with Tallinn, just across the Gulf of Finland, then a port controlled by the Hanseatic League. A first fledgling settlement was erected on the mouth of the Vantaa River at the innermost point of the Helsinki Bay – a little northeast of where Helsinki stands today. In order to populate the town of Helsingfors ("Helsinge", the local parish, plus "fors", Swedish for "rapids"), Gustav Vasa simply ordered citizens from Porvoo, Ulvila and Rauma to move to the new town.

The new port proved, however, to be not only unpopular but a money-loser as well, once the shallow inner bay became shallower and impossible to navigate. It languished for nearly a century until a visiting governor general named Per Brahe recommended it be moved further south towards the open

The Koff Bar Tram (mid-May–Aug) follows a scenic route around the inner city and has two beer taps on board to help you relax. Stops include Kauppatori, Railway Square and the Opera House.

sea. In 1640 a second site was designated on the section of present-day Helsinki called Kruununhaka, and the citizens again moved. On this new site Helsinki finally began to grow, though it still wasn't much more than an outpost for fishermen and farmers. Then the Russian Empire stirred against Sweden, and the town's small fortunes began to go downhill. After battling against the Great Famine in 1696, the Northern War from 1710 to 1721 and the Great Plague in 1710, Helsinki was reduced to ashes and the population to some 150 hardy souls.

Helsinki prospers

Sweden's decision in 1746 to build Suomenlinna Fortress off the shore of Helsinki (*see page 179*), to protect what remained of its Finnish territory, is, ironically, what saved – and rejuvenated – the city. Construction of the fortress drew attention to the port and brought it its first taste of wealth. Merchants constructed a clutch of stone houses and, although streets were still unpaved, some semblance of European cultural life took root.

Russian money, and the talents of German architect Carl Ludwig Engel, were poured into the creation of administrative halls and a cathedral. As the city began to enjoy steady prosperity from around 1850, workers' homes were mostly replaced with stone ones. By 1900, Helsinki was a new place. In half a century it grew from a small port with some 20,000 inhabitants into a bona fide capital city. The population soared to 100,000, a railway was built, and gasworks, electricity and water mains all laid down. At the same time, Helsinki became the seat of the nationalist movement. Native architects, such as Eliel Saarinen, then Alvar Aalto, emerged; after independence in 1917, the more Finnish Functionalism replaced Jugendstil (the German version of Art Nouveau) as Helsinki's predominant architectural style.

Unfortunately, nothing could protect the city from the massive Russian air raids of 1944 – nor from fervent, and not always aesthetically pleasing, post-war reconstruction. But Helsinki's position on the sea resurfaced to help it regain and then increase its stature.

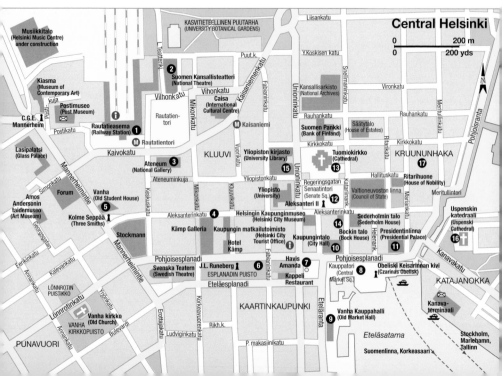

not only as a major port but eventually also as the important site for shipbuilding, international conferences and tourism it has become today.

The city today

Modern Helsinki is a tranquil but still growing city with some 580,000 inhabitants – many of whom are second-generation city dwellers. Gone are the marshes and wooden houses, but the faces of the fishermen who sell their catch straight from the docks are reminders that this capital's urbanisation is relatively recent. Helsinki isn't a frivolous city but the Finns have let their innate artistry flavour their capital. Statues stand on every other corner, and even the most functional of buildings are notable monuments to Finland's architectural history.

Consider the **Railway Station ❶** (Rautatieasema). A busy place that connects Helsinki with numerous commuter cities as well as the rest of Finland, it also contains both a metro station stop and an underground shopping complex. Recently renovated, the station is a strikingly stylish, round-edged structure in pinkish granite with green trim, a black roof and a 48-metre (160ft) green clocktower.

Designed by Eliel Saarinen in 1905 but not completed until 1919, it links two of Helsinki's most prevalent styles: National Romanticism and Functionalism *(see page 86)*. It also incorporates work by several other well-known Finns. Thanks to Emil Wikström, pairs of solemn-faced, muscular giants hold translucent lanterns on either side of the station's impressive front doors. A large painting by Eero Järnefelt looks over the Eliel Restaurant inside.

The railway station has a more metropolitan focus compared to the somewhat rustic harbour. It is a good reference point for a city tour; most places of interest to visitors are within walking distance of here.

Exploring the city

The first thing to do before beginning a tour of Helsinki, however, is to find your directional bearings. These are not immediately obvious because much of central Helsinki lies on a peninsula, jutting southward into the

All Helsinki road signs are shown in both Finnish and Swedish.

BELOW: Wikström's massive figures adorning Helsinki Railway Station.

BELOW: trams make it easy to get around.

Baltic. Being by the sea, therefore, doesn't automatically mean you are in the south of the city. In fact, the peninsula has only a brief southern shore but extended longitudinal coasts on both its eastern and western sides.

Don't rely on geographical names either, which can be deceiving, particularly if they belong to the time not so long ago when the city was much smaller. The "South" Harbour actually lies on the peninsula's eastern side. It is, however, south of Kruununhaka – the old city centre. Keep in mind that the railway station is effectively right in the middle of the peninsula; the tiny *Keskusta*, or centre, runs east–west below it; and the other neighbourhoods of central Helsinki radiate around them.

More confusing, though, is a visitor's initial glance at the city. Helsinki doesn't follow any of the rules of European capitals. It isn't quaint; it isn't regal; it isn't even terribly old. Nearly every wooden structure that predated 1808 was burnt to the ground, and little more than a century ago, there were still animals wandering the streets.

Step out of the railway station and you'll be greeted by two monolithic commercial complexes side by side: one "modern" and bedecked with neon signs, a second known for the lengthy tubular balcony winding about its facade. Don't let this put you off: Helsinki is an immensely compelling place for urban exploration, in a quintessentially Finnish way: reserved and modest, enigmatic and stylish.

The **National Theatre** ❷ (Suomen Kansallisteatteri; tel: 09-173 311), to the immediate east of the station and at the northern head of the cobbled railway square, is visually striking. This small castle in white granite with green trim and a red roof was conceived in National Romantic style. Productions are in Finnish but the pensive statue of Aleksis Kivi, Finland's national writer, in front of it, transcends any linguistic barriers.

Directly across the square from the theatre is the **Ateneum** ❸ (tel: 09-173 361; Tue and Fri 10am–6pm, Wed–Thur 10am–8pm, Sat–Sun 11am–5pm; charge). Built in 1887, the Ateneum's gilt yellow-and-white facade might

em reminiscent of St Petersburg but is the site of Finland's National Gallery of Art, one of the first manifestations of Finland's struggle for independence. The museum's collection of Finnish paintings, sculpture and graphic art covers the years 1750 to 1960 and includes works by such famous Finns as Akseli Gallén-Kallela and Albert Edelfelt.

The Ateneum lies on the east side of Makkaratalo. Wedged in between Kaivopiha and the north–south-running **Mannerheimintie** (Helsinki's main thoroughfare and the longest street in Finland) is the handsome though slightly faded Seurahuone Hotel. Inside, the luscious red-velveted, high-ceilinged Bar Socis is a perennial favourite with locals and resident foreigners, especially late at night.

hops and students

ehind these buildings stretch three locks containing one of Helsinki's most important shopping districts. **leksanterinkatu ❹** (better known as leksi), running parallel to the railway ation, is the main thread of this area,

but intersecting streets also contain shops. An elegant shopping centre, **Kämp Galleria** – with its specialised shops, boutiques, cafés and restaurants – is also on Aleksi between Mikonkatu and Kluuvikatu. On the same block sits the legendary five-star Hotel Kämp, originally opened in 1887 and Helsinki's first luxury hotel. It has witnessed important political events, while great Finnish artists such as Jean Sibelius, Eino Leino and Akseli Gallén-Kallela were regular visitors.

Aleksi leads up to Mannerheimintie and **Old Student House ❺** (Vanha). Built in 1870, Vanha's own stairs are a favourite meeting place for pretty young things in leather jackets on a night out, and its interior now houses a performance hall, café-bar and exhibition quarter. Numerous student organisations are based in the New Student House, on the other side of the Kaivopiha steps.

Vanha lies on the intersection of Aleksi and Mannerheimintie, and a trio of naked men with fine pectorals – the statue of the *Three Smiths*, or *Kolme Seppää* – dominate the triangular square

Finland's National Gallery of Art is housed in the 19th-century Ateneum.

BELOW: rye bread on sale at the Old Market Hall (Kauppahalli).

The stylish Kappeli restaurant by Esplanade Park.

beneath it. As soon as the snow melts in spring, musicians use this square to serenade the passing crowds, ice-cream stands open for business and even some café tables appear.

Finland's largest department store, **Stockmann**, lies on the other side of Three Smiths' Square from Vanha. Beside it, on Keskuskatu, is Scandinavia's largest bookshop, Akateeminen Kirjakauppa *(see page 319)*. Upstairs is a stylish café designed by Alvar Aalto.

Esplanade Park

The bookshop looks onto another Helsinki landmark, **Esplanade Park ➏** (Esplanadin puisto). Planned by Ehrenström (who was also responsible for the 19th-century city plan), it was first laid out in 1831 and runs east–west between Mannerheimintie and the South Harbour.

The **Swedish Theatre** (Svenska Teatern), an elegant semicircular stone building dating from 1866, commands Esplanade Park's western head on Mannerheimintie. Back to back with it and facing into the long and narrow park is a trendy restaurant called Teatteri. Its

BELOW:
Esplanade Park.

terrace is always filled with relaxed beer drinkers in warm weather, while the Cafe Kafka, inside the theatre, is a great place to take in some of the theatregoing atmosphere come evening.

Places to meet

An old-fashioned promenade stretches from here across the length of the park between well-sculpted patches of lawn, past the central statue of J.L. Runeberg, Finland's national poet, to the Kappeli Restaurant at its eastern end. This park is still a popular meeting place and is the scene of the Christmas Fair and the Night of the Arts in August. On May Day Eve it is given over to widespread lunacy, gallivanting and inebriation.

Kappeli is also an important spot for a rendezvous, and the tall, lacy windows and a whimsical roof give it a Chekhovian, gazebo-like feel – the older parts of the café date from 1867. The summer terrace allows patrons to enjoy simultaneously fresh air, drink and musical performances (June–Sept) from the bandstand opposite.

Flanking the bandstand are two pretty little "ponds" graced by statues

f cavorting fish boys and water nymphs. But they cannot compete with the **Havis Amanda fountain ❼** in the small square that separates the eastern end of the park from the South Harbour amid a constant swirl of traffic and trams. The sensuous bronze Amanda created quite a stir when first erected in 1908. Surrounded by four sea lions spouting water, she represents the city of Helsinki rising from the sea, innocent and naked. On May Day Eve, at least, she gets something to wear – a white student cap – while a champagne-happy chaos of clustering human cap-bearers cheer. This square is also the site of an outdoor produce, handicrafts and flower market (Mon–Fri 6.30am–2pm, Sat 6.30am–4pm, also Sun 10am–4pm mid-May–Sept).

Venerable buildings and tourist office

Two boulevards stretch east–west alongside either side of the park. Nowadays, the fine 19th-century stone buildings along Pohjoisesplanadi mostly house design shops like Marimekko and Aarikka, the latter featuring, among other things, some distinctive wooden jewellery. No. 19 is an exception. The extremely modern and helpful **Helsinki City Tourist Office** (tel: 09-3101 3300; www.visithelsinki.fi) occupies its first floor, offering extensive selections of maps and brochures. The Helsinki Expert Tour Shop here sells tickets for sightseeing tours and public transport.

Still more venerable houses line the Southern Esplanade, most of which function in some type of official or commercial capacity. The oldest is Engel's Empire-style former Council of State, dating from 1824. During the period of Russian rule, it was the palace of the governor general.

Going to market

The **Central Market Square ❽** (Kauppatori), across from Havis Amanda on the South Harbour, exudes a much earthier type of appeal. A busy market makes its home here year-round (Mon–Fri 6.30am–6pm, Sat until 4pm, Sun during the summer only until 4pm). Going to market is still an important part of the daily routine in Helsinki, partly because the shift to urban life is

TIP

Karaoke Taxi
If singing karaoke while zooming round town sounds like your idea of a good time, you'll love this roving karaoke van that drives throughout Helsinki – and beyond if you wish. Prices start at around €85 per hour. (tel: 040-500 6070; www.karaoketaxi.fi).

BELOW:
a classic example of Art Nouveau (Jugend) style in Katajanokka.

Art Nouveau

At first sight they are just city buildings, but the elements are unique: visually striking windows, heavy ornamentation, grey granite, natural colours and castle-like features. Some of the most famous tourist attractions in Helsinki are Art Nouveau – the National Museum, or the Hvitträsk House in Kirkkonummi. But Art Nouveau, or Jugend as it is called in Finland, is far more common in Helsinki than first seems to be the case.

Art Nouveau is also called National Romanticism. Its roots go back to the great epic *Kalevala*, which inspired the composer Sibelius and the artist Gallén-Kallela. Architects Gesellius, Saarinen and Lindgren soon followed suit, going back to the roots of Karelianism, forests, bedrock – the key elements of Finnishness.

One of the best areas to look for their designs is Katajanokka, a few blocks east of Senate Square. Eira is another area – see Lars Sonck's hospital at Laivurinkatu 27. Hotel Linna (Lönnrotinkatu 29) by Lindahl and Thomé is typically Art Nouveau with a granite facade, as is their Otava House (Uudenmaankatu 10), Pohjola House at Aleksanterinkatu 44 (by Gesellius et al) or the Tarjanne's National Theatre. Even Saarinen's railway station has hints of Art Nouveau. Arrive in good time before your train leaves and take a look around.

Fresh, garden-grown vegetables are a good buy at Helsinki's Central Market.

a comparatively recent experience for many formerly agrarian residents.

Peninsular Helsinki has no fewer than four open-air markets. Of these, the Central Market is both the one most aimed at visitors and the most expensive, but locals on lunchbreaks from nearby shops and offices and housewives from the affluent southern suburbs still favour it. A multitude of ruddy-faced merchants gather to serve them and, after the ice melts, boat owners also get involved, tying their vessels to the end of the harbour and selling fish and root and other vegetables straight from their prows.

The north part of the market square is reserved for Finland's delicious fresh produce. Offerings very much follow the seasons and, in summer, become irresistible: sweet baby peas and mounds of deeply flavoured berries. No wonder that, by July, every Helsinki dweller can be seen clutching a small paper bag filled with something juicy and colourful. The coffee tent attracts locals and tourists; even presidents have been known to pop out from the nearby palace for a quick snack.

BELOW: restaurant in Kauppahalli, the Old Market Hall.
BELOW RIGHT: traditional Finnish dolls are popular souvenirs.

Handicraft stalls

Further down, around the bellicos **Obeliski Keisarinnan kivi** – whos imperial, doubled-headed golden eag was ripped off during the Russian Re olution and not restored until 1972 the market veers away from food. Som of these stands proffer interesting good and handicrafts, but if you are lookin for authenticity, be aware that mo: Finns stopped wearing fur hats quite while ago. Women wearing high hee' might also want to bear in mind tha the spaces between the cobbleston(are particularly treacherous here.

The water in this part of South Ha bour is overrun by gulls, geese and pa senger ferries and not the cleanest o bays, but don't let that stop you fror sitting with the locals on its storie docks in the sun, and enjoying a pu net of Finland's fabulous strawberrie

Old Market Hall

However, if it is cold or raining, yo might prefer to duck into the yellov and-red-brick **Old Market Hall** ((Vanha Kauppahalli; Mon–Fri 8am 6pm, Sat 8am–4pm). Having traded fc

ore than 100 years, the Old Market [H]all is not only Helsinki's most cen-ally located *kauppahalli* but its old-st. It knows its advantage. The terior is polished to the gills, and e price of even simple *piirakka* can e high. As well as reindeer cold-cuts d rounds of Oltermanni cheese, you n buy ready-made snacks from an xcellent Russian-style kebab stand or xcellent pastry breakfasts at the small utdoor market café.

ivic triumphs

he Central Market sprawls before me of Helsinki's most important dministrative buildings. An austere w lies directly across at the end of ohjoisesplanadi: the long, blue City [H]all, designed by Engel in 1833, with a innish flag flying above it; the sensi-le brown Swedish Embassy, impor-ntly placed, and with a Swedish flag; e Supreme Court, dating from 1883; d the Presidential Palace.

The **City Hall** ⑩ (Kaupungintalo; osed to the public) started out with a ifferent purpose. Until 1833 it was me to the Seurahuone Hotel (now

across from the railway station). Its first opening was celebrated by a masquer-ade ball, so that women could attend – although they had to leave by 4.30am. It is now an elegant venue used for offi-cial functions.

The **Presidential Palace** ⑪ (Presi-dentinlinna) was designed in 1818 as a private home and turned into a tsarist palace by Engel in 1843. The Finnish president no longer lives here, but the new official residence, Mäntyniemi, not far from Seurasaari, is occasionally open for visitors.

Helsinki's piazza

Helsinki's third major landmark, **Sen-ate Square** ⑫ (Senaatintori), stands one block north of here, back along Aleksi. There is something fateful about Senate Square. As early as the 17th century, the same spot housed a town hall, church and central square. It was flattened by the following century's continuous bat-tles, but the merchants made rich by Suomenlinna soon rebuilt it, erecting the city's first stone buildings about its southern perimeter. The 1808 fire destroyed everything wooden, but

Helsinki Cathedral dominates Senate Square.

BELOW: inventive ways with salmon.

New Finnish Cuisine

Any gastronomy snobs who think Finnish cuisine is bland, boring and inferior just haven't eaten in the right places. Over the past two decades the idea of what comprises typical Finnish food has been changing radically. A number of local chefs have become outspoken advocates of the use of organic local products in Finnish cuisine and have jumped on a cam-paign to revise the definition of Finnish – and Nordic – food.

While the buzzword in many restaurants across Europe these days is still "fusion" – applying continental techniques to native ingredients to reinterpret traditional dishes – the cutting edge of Finnish cuisine is more a case of back to basics. Many chefs have become avowed champions of the Slow Food movement, which seeks to preserve local and regional products and cuisine, and stresses the importance of food traditions passed down through generations.

Unlike countries such as France and Italy, the Nordic nations never maintained a strong bourgeoisie, whose affluence and leisure time allowed for the development of rich culinary tradi-tions. Rather, Finland's austere gastronomic culture developed in the 18th and 19th centuries as a result of the country's

isolated rural economy and its unforgiving climate. Animals were only put out to pasture during short summers, while long winters meant that harvest stores had to last for six or more months. Finns depended on dried, smoked and pickled meats and fish dishes that would keep for several seasons.

Naturally, Helsinki is the best city in the country to sample some of the new directions in Finnish food; if your budget allows, try Chez Dominique, which has two Michelin stars. See pages 310–14 for other recommendations on the best places to eat, and pages 127–31 for more on food and drink.

Statue of Tsar Alexander, standing proud on Senate Square.

BELOW: the mighty Helsinki Cathedral.

immediately afterwards Russia commissioned architect C.L. Engel to rebuild the square as the municipal centre of their new city plan for Helsinki. Eventually, so many important institutions made their home here that Senate Square became a national centre for the country – the equivalent of Russia's Red Square or Beijing's Tiananmen.

Encompassing some 7,000 sq metres (75,350 sq ft), this impressive square is covered by no fewer than 400,000 grey and red cobblestones of Finnish granite. Nowadays, the Senate Square functions principally as a byway. The main building of Helsinki University, which occupies the square's entire western border, has a new entrance at the back that lures student activity away. The current Council of State, directly opposite, receives few visits from the average citizen. The former town hall, on the south side, is used for entertaining official guests, and the flux of boutiques around it cater mostly for visitors.

But the city remembers. Senaatintori becomes the centre of activity on important occasions such as Independence Day in December, when the wind-

swept square is a sea of candles held b[y] students who march here from Hie[ta]aniemi Cemetery in the midwinte[r] dark. Locals gather again one mont[h] later to listen to the mayor's tradition[al] New Year's Eve speech and watch fir[e]works, and again for May Day.

A self-important statue of Tsar Alex[-]ander II, erected in 1894, stands in th[e] centre of all this. At his feet, four add[i]tional figures tell the square's story[:] *Lex*, or law (facing the government pa[l]ace); *Lux*, or light (facing the sun[);] *Labor* (facing the university); and *Pa[x]* or peace (facing the cathedral).

Helsinki Cathedral  (Tuomi[o]kirkko; June–Aug daily 9am–midnigh[t] Sept–May Mon–Sat 9am–6pm, Su[n] noon–6pm, subject to services), up [a] bank of steep steps on the north side, [is] a point of pride for Finns, and the exte[ri]or – with its five green cupolas, whit[e] Corinthian columns and sprinkling [of] important figurines posing on its roo[f] – is decidedly impressive. The interio[r], in contrast, is severe. Apart from th[e] gilded altarpiece and organ, only statu[es] of Luther, Mikael Agricola and Melanc[h]thon disturb its white symmetry.

Engel's triumph

A walk around Senate Square can also reveal a lot about Helsinki's history. The city's oldest stone building, dating from 1757, is the small blue-grey Sederholm House on the corner of Aleksi and Katariinankatu. Across the street is the **Bock House** ⑭ (Bockin talo; closed to the public), also 18th-century, which became the meeting place for Helsinki's City Council in 1818, as a plaque by its door proclaims. It also served briefly as the governor general's residence after Engel had it embellished with Ionic pillars and a third floor. Around the corner and towards Unioninkatu is Sofiankatu, a street museum with pavements and street furniture from the late 18th century to the 1930s. Situated in Sofiankatu is the main building of the **Helsinki City Museum** (Helsingin kaupunginmuseo; tel: 09-3103 6630; Mon–Fri 9am–5pm, Thur until 7pm, Sat–Sun 11am–5pm; charge), which presents a solid overview of the city's history, covering three periods: the Swedish era, the Russian era and the era of Finnish independence.

The rest of the square is pure Engel, making it not only a beautiful but an unusually consistent example of neo-classical design. In 1832, the oldest part of the main building of Helsinki University (it was extended later to cover the entire block) was completed under the architect, on the western side of the square. Ten years earlier, he had designed the Council of State, along the entire eastern side of the square. The Finnish government still has its seat here. Engel drew the plan for the cathedral as well, although he died 12 years before its completion in 1852.

Across Unioninkatu, the **University Library** ⑮ (Yliopiston kirjasto; Mon–Fri 9am–8pm, Sat 9am–4pm, closed Sat in July) is decidely ornate. Not only do white Corinthian columns line every inch of its yellow facade, but inside the splendour continues. In the central room, more columns (now marble with gold tips) support a dark-wood second tier, beneath a painted cupola ceiling. Yet this is still a working library, and visitors are expected to leave their coats at the door, sign in and, above all, respect the quiet and no

Helsinki has plenty of bars and a young population happy to fill them.

BELOW: facade of the University of Helsinki Library.

The ornate interior of Uspenski Cathedral.

BELOW: sailing ship in the harbour at Katajanokka.

entry signs. But don't let this discourage you from enjoying the public parts of this most beautiful of Engel's works, dating from 1844.

Katajanokka

After exploring Helsinki's *Keskusta* (centre), venture into one of the surrounding districts, each of which has its own very particular character, though borders are not always clearly defined.

One of the most attractive is **Katajanokka**, which lies on a small promontory sticking out into the sea a few blocks east from Senate Square. Katajanokka is connected to the centre by two short bridges where locals like to cast their fishing rods. A restaurant complex opened a few years ago, injecting new life into this area. After a snowstorm or on a brilliant spring day, its elegant streets are pure serenity. Unfortunately, the first thing you see crossing the Kanavakatu Bridge on to Katajanokka is one of Alvar Aalto's least successful efforts: the dirty white marble Enso Gutzeit Office Building (the "sugar cube"), dated 1962. Fortunately, Katajanokka has better sights to offer.

Russian style

The **Uspenski Cathedral** ⓰ (Uspen skin katedraali; Mon–Fri 9.30–4pm Sat 9.30am–2pm, Sun noon–3pm closed Mon Oct–Apr), across the stree at the top of a sudden grassy knoll gives supreme proof of this. Russian Orthodox, built in 1868, dedicated t the Virgin Mary and undeniably glam orous, Uspenski makes a striking excep tion to Helsinki's general architectura style. Its red-brick conglomeration o cross-tipped spires and onion-shape domes has undoubtedly helped con vince many filmmakers to use Helsink as a surrogate Moscow (for example, i *Reds* and *Gorky Park*). The cathedral interior is also both impressive an atmospheric, with a glittering iconosta sis. Services in Old Church Slavoni are held at least twice weekly.

Appropriately enough, a Russian re taurant called the Bellevue sits at th base of the cathedral, across from Kat janokka Park. The Bellevue, howeve has a slightly unorthodox political hi tory. The restaurant was founded th year Finland declared independenc from Russia (1917). One of its golde

walls also displays a thank-you note received in 1990 from America's former First Lady, Barbara Bush.

The Russian motif is echoed elsewhere on Katajanokka, and flirtatious basilic motifs appear over many doorways. Red brick also gets more use, particularly in the recently built residences on the tip of the promontory. But central Luotsikatu is one street where Jugendian (Art Nouveau) style rules. Many of the buildings on this and nearby streets were designed by the architectural team of Gesellius, Lindgren and Saarinen at the turn of the 20th century and abound with little pleasures. Don't miss the charming griffin doorway at No. 5.

Turning north from Luotsikatu on to Vyökatu takes you to the northern waterfront. A narrow flight of stone steps leads down to an ageing gateway, which until 1968 blocked the way to the **Naval Barracks** (Merikasarmi). These long, yellow buildings have since been restored and now house the Finnish Foreign Ministry. Some have been reconstructed but follow Engel's original design. You can stroll along the avenues that run between them.

The southern side of Katajanokka is where the huge Viking Line ships come in from Stockholm, disembarking crowds of passengers. Conversions have already been completed on the block of old warehouses at Pikku Satamakatu, beside the Viking Line Terminal, and the so-called Wanha Satama now entertains a clutch of eating spots, exhibition halls and stores. Two more warehouses nearby have also been earmarked for renovation but the Customs and Bonded Warehouse, however, should not change. Even if you don't have any business to attend to here, it's worth passing by to view its inventive Jugendian style, as designed by Gustaf Nyström in 1900.

The Old City

Following Kanavakatu back west will return you to Helsinki's oldest district, **Kruununhaka** **⑰**, whose name means

"the Crown's Paddock"; not so many centuries ago it was primarily a home for cows. Senate Square is at the lower end of this area, which is now favoured by the well-heeled and offers a large collection of antique furniture, book and clothing shops and art galleries.

Central Helsinki's second-oldest building lies in the southeastern corner of this district, at the juncture of Aleksanterinkatu and Meritullintori. The modest squat structure was erected in 1765 as a customs warehouse, but now houses everyday offices. Other venerable leftovers of an earlier age hover nearby, such as the deep red Lord Mayor's Residence at No. 12 Aleksanterinkatu (next to Helsinki's Theatre Museum) with its gorgeous blown-glass windowpanes, and the mid-19th-century, neo-Gothic Ritarihuone ("House of Nobility") situated one block north on Hallituskatu.

A few particularly nice pedestrian streets crown the crest of hilly Kruununhaka. Solid stone buildings cut into exposed rock cliffs, insulating the end of the district from the Siltavuori Strait flowing directly below.

Striking architecture in Katajanokka.

BELOW: bookworm's heaven in the town centre.

Pukkisaaret

Seurasaarentie

Seurasaarensalmi

Paciuksenkatu

MEILAHDEN PUISTO

Messeniuksenk.

Nordenskiöldinkatu

Mannerheimintie

Olympia-stadion

Stenbäckenkatu

Tavaststjernank.

Töölöntori

Linnankoskenkatu

M. Lybeckink.

Topeliuksenkatu

Humalistonkatu

Eino Leinon k.

Helsinginkatu

Rajasaarent.

Ruusulankatu

Humallahti

Ulkomuseo
★ (Open-Air Museum)

Rajasaari

SIBELIUKSEN
PUISTO

Sibeliuksenk.

Kivelänk.

Mannerheimintie

Töölönkatu

39

Seurasaari

Sibeliusmonumentti

Mechelininkatu

Kesäk.

Vaisaarenkatu

TAKA-TÖÖLÖ

25
Suom
Kans
(Finnis
Opera

Taivalluoto

Pohj. Hesperiankatu

Pohj. Hesperiankatu

Apollonk atu

Finla
(Finla

Kansallismu
(National Muse

Mustasaari

Seurasaarenselkä

Eläinen. Hesperiankatu

Caloniuk.

Museokatu

Oksasenkatu

Runeberginkatu

Tunturin.

27

Haka
Edusk
(

Porsas

Hiekkarannantie

Hietaniemenk.

Krematorion.tie

Sammonk.

Temppelik.

30 ✝
Temppelinaukion
kirkko

29
Luonnontieteellinen museo
(Natural History Museum)

Ourit

Pieni-Porsas

HIETANIEMEN
HAUTAUSMAA

Hietaniemenk atu

Hietaniemenkatu

Lappsuork.

Tennispalatsi
(Tennis Palace)

Fredrikink

Lapinlahti

Pohj. Rautatiekatu

Malminkatu

M
Kampp

Länsiväylä

Lapinlahdentie

Töölönl.

Lapinlahdenk.

Lastenk k

Länsiväylä

Länsiväylä

SALMISAARI

Lapinlahdentie

Ruoholahdenk.

Abrahamink.

Pohjoiskaari

Norsvängen

Salmisaarenranta

Taipalenkatu

Porkkalankatu

Kortenk.

Aleksanterin tea
(Aleksander Theat

Klaaräntie

Itämerenkatu

Ruoholahti M

Santakatu

Hietalahdenranta

Hietalahdentori
(Hietalahti Market) 33

Lauttasaarentie

LAUTTASAARI

Tallbergin.katu

Kellosaarenkatu

RUOHOLAHTI

Selkämeren katu

Sinebrych
Taidem

Kauppaneuvoksentie

Tammasaarenlaituri

Tammasaarenranta

Jaalaranta

Hietalahti

PUN

Pajalahdentie

Lauttasaarensalmi

Messityönkatu

Lavapojankatu

Tallbergin puistotie

Haahkatie

Merikylläntie

Lohiapajanlahti

Länsisatamankatu

Mattaajankuja

Lahminen vaihdekuja

Italainen raidekuja

Tarmonk.

Munkk
Herne

Perttulantie

Heikkiläntie

Kiviaidank.

Lahminen vaihdekuja

Makakakuja

Helsinginlahdenkatu

Hyväkenpoytäkuja

Wavulinint.

Vattuniemenkuja

Matalasalmenk

VATTUNIEMI

Melkonkatu

Nahkahoususntie

Vattuniemenkuja

Venermäkijalärie

Melkonkatu

Italahdenkatu

Vattuniemenkuja

LÄNSISATAMA

Poseidoninkuja

Kellosaarenkuja

Länsi-
terminaali

MUNKKISAARI

ULKOILUPUISTO
FRILUFTSPARK

Pihlajasaari

Tallinn

Pihlajasaari

Helsinki

0 — 500 m
0 — 500 yds

Väenasuntomuseo
(Museum of Worker Housing)

Aleksis Kiven katu

Porvoonk.
Sturenkatu
Fleminginkatu
Teollisuuskatu
Hämeentie
Lautatarhankatu
Työpajakatu
Varastok.

HARJU
Vaasankatu
Harjuk.
Pääskylänkatu

(M) Sörnäinen

Helsinginkatu

Linnanmäki

Singinkatu
Alppikatu
Kaarlenkatu
Franzénk.
Torkkelinkatu
Pengerkatu

Vilhonvuorenk.

SÖRNÄINEN

Itäväylä

Alppikatu
Neljäs linja
Agricolank.
Hämeentie
Käenkuja

Ensi linja
Wallininkatu
Castreninkatu
Kolmas linja
Toinen
Suonio linja
Vides. linja
Kaikukatu
Lintulahdenk.
Sörnäisten raitatie
Hanasaarenkatu
Parrukatu
Kaasutehtaankatu

Kaupunginteatteri
(City Theatre)

KALLIO 22

Hämeentie
Näkink.
Haapaniemenkatu

Eläintarhanlahti
Hakaniemi
(M)
Hakan.k.
Näkinsilta

HAKANIEMI 21

Säästö Ranta
Pitkänsillanranta
Hakan. torik.
Hakaniemenranta

SOMPASAARI

MUSTIKKAMAA

Sompasaarensalmi
Mustikkamaansalmi

EMI
Kaisaniemenranta
Siltavuorenranta
Sörnäisten satama

Kasaniemenranta

KASVITIETEELLINEN
PUUTARHA
(UNIVERSITY BOTANICAL
GARDENS)
20

Ruiskumestarin
talo
(Burgher's House) 18

Kristianink.

Sotamuseo
(Military Museum)

Maurink.
Liisankatu

Tervasaarenkannas

Maneesikatu
Mariankatu
Meritullinkatu
Pohjoisranta

Tervasaari
19

Korkeasaaren
eläintarha
(Zoo)
★

KORKEASAARI
38

Unioninkatu
Fabianinkatu
Vironk.

Rautatieasema
Järnvägs-
stationen
Kaisaniemenkatu

KRUUNUNHAKA

Vilhonkatu
Snellmaninkatu

Rauhankatu
Kirkkokatu
Ritarikatu

Hylkysaarensalmi

Hylkysaari

(M) Rautatientori
Kaivokatu
Kaisaniemi

Tuomiokirkko ✝
Yliopistonkatu

Yliopisto
Senaatintori

Keskuskatu
Aleksanterinkatu
Aleksanterinkatu

Presidentinlinna

Pohjoisesplanadi
Eteläesplanadi

Uspenskin
katedraali ✝

Pohjoissatama

Laivastokatu
Luotsikatu

Merikasarmi
(Ex-Naval Barracks)

Kaup.k.
Vyökatu
Merikasarminkatu

Eteläranta
Unioninkatu

Katajanokan laituri
Kruunuvuorenkatu
Kanavakatu
Linnankatu

Kanavatermi-
naali

Korkeavuorenkatu
Kasarmikatu
Erottajankatu

KATAJANOKKA

Katajanokanranta

Designmuseo
(Design Museum)

Suomen
Rakennustaiteen
museo
(Museum of Finnish
Architecture)

Makasiini-
terminaali

Eteläsatama

Katajanokan
terminaali

Katajanokanluoto

Ratakatu

Johanneksen
kirkko

Tarkk'ampujankatu

Tähtitorni
(Observatory)

Olympia-
terminaali
36

Laivasillankatu
Kasarmikatu

Jääkärinkatu

ULLANLINNA

Yrjö-Vuoriemenk.

Pyhän Henrikin
kirkko

Cygnaeuksen
galleria

Itäinen Puistotie
Kallio-
linnantie
Puistotie

Valkosaari
Blekholmen

Luoto

Ryssänsaari

Kruunuvuorenselkä

Suomenlinna ←

Mannerheim-
museo
35

Kaivopuistontie

Tähtitorninkatu
Puistokuja
Iso puistotie

Siltatie

34

KAIVOPUISTO

Pietarinkatu
Neitsytpolku
Laivanvar.k.

Puolimatkansaari

Merisatamanranta

palesalmi
Ehrenströmintie

Merisatama

Uunisaari

Lonna

Pormestarinluodot

★

ari

Liuskasaari

Harakka

Särkkä

Pikku-Musta

Vanha-Räntty

Länsi-Musta

Rostock, Stockholm, Tallinn, Mariehamn →

37

SUOMENLINNA

N ↑

They also shelter the city's oldest extant wooden buildings at Kristianinkatu 12, the **Burgher's House** (Ruiskumestarin talo; tel: 09-3107 1549; Jan–Apr, June–Aug and Nov–Dec Wed–Sun 11am–5pm; charge). The Burgher's House was built in 1818, shortly after the Great Fire, by a wealthy merchant who unfortunately wasn't quite wealthy enough to use stone as a building material. A high wooden fence encloses it with a second mustard-coloured house and a weatherbeaten red shed, all huddled round a small earthen courtyard filled with the pungent scent of wood smoke. The main house itself remains exactly as it was when first built, and its gorgeous slats of wooden flooring are completely original. The furniture, meanwhile, has been assembled from different periods starting from 1860. To top off the period atmosphere, guides dress in old-fashioned garb.

Outside the city centre

If it's a warm day, you may want to head east down to **Tervasaari** ⓳. This little island, now connected to Kruu-

nunhaka by a man-made isthmus, used to be the city's storage place for tar – an important early export (Tervasaari means "tar island"). Modern times have turned it into a nice park for summer sunning, with a dog run and laid-back terraced restaurant.

Although Finland has not won strictly speaking, any of the wars it has fought, the **Military Museum** (Sotamuseo; Maurinkatu 1; 0299-530 258; Tue–Thur 11am–5pm, Fri–Sun 11am–4pm) is worth a look, especially as wars have been so tragic for the nation in its struggle to defend its independence against Soviet aggression.

Walking west now brings you down to Kaisaniemenkatu, the street that begins in front of the railway station and frames the west of Kruununhaka. An attractive park squeezes between it the station and Kaisaniemi Bay.

Kaisaniemen puisto is a sort of multipurpose park, with sloping stretches of grass, a variety of playing fields that turn into ice-hockey rinks in winter, an open-air restaurant and the **University Botanical Gardens** ⓴ (Kasvitieteell inen puutarha; Unioninkatu 44; tel

ervices). It is not only an architectural oddity – built directly into the cliffs, with inner walls of stone – but also the ite of many excellent concerts during he year. A service for English-speakers s held here weekly.

Helsinki's expanding heart

he whole neighbourhood has evolved ased on an original plan by Alvar aalto. **Kiasma** ③ (tel: 09-1733 6501; Tue 10am–5pm, Wed–Sun 10am–.30pm; charge), Helsinki's reigning museum of contemporary art, is situated on Mannerheiminaukio, just across rom the Parliament Building and adjacent to Finlandia Hall and the Musiikitalo site. This remarkable machine-like tructure by American architect Steven Holl is a symbol of a new Helsinki, whose cultural centre is gradually migrating to this area from Senate quare. The curving asymmetrical buildings harmoniously interacts with its surroundings – the oddly shaped windows afford good views of the key landmarks of Helsinki. The bold exhibitions vary from astounding to macabre.

A triangle of Functionalist architec-

ture has emerged with a new role in life: Kiasma, closest to the railway station, Lasipalatsi ("Glass Palace") across Mannerheimintie and the former Tennispalatsi ("Tennis Palace") further up on Salomonkatu 15.

Lasipalatsi is one such Functionalist structure that has been rejuvenated with utmost care to create a welcoming media centre with an internet library, two TV studios (for live programming), a cinema, other media companies and fine cafés and restaurants.

Tennispalatsi, once something of an eyesore, was used during the 1952 Olympic Games, and now houses Finland's largest cinema complex (14 screens) and two museums: the **Helsinki City Art Museum** (Helsingin Kaupungin Taidemuseo; tel: 09-3103 6630; Mon–Fri 9am–5pm, Thur until 7pm, Sat–Sun 11am–5pm; charge) hosts interesting temporary exhibitions including contemporary art and popular culture, while the **Museum of Cultures** (Kulttuurien museo; tel: 09-4050 9806; Tue–Thur 11am–8pm, Fri–Sun 11am–6pm; charge) documents different peoples of the world.

Buskers are heard and seen in downtown Helsinki during the city's brief summer.

BELOW:
Temppelinaukio church is built into the rock.

You'll find interesting antique shops in Punavuori.

BELOW LEFT AND RIGHT: architectural glories along Bulevardi.

The greatest change to the area has been the construction of the Kamppi shopping centre and the move of the long-distance bus station to underneath this structure. At ground level are office buildings, shops, restaurants and a market square – further proof that this area is fast becoming the city's new heart.

Hip, happening and historical

Another district in southwestern Helsinki worth exploring is **Punavuori** ㉜, a bohemian chic area south of Esplanade Park and the city centre. The main street here is **Bulevardi**, one of Helsinki's most beautiful avenues, which begins at a perpendicular angle from Mannerheimintie (just a couple of blocks before its end) and leads down to Hietalahti shipyard. Most of the buildings date from between 1890 and 1920 and were formerly home to Helsinki's turn-of-the-century patricians. Vanha kirkko (The Old Church), however, between Annan and Yrjön streets, is a stray from Engel. Dating from 1826, it was the first Lutheran church to be built in the new "capital".

The former National Opera House – now the Aleksander Theatre – lies a few blocks further west on Bulevardi. This delightful red building was erected in 1870 as a theatre for Russian officers and for decades it housed the national opera, until the construction of the new opera house (*see page 172*). The inside is plush and ornate, and the building now functions as a musical theatre and school.

As you reach the end of Bulevardi, you will come to the buildings of the former Sinebrychoff Brewery, which was established in 1819 and is the oldest brewery in Finland. The **Sinebrychoff Art Museum** (Sinebrychoffin Taidemuseo; tel: 09-1733 6460; Tue and Fri 10am–6pm, Wed–Thur 10am–8pm, Sat–Sun 11am–5pm; charge), which specialises in old European art, is housed at Bulevardi 40, and includes several grandiose rooms containing Old Masters and miniatures.

Don't miss the **Hietalahdentori** ㉝, best known for its flea market. The goods are usually just bric-a-brac and

...othes, but this market is one of the ...est places in Helsinki to watch large ...umbers of locals in action during the ...ay. On the side of the square, the mar-...et hall is now occupied by the ...ntiques and Art Hall (Mon–Fri 10am–...om, Sat 10am–3pm).

...Bulevardi does, however, hold many ...shionable art galleries and boutiques, ...hich spill into neighbouring streets. ...ne of the intersecting streets, **Fre-rikinkatu** (known locally as Freda) ...as several trendy boutiques and design ...ops. One block south and parallel to ...ulevardi is Uudenmaankatu and the ...edestrianised Iso-Roobertinkatu, ...hich form a part of the "bar-hopping" ...istrict for the young and trendy. ...nother two blocks further on is the ...hannes Church. This rather regal ...fair with two piercing stiletto spires ...the largest church in Helsinki and a ...articularly popular place for choral ...oncerts, with excellent acoustics. ...cross the street, at Korkeavuorenkatu ...3, the **Design Museum** (Designmu-...o; tel: 09-622 0540; June–Aug daily ...am–6pm, Sept–May Tue 11am–8pm, ...ed–Sun 11am–6pm; charge) is an

essential stop; it showcases Finland's famed skills in *objets* and furniture design, including Aalto furniture, Lapponia jewellery and many new names to various aspects of the design scene (*see pages 88–91*).

In the same block is the **Museum of Finnish Architecture** (Suomen Rakennustaiteen museo; Kasarmikatu 24; tel: 09-8567 5100; Tue–Fri 10am–4pm, Wed until 8pm, Sat–Sun 11am–4pm), which has an excellent archive of architectural drawings, and changing exhibitions focusing on Finnish architectural movements (including National Romantic, neoclassical, Jugendian, Functionalist and modern).

High-class life

Heading directly south from here you come upon Eira, historically Helsinki's most exclusive neighbourhood. On the southernmost end of the peninsula the coastline below Eira is lined by parkland. After the ice melts, small boats dock all along the coastline and Sunday cyclists take to the paths. While the sea is still frozen, you can actually walk out over the ice to some of the

Neoclassical stone detail in the Eira district.

BELOW: Helsinki's shopping area is Aleksanterinkatu.

Statue of General Mannerheim, distinguished Commander-in-Chief of the Finnish army in World War II.

BELOW: the Ilmatar and Sotka statue in Sibelius Park.

closer offshore islands. Towards the northeast and the centre, this strip of green grows into Helsinki's best park, **Kaivopuisto** ㉞. In summer, the city sponsors free concerts here and Kaivopuisto overflows with happy sunbathing locals. Kaivohuone, a former spa in the park, is also one of the city's most popular places to meet and hear music. The recently refurbished nightclub features hot Finnish bands, but due to complaints about noise on its terrace, it can currently stage rock 'n' roll only on agreed evenings.

Embassies fill the well-heeled Ullanlinna district. Most noticeably, the Russian Embassy commands almost a block opposite St Henrik's, one of Helsinki's two Catholic churches. Above them rises **Observatory Hill** (the Finnish name *Tähtitorninmäki* literally means "star tower hill"). From here you can look down over the city centre and Katajanokka to the north.

The fine **Mannerheim Museum** ㉟ (Mannerheim-museo; tel: 09-635 443; Fri–Sun 11am–4pm; guided tour obligatory; charge) is tucked away between embassies at Kalliolinnantie 14. It was

the home of General C.G.E. Mannerheim, perhaps the most respected figure in Finland's history (*see page 57*). His achievements include a two-year expedition to Asia, when he travelled 14,000km (8,700 miles) on horseback along the Silk Road. Some of his souvenirs from his lengthy travels are on display here.

Not far away is **Cygnaeus Gallery** (Cygnaeuksen Galleria; Kalliolinnantie 8; tel: 09-4050 9628; Wed 11am–7pm, Thur–Sun 11am–4pm; charge) a tiny, exquisite wooden summer home of a local poet and art collector. Inside the house is his remarkable display of 19th-century Finnish painting and sculpture.

Directly below to the east is the **Olympia Terminal** ㊱ (Olympiaterminaali), the port of call for huge Viking and Silja Line ships and a reminder that the sea has brought prosperity to Helsinki, the "Daughter of the Baltic".

Suomenlinna

Literally hundreds of islands dot the city's coastline. Some, like Lauttasaari and Kulosaari, have been so integrated

TAMAN KALEVALA-AIHEISEN PATSAAN
LAHJOITTI VUONNA 1930 LEO JA REGINA
WAINSTEININ SÄÄTIÖ HELSINGIN

y bridges and metro lines that they re almost indistinguishable from the mainland. Others are reserved for weekend cottages, reached over the ice in winter or by motorboat in summer.

Suomenlinna ㉞ ("Finland's castle") is undoubtedly the most important of the latter and a popular picnic place among the locals. In reality it consists of five islands, over which the ruins of naval fortress and its fortifications are spread. Suomenlinna has played an integral part in Helsinki's life since its construction in 1748, under Count Augustin Ehrensvärd. It is a unique architectural monument, listed by Unesco as a World Heritage site.

Suomenlinna has a complicated identity. It began as a naval post, and still houses Finland's Naval War Academy, but it is hardly just a military enclave. A thriving local artists' community, which uses restored bastions as studios and showrooms, is more visible. Marine repairers and ship restoration workers also live on the island.

Getting to the island is both cheap and easy. Water buses leave from Market Square every 20 minutes, year-round, and cost the same as a metro ticket. They dock on Iso Mustasaari and from here, a hilly path leads up through **Jetty Barracks** (Rantakasarmi), which now house art exhibitions and an interesting restaurant and microbrewery by the name of Panimo (tel: 09-228 5030).

Island museums

Continuing past wooden houses, the Lutheran church sometimes stages concerts. This part of Suomenlinna has permanent residents living both in new houses and formerly Russian-era military houses. This island also has three museums of interest. The **Suomenlinna Toy Museum** (Suomenlinnan Lelumuseo; tel: 09-668 417; Apr Sat–Mon 11am–5pm, May Mon–Fri 10am–3pm, Sat–Sun 11am–5pm, early–mid-June daily 10am–5pm, mid-June–early Aug daily 10am–6pm, early Aug–late Aug daily 10am–5pm, Sept

Sat–Sun 11am–5pm; charge) contains thousands of dolls and toys from the Helsinki region from the 1830s to the 1960s, collected during the last 30 years. It is a private collection, the achievement of Piippa Tandefelt, an energetic lady who also prepares apple pies for the museum café.

The large **Suomenlinna Museum** (tel: 09-4050 9691; daily May–Sept 10am–6pm, Oct–Apr 10am–4pm; charge) is the main historical exhibition of the islands. A fine, multivision programme is shown regularly to fill you in on the details, and the building also houses the main information centre (tel: 09-684 1880) for Suomenlinna. The Military Museum exhibits heavy equipment – authentic artillery and other war machines, with roots in Swedish, Russian and Finnish history.

Crossing the bridge leads to the rambling remains of the **Ehrensvärd Crown Castle** (Kruunulinna Ehrensvärd; tel: 09-6841 1850; Apr Sat–Sun, May–Sept daily; charge) and gardens. The castle courtyard is the best-preserved section of the fortress and contains the 1788 sarcophagus of the

EAT

One of the most popular eating places on Suomenlinna is the Café Piper, in a park just south of the Ehrensvärd Crown Castle. The café has a delightful setting, and offers alfresco dining with a view.

BELOW: Kaivopuisto Park.

Try your hand at dinghy sailing around Helsinki's islands.

BELOW: an 1842 stable in the Seurasaari Open-Air Museum.

Count himself. His former home is now a museum, with old furniture, arms and lithographs.

The rest of Suomenlinna is split between residences and the fortress fortifications, which spread across Susisaari and the southernmost island of Kustaanmiekka. From the highest outcrop on this windswept last island, close to an atmospheric summer restaurant called Walhalla, it is possible to see Estonia, some 80km (50 miles) away, on a clear day. The might of larger-than-life passing ferries, on their way to Estonia or Sweden, is a spectacular view. There is also the Rannikotykisto museo (Coast Artillery Museum), and the Vesikko Submarine.

Helsinki's offshore islands

Korkeasaari ❸ is a popular tourist attraction, with the zoo dominating this rocky outcrop just a few steps away from the mouth of Sörnäinen Harbour. You can reach it by boat from Hakaniemi or from the Market Square. **Helsinki Zoo** (Högholmen; tel: 09-310 1615; www.korkeasaari.fi; daily May–Aug 10am–8pm, Apr and Sept until 6pm,

Oct–Mar until 4pm; free), perhaps no surprisingly, specialises in "cold climat animals", although there's a very inter esting enclosure which is home t South American animals. However, i you want to learn about indigenou Finnish fauna, you'd probably do jus as well at the Natural History Museun *(see page 174)*.

Seurasaari ❸ is also an atmospheri island and popular among sea-lovin; Helsinki dwellers and visitors alike. / pretty, forested place, its northeaster side has been made into an **Open-Ai Museum** (Ulkomuseo; tel: 09-405 9660; mid-May–end May and early mid-Sept Mon–Fri 9am–3pm, Sat–Su 11am–5pm, June–Aug daily 11am– 5pm; charge), with wooden building from provinces all over Finland. Th transplanted houses date from the 17t to 19th centuries and include farm steads and a church. Bonfires are hel near here to celebrate traditional fe tivities for Midsummer and Easter, du ing which local Finnish children dres up as "Easter witches". The other side c the island is a national park. Seurasaa also has one of Helsinki's naturi

beaches. Here there are separate sections for both sexes, whereas on the island of Harakka (*see right*) the beach is shared by men and women.

The island is connected to the Helsinki shore by a wooden footbridge, so here's no need for a boat. Just take either bus No. 24 from the centre or cycle along the Meilahti coastal drive which takes you past Sibelius Park and the silvery tubular Sibelius Monument) to the bridge. Admission to the island is free but, to enter any of the houses, you'll need to buy a ticket.

Less well-trodden are the smaller islands that form a string around Helsinki's southern peninsula. Across the "Olympic Harbour" are Luoto and Valkosaari, popular restaurant islands with romantic villas as dining spots. A long pier outside Kaivopuisto (*see page 178*) offers a boat service to Särkkä, another island with a popular restaurant, and Harakka. **Uunisaari** is accessible at the southern end of the street Neitsytpolku. It's a popular recreational island with a beach, a sauna and a restaurant, and is very popular with young Finnish couples. The Finnish

Sauna Society situated on the beautiful island of **Lauttasaari** offers wood-fired saunas and massage (tel: 09-686 0560; www.lauttasaari.fi).

Helsinki residents' favourite island for swimming is undoubtedly **Pihlajasaari**. Literally meaning Rowan Island, Pihlajasaari actually comprises two islands, with a sandy beach, café and changing cabins on the larger island's western shore. The nudist beach is on the smaller island, which also hides wartime bunkers. Boats to Pihlajasaari depart in summer every 15 to 30 minutes, just outside Café Carousel in Eira.

The very special **Harakka** ("Magpie") island (www.harakka.fi) is now a wildlife reserve but, up until 1990, was reserved for military purposes; this helps explain why it is still absolutely pristine. A network of paths (marked by signposts giving information in Finnish and Swedish) circle the tiny island, and visitors are asked not to stray from these paths or remove plants. You can reach Harakka by boat in the summer or, in the winter, by crossing the ice from Eira (*see page 177*). ❏

The tubular Sibelius Monument by Eila Hiltunen honours Finland's finest composer.

BELOW: old ships and historic buildings within Helsinki's harbour.

Visiting Russia and the Baltics

Finland is relatively close to the continental mainland, and a visit to Russia or one of the Baltics is surprisingly easy.

As the Finnish economy started to grow stronger in the 1970s, affluent Finns and Swedes enjoyed more leisure time and took advantage of their unique geographical location to visit cities such as Tallinn and St Petersburg, popularising the 24-hour mini cruise for "quick" foreign holidays. For foreign visitors too, ferries and trains around the Baltic are an easy way to combine a visit to different countries *(see page 300 for details)*.

The ships ply the Baltic sea lanes to and from Sweden, via the Åland Islands, and several sail under the Swedish and Estonian flags. Any preconceived ideas about car ferries will vanish as soon as you board one of these magnificent ships operated by either of the top players, Viking Line (white and red) and Silja Line (white and blue). They are fun, value for money, and cruise through the most beautiful seascapes in the world.

St Petersburg

Some of the most popular ferry trips from Helsinki are across the Bay of Finland to the gorgeous, historically rich cities of Russia. Most popular of all is the two-day excursion to St Petersburg: accommodation is often provided on the boat. Largely built by European architects in the 18th century, St Petersburg is the least Russian of all the country's cities. Situated on 40 islands in the Neva River Delta, its Italianate palazzi and numerous waterways draw comparisons with Venice and Amsterdam.

It is European art that draws the crowds to the city's Hermitage gallery, for the highlights of the collection are concentrated in the rooms devoted to Western painting, from private collections nationalised after the Revolution: masterpieces by Rembrandt, Poussin, Cézanne, Van Gogh and Matisse are all here.

St Petersburg is a rewarding city for walking and absorbing the street life. The city is particularly lively during the "white nights" of June, when everyone comes out to watch the lingering sunsets. A walk from the Hermitage, through the archway of the General Staff building, will take you to Nevsky Prospekt, the city's main thoroughfare. Men still play chess here and street musicians perform. Also visit the enclosed market off Nevsky for a slice of daily life. The Kafe Literaturnoya (18 Nevsky) has a Viennese atmosphere: coffee and cakes, and occasional poetry readings or chamber concerts. Pushkin ate his last meal here in 1837, before fighting a fatal duel.

Arts Square, round the corner, offers music at the Philharmonia Bolshoy and the Glinka Maly halls, and opera and ballet at the Mariinsky Theatre. Gostiny Dvor (35 Nevsky) is the largest department store, where home-produced consumer goods sit beside modern Western imports.

Petrodvorets

A trip to Petrodvorets, 28km (18 miles) west of St Petersburg, is a must. This is Peter the Great's answer to Versailles and he invited all the European rulers to attend its gala opening. The centrepiece of the Great Cascade is a statue of Samson tearing open the jaws of a lion, which symbolises Peter's victory over the Swedes in 1709. Equally revealing of his character are the trick fountains scattered around: be careful when choosing a seat – some will send up a shower of water.

LEFT: city spires in Tallinn, capital of Estonia.
RIGHT: open-air ethnographic museum in Riga, Latvia.

Tallinn

Tallinn, the capital of Estonia, is another extremely popular ferry destination, and from here you can set off to explore all three independent Baltic states: Estonia, Latvia (capital Riga) and Lithuania (capital Vilnius). Tallinn lies directly opposite Helsinki, 80km (50 miles) across the water, and large numbers of Finnish tourists visit the city – many for the capital's lively nightlife and inexpensive alcohol rather than for its beautiful medieval Old Town. Here, cobbled alleys ascend from the 14th-century castle and the Gothic architecture reminds you that Tallinn was once an important port of the Hanseatic League. In recent years, Tallinn's popularity has grown immensely thanks to discount airlines and the affordability and exoticism of holding stag and hen dos here. A number of new boutique hotels add to the appeal, although some of the charm of the Old Town may get lost in the swarms of visitors that descend in the warmer months.

Riga

Latvia's capital, Riga, a city founded by merchants, is also rich in history but receives far fewer tourists, making it arguably a better option to visit. The city is well known for its Jugendstil (Art Nouveau) architecture, and its historic centre is a Unesco World Heritage site, with a dozen churches, a castle and a tower that is a survival from the original city walls. The 13th-century Romanesque cathedral is lined with the tombs of bishops, knights and landmeisters. The organ is the fourth-largest in the world, and most evenings you can hear performances of Bach or Mozart here.

Vilnius

In Vilnius, meanwhile, three things impinge on every visitor: the ubiquitous jewellery shops selling amber, for which Lithuania has long been famous, the medieval streets clustering below the city's towering castle, and the festive atmosphere that prevails since independence arrived.

The increasing popularity of these trips and, in turn, the increased size of the ferries is, however, causing some concern for the erosion of the shorelines, the islands of the inner archipelago and the seabed. Another environmental concern is the pollution caused by heavy traffic near ferry terminals. The ferries carry well over 1 million passenger cars, coaches and trailers every year. At the same time the ships are a vital link in Finnish-Swedish trade and one of Finland's lifelines to Europe. Much of Finland's foreign trade travels by ferry.

But on a still summer night, as tiny points of light fade away with the ferry's white wake, these issues are unlikely to trouble a passenger leaning over the deck rail and gazing out to a darkening sea. ❑

WEST OF HELSINKI

Many of the artists and architects who created Helsinki's image chose to reside in the city's western suburbs, which are also still home to a few rural and traditional communities

The 19th-century search for a rural Finnish identity has left a collection of museums and buildings dotting the landscape – a space that has become the glorified suburbs of the capital, albeit in rather more bucolic settings that you would expect. If you have time to leave Helsinki for a day, the places mentioned in this chapter are worth a visit, offering something completely different from the city centre.

A garden "city"

Leaving Helsinki, the next settlement of any size you come to is **Espoo ❶**. While Espoo is, strictly speaking, a "city", it feels much more like a huge, spread-out municipality. Populated largely by wealthier Finns who commute to Helsinki, Espoo is a strange mix of rural farm areas and genteel, leafy suburbs that offer a large and colourful palette of Finnish residential architectural styles.

Espoo's Tapiola area is renowned as the planned garden suburb of the 1950s, in which leading architects of the age aimed to create a harmonious mix of housing, from flats to family houses, set around a central pool. Yet despite all this sleek Modernism, the area has been settled since 3500 BC, and Espoo's parish church dates as far back as the 15th century. In addition, many artists and architects have made their homes in the area. Only a handful of wooden houses and scenic rapids now mark the original settlements, but

the river paths are beautifully tended and lead to some spectacular Finnish countryside only moments away from Helsinki's centre.

National Park

Around 16km (10 miles) north of Espoo is **Nuuksio National Park ❷** (Nuuksion kansallispuisto), a great place to come for a short hiking trip of a day or two. The park is one of the most important conservation areas in Finland, with cool, herb-rich forests, lakes and mires that are home to a

Main attractions
ESPOO
TARVASPÄÄ
HVITTRÄSK
SAMMATTI
SALO
PUKKILA MANOR HOUSE
   MUSEUM
KUUSISTON CASTLE
PARGAS

PRECEDING PAGES: golden wheatfields.
LEFT: steeple on the western road.
BELOW: an agricultural life.

TIP

You can reach Nuuksio National Park and trails from Espoo via bus 85(A); get off at the fork of the road to Haukka-lampi, then walk 2km (1 mile) to the park's main information point.

number of threatened species, including the wood lark, European nightjar and various flying squirrels.

Some 20km (32 miles) west of Espoo off Road 1 (E3) is the town of **Lohja**, full of pretty gardens and with a medieval church at its centre. Numerous cultural festivals, carnivals and markets are held here throughout the year.

Finland's national artist

At the start of the route from Helsinki to Turku is **Tarvaspää ❸**, the home of Finland's national artist, Akseli Gallén-Kallela (*see box, right*). To get there by car, leave Road 1 (E3) 200 metres/yds past Turunväylä (Tarvontie). Almost at once, a road marked Tarvaspää takes you to the museum. Alternatively, travel on tram 4 and enjoy the scenic 2km (1-mile) walk from the last stop.

Gallén-Kallela was already well established when, between 1911–13, he built a studio-home around the Linudd Villa on the old Alberga Manor ground. The studio has been converted into the **Gallén-Kallela Museum** (Gallén-Kallenlatie 27; tel: 09-849 2340; Jan–mid-May and Sept–

Dec Tue–Sat 10am–4pm, Sun 10am–5pm, mid-May–Aug 10am–6pm; charge; guided tours by arrangement), a peaceful oasis consisting of a studio wing, tower and main building, with a coffee house and a terrace restaurant. Concerts are occasionally held here.

The studio was designed by Gallén-Kallela himself, whose forceful personality is etched throughout, along with his own hard physical work. Architect Eliel Saarinen, a close friend, participated informally in the studio project as technical adviser.

The museum holds some 100 illustrations for the *Kalevala* which decorated the Finnish Pavilion at the Paris World Exhibition in 1900. The paintings are on display at the Ateneum in Helsinki (*see page 158*) and Turku Art Museum, where Gallén-Kallela's work sometimes features in temporary exhibitions. Also on view are paintings for his frescoes in the Juselius Mausoleum in Pori (*see page 241*), which commemorated Sigrid Juselius, the 11-year-old daughter of a Pori businessman. Working on these frescoes was a poignant task for the painter, because his own young daugh-

BELOW: part of the artistic mecca at Hvitträsk.

ter had died a few years earlier. There are also relics of his time spent in Africa, Paris and further afield.

Art Nouveau in the woods

Another must-see artistic mecca is Eliel Saarinen's home at **Hvitträsk ❹**, some 20km (14 miles) west of Helsinki in Kirkkonummi municipality (tel: 09-4050 9630; May–Sept daily, Oct–Apr Tue–Sun; charge; guided tours by arrangement). It can be easily reached by Road 1 (E3), taking junction 3 left for Jorvas, and following the signs for Hvitträsk. It can also be reached by bus (No. 166 from platform 60 at Helsinki bus station) or train (L or U train: Helsinki–Luoma; 3km/2-mile walk).

You would expect the studio home of three of Finland's most famous architects to be at one with its surroundings, but at Hvitträsk this is quite literally interpreted. The stone and timber buildings seem to blend right into the forest, the great cliffs and the lake (White Lake) that gives the house its name. Inside, architecture, interior designs and furniture all blend together. The partnership of Eliel Saarinen, Herman Gesellius and Armas Lindgren was responsible for many important buildings – the studio, now a museum, presided over some 70 individual architecture projects. Hvitträsk celebrated one of the architects' earliest triumphs, the Finnish Pavilion at the Paris World Exhibition in 1900. The dining-room ceiling, like the pavilion decoration, is the work of Gallén-Kallela. Saarinen, who disliked long meetings, designed the hard black table and chairs; reproductions of his furniture designs are still on sale today.

The harmony of working partnerships did not always extend into the private lives of the little community, however. Proximity, perhaps, turned the gaze of Saarinen's first wife, Matilda, towards his partner, Gesellius, and she simply crossed the garden and changed houses. Apparently bearing her no grudge, Saarinen married Gesellius' sister, Loja, two years later. But the triumvirate broke up in 1906, and by

Old windmills still dot the landscape.

BELOW: self-portrait of Akseli Gallén-Kallela on display at Tarvaspää.

Akseli Gallén-Kallela

Akseli Gallén-Kallela (1865–1931) is considered by many to be Finland's greatest national artist. After studying at the Finnish Society of Fine Arts, he made his debut in the 1880s to popular acclaim, with his realistic images of everyday Finns. Between 1884–8 he lived in Paris and painted images of Parisian bohemian life, but was soon to be drawn back to his native country. Gallén-Kallela had become fascinated with Elias Lönnrot's epic collection of poetry, the *Kalevala,* and wanted to capture in paint its mythical heroes. Returning to Finland, he devoted his time to researching themes from the epic poems.

In 1890 Kallela married Mary Slöör and they honeymooned in eastern Finland and Karelia, the regions in which the folk poems were set. The *Kalevala* paintings were to become the best known of Kallela's works. In 1909–10 the family lived in British East Africa (now Kenya), where he painted some 150 works and gathered ethnographic and zoological material. In 1911, Kallela designed and built his studio at Tarvaspää, and in 1918 he was appointed aide-de-camp to General Mannerheim. During the 1920s, the family lived in the United States for three years, during which time Gallén-Kallela created the *Great Kalevala*, a lengthy series of illustrations based on the mythology of the *Kalevala*, which he continued to work on throughout his life.

A coat of arms shows the region's Swedish influence.

BELOW: wild flowers in the Finnish springtime.
RIGHT: the flat landscape and quiet, rural roads make the area ideal for cyclists.

1916 Saarinen was working at Hvitträsk on his own.

In 1922, after winning a major prize in a competition in New York, Eliel Saarinen moved to the United States, was made Dean of the Cranbrook Academy of Art and became as well known abroad as he was in Finland. He continued to visit Hvitträsk each year until his death in 1950, and his grave now overlooks the lake.

Leased to Russia

The whole Kirkkonummi municipality was once a large rural Swedish-speaking area. However, at the end of World War II, Finland was forced to lease the Porkkala Peninsula in the south to the Soviet Union as a naval base, a situation that remained until 1955. The Russian cemetery here, in typical Soviet scale, is an ageless reminder of that time – 7,000 Finns had to leave their homes at 10 days' notice to make space for it.

Today Porkkala has a Finnish naval garrison in **Upinniemi**, with a remarkable sea chapel, designed by Marianne and Mikko Heliövaara, that is shaped like a boat with open sails and overlooks the sea. An impressive number of bird migration routes pass over the Porkkala Peninsula, and spring and autumn draw ornithologists here to gaze at flocks of cranes, swans and geese. In summer, sailing boats and beach cabins dot the spectacular Baltic coastline.

Back on Road 1 and heading west, the area of lake and ridge is part of the Salpausselkä Ridge, formed at the end of the Ice Age. The next major stop is **Sammatti ❺** (tel: 019-356 659; mid-May–mid-Sept 11am–5pm), just south of the road. Look out for the sign to *Paikkarin torppa* (Paikkari Cottage), the home of Elias Lönnrot, who collected the old legends and tales for the *Kalevala (see page 103)*. The building is typical of a worker's home in 19th-century southwest Finland. Outside is a statue of Lönnrot by Halonen and Räsänen. Not far away stands Lammi House, where the writer died.

At **Salo ❻**, some 115km (80 miles) from Helsinki in the heart of the apple-growing Salojoki Valley, it is worth turning off the main road to stop in

he town centre. Dominated by a triad of churches – the Lutheran Uskela (Engel, 1832), the Greek Orthodox Tsaouna at its foot, and the stunningly modern Helisnummen (Helisnummi Church) about 4km (2½ miles) outside the town – Salo still has a very lively market, held every day except Sundays. Along the Uskela River there are some beautiful residential garden districts.

Many of Nokia's mobile phones are manufactured in Salo – the only major remaining mobile handset factory in Western Europe.

Tyrant's carriage

At Piikkiö, only 15km (10 miles) from Turku, turn right for the **Pukkila Manor House Museum** ❼ (Pukkilan kartano; tel: 02-479 5320; June–mid-Aug Wed–Sun 11am–5pm; charge), where the rococo-style mansion is furnished as the home of a state official.

The town church dates back to 1755, built partly of stones from the ruins of **Kuusiston Castle** ❽. This medieval bishop's castle is worth a detour to the Kuusisto Peninsula, just west of Piikkiö – take the road to Pargas (Parainen) and

branch onto a secondary road to the ruins. The 14th-century castle stood stoutly until Gustav Vasa ordered its demolition in 1528, but enough remains to have encouraged recent attempts at restoration.

Having come this far, you may like to continue to **Pargas** ❾ (Parainen), which has a beautiful view over the islands of the archipelago and is famous for its large limestone quarries. Pargas has one of the most stunning medieval greystone churches in Finland, Harmaa Kivikirkko, dedicated to St Simon. Built in the 1320s, it is unusual for the spreading brick columns that support the interior and contrast with the light-blue trim of the pews. Notice, too, the panel paintings of Old Testament figures running around the porch where the organ sits. Pargas has a good marina, and a charming series of wooden buildings scattered around the church which form a kind of extended folklore museum; weaving still goes on here. From here it is a short drive northwest to the old city of Turku (see page 205). ❏

Oil painting of Jean Sibelius by Akseli Gallén-Kallela.

BELOW: architect Eliel Saarinen's home at Hvittråsk.

THE TRADITIONAL FINNISH SAUNA

An old Finnish proverb says: "First you build the sauna, then you build the house"; even today, there's nothing so uniquely Finnish as a sauna

There are some things along the way that a traveller does not forget – and a real Finnish sauna is one of them. Although its origin is obscure, the sauna came to Finland over 2,000 years ago, and it is a rare Finn who admits to not liking one. Official statistics estimate that there are more than 2 million saunas in Finland – that's one for every 2.5 Finns – and many of these are in the summer cottages and cabins that dot the shoreline of the country's lakes (*see page 255*). The sauna is a national institution, and a way of life for country people.

Business and Pleasure

The sauna outgrew its rural roots long ago. Today, be it in a city or a village, you will find public saunas everywhere, and it is safe to assume that every new apartment block has a sauna for its tenants. Many companies also maintain saunas for their employees.

A Finnish sauna is not a meeting place for romance or sexual encounter, as it may be in some countries; codes of behaviour are strict. Titles and position are, they say, left hanging in the changing room with the clothes. It is not unusual for board meetings and government cabinet meetings to be held in a sauna – perhaps because swearing or raising one's voice is a cultural no-no once inside.

LEFT: water thrown over hot stones creates a dry steam *(löyly)*, which makes the heat more tolerable.

RIGHT: the sauna is an integral part of Finnish life and there are "designer" outlets geared towards sauna accessories.

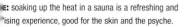
E: soaking up the heat in a sauna is a refreshing and 'ising experience, good for the skin and the psyche.

not for the faint-hearted; this instant sauna in Lapland has out together out of ice blocks.

HOW TO TAKE A SAUNA

There is no "right way" to take a sauna – temperature and style vary. The ideal temperature is between 80–100°C (175–210°F), although it can be a cooler 30°C (85°F) on the bottom platform, reserved for children. A common practice is to brush oneself with a wet birch switch, called the *vihta*. This not only gives off a fresh fragrance but increases blood circulation and perspiration.

How long you sit in the sauna is entirely up to you. When you have had enough, you move on to stage two: cooling off. A cold shower is the most common way but, if the sauna is by a lake or the sea, a quick plunge into the cool (or often freezing) water is stimulating.

The final stage is to dry off, which should be done naturally, to avoid further perspiration. It is also time for a beer or coffee and a snack to complete the ritual.

But there is more to the sauna than just getting clean. It is a social event and a ritual – a time to meet friends or family, to share gossip and news.

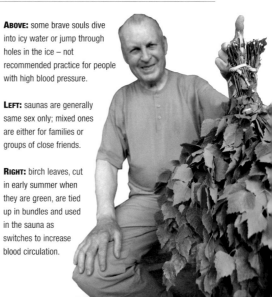

ABOVE: some brave souls dive into icy water or jump through holes in the ice – not recommended practice for people with high blood pressure.

LEFT: saunas are generally same sex only; mixed ones are either for families or groups of close friends.

RIGHT: birch leaves, cut in early summer when they are green, are tied up in bundles and used in the sauna as switches to increase blood circulation.

SOUTHERN FINLAND

From Swedish-speaking farming communities to bastions built to protect the Finnish-Russian border towns, the south coast has an atmosphere quite distinct from the rest of the country

Helsinki

Main attractions
TURUNMAAN ARCHIPELAGO
HANKO
EKENÄS
RAASEPORI
PORVOO
LOVIISA
KOTKA
HAMINA

LEFT: detail of Loviisa's wooden houses. **BELOW:** Russian-style villa in Hanko.

o follow the south coast of Finland from west to east is to follow a route once travelled by Nordic kings and princes to St Petersburg, known appropriately in Finnish as *Kunikaantie*, or the King's Road. It is mainly flat, coastal country covered with farmland and densely grown forest. And, because proximity to the coast has always given extra value to land – in addition to the beneficial, warming effects of the Gulf of Finland – this area has traditionally been heavily settled by Finnish peasants and manual labourers.

It is also heavily Swedish-speaking. From Pargas *(see page 191)* south of Turku at the head of the Turunmaa Archipelago, through Ekenäs (Tammisaari), Karis (Karjaa), and further east through a cluster of small villages on the approach to Kotka, you will hear a great deal of Swedish and see it as the first language on signposts. This is all part of the democracy of bilingualism in Finland: in any town with a majority of Swedish-speakers, the Swedish name will take precedence.

Farms and fortresses

The landscape changes only very subtly from west to east. The low farmland tends to be misty in the early morning and late evening. While not as rich in lakes as the country north of here, it is sufficiently irrigated by local meandering rivers and streams, and there are plenty of good walking trails.

The green of ripening wheat and the golden hue of rape seed dominate in late spring, after which the wheat matures and the wild flowers explode into bloom. The grassy strips at the roadside are first overrun with cowslip and lupin, a midsummer flower with tall purple, pink and white spindles. When the lupin fades, the landscape is overtaken by *maitohorsma*, a tall, spindly flower, its magenta petals filling not just the edge of the road but entire forests and fields. Autumn is slightly more colourful in the west, where the

The harbour at Hanko, Finland's southernmost town.

linden adds bright colour to the golden hue of the birches. The west is also hillier than the east, and set against this backdrop are clusters of attractive old farm buildings, stained dark red, and manor houses painted a rich ochre or brilliant yellow.

The eastern section of the coast, beyond Helsinki, is scattered with fortifications, a telling reminder of Finland's chequered past. For the Swedes, then the Russians, and finally the independent Finns, the Russian border has served as a critical dividing line, for centuries separating nations, cultures and peoples.

The Finnish-Soviet borders still have a no-man's land running between them, and although travel between the two countries has become far simpler and more popular since the break-up of the USSR, there is a definitive change in atmosphere after you've crossed from west to east: a somewhat sterner attitude in Russian customs guards and a noticeable change in road condition and land upkeep. Plan ahead if yo intend to travel into Russia as you' need a visa *(see page 201).*

Exploring the islands

Richly vegetated but sparsely popu lated, the **Turunmaan archipelago** ❶ (Turunmaan saaristo) is quieter tha the Ålands in terms of tourism *(se page 231),* and the islands are easier t reach from the mainland, as they ar linked by a series of bridges and ferrie Boats also service some of the smalle islands that spin off south from th main chain, while local buses connec the larger towns.

Turunmaa's finest harbour is on th northeast spur of **Nagu**. An ol wooden house overlooking the marin has been made into a guesthouse-sty hotel, with a French brasserie and chic restaurant, L'Escale, next doo Also to be found in Nagu is the **Fol Museum** (tel: 02-460 5500; June an Aug Tue, Thur, Sat 11am–3pm, Ju Tue, Fri–Sat 11am–4pm) and the 14th century St Olof's Church (June–Au Tue–Sun noon–5pm).

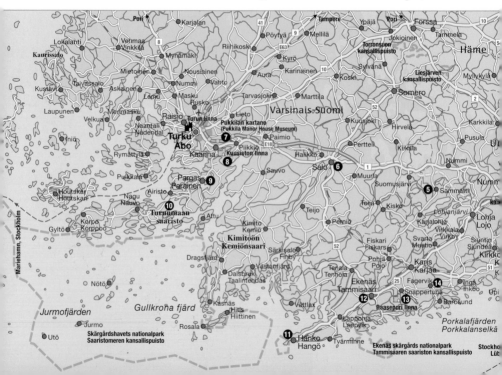

owns. It was a busy trading post from 346 and, ultimately, was where the Diet of Porvoo (1809) convened to transfer Finland from Swedish to Russian hands *(see page 41)*. The striking **Porvoo Cathedral** (tel: 019-66111; May–Sept Mon–Fri 10am–6pm, Sat 10am–2pm, Sun 2–5pm, Oct–Apr Tue–Sat 10am–2pm, Sun 2–4pm; free), where this momentous event took place, dates to the 15th century. Sadly, much of the church was destroyed by arson in 2006 – the culprit being a teenage boy – though it was renovated and reopened in 2008.

Porvoo's rich history made the town important; **Holm House** (Välikatu 11; tel: 019-574 7500; late Mar–Apr Tue–Sun 10am–4pm, May–Aug Mon–Sun 10am–4pm, Sept–Dec Wed–Sun noon–4pm; charge) is a 1763 merchant's house now converted into a museum that shows how well-off tradesmen lived at the turn of the 18th century. It contains several spacious rooms – a living room, salon, smoking room and bedroom – with many antique furnishings.

For scenery, Porvoo also has few rivals: its trim riverbanks are lined with fishing cottages, and the pastel-coloured houses of the Old Town provide a charming backdrop. Furthermore, the town has a palpable artistic energy, alive with the work of artists and writers who live here.

East of Porvoo, the landscape becomes more rural and less populated, with only the occasional village to break up the vast spread of forests, wheatfields, hillocks and wild-flower beds (in spring and summer). There are just two more towns and one sizeable city, all in fortification country.

Loviisa ⓱, a pretty, provincial town with an esplanade headed by the New Gothic Church, is the smallest of these. A town museum tells of local history, including the role of the Rosen and Ungern bastions, built in the 18th century to safeguard the important trade route between Vyborg and Turku.

Further east, the frequency of both rivers (originating in the great lake area immediately to the north) and Orthodox churches begins to increase. After the old towns of Ruotsinpyhtää *(see margin)* and Pyhtää is the broad Kotka Delta, at the centre of which is Kotka

(see page 41); *(see margin)*

TIP

Ruotsinpyhtää is known for its 17th-century ironworks, unique octagonal wooden church and annual bluegrass festival (www.bluegrass.fi). Held in early April, this is one of the best opportunities in the country to catch a jamboree in the great outdoors.

BELOW LEFT: the Town Hall and wooden houses of Porvoo. **BELOW:** main street, Porvoo.

This is big sky country. The Kotka tourist board can point out nature-protected paths and rivers, as well as arrange other trips and activities (with guides, if needed).

BELOW: interpreters at the tsar's fishing lodge, Langinkoski.

– at first unappealingly industrial, but on closer inspection one of the most beautifully situated cities in Finland.

Delta fishing

It is around **Kotka** that the Kymi River divides into five branches before emptying out into the sea, creating excellent conditions for salmon and trout fishing. The closest of the spray of islands along the coast can be reached by bridges, the rest by ferry. Focused around an esplanade, Kotka has a brick buttressed Lutheran church at Kirkkokatu and Koulukatu, while the imposing Orthodox church complex and park runs along Papinkatu. Kotka has frequent boat services to

nearby islands, some of which have old fortifications. The pleasant Sapokka harbour, with a high (artifical) water fall, is home to one of the finest parks in Finland.

Apart from the Kotka islands, the **Kymenlaakso** (Kymi River Valley) extends further inland, where there are gorgeous forest paths. Details are available from the Kotka tourist office at Keskuskatu 6; tel: 05-234 4424.

The famous fishing lodge of Tsar Alexander III is at **Langinkoski** (signposted from Langinkoskentie). The tremendous log building and its furnishings are now preserved as a museum (tel: 040-596 5215; www.langinkoskimuseo.com; daily May 10am–4pm, June–Aug 10am–6pm, Sept–Oct Sat–Sun 10am–4pm; charge). The cabin was crafted by the Finns for the tsar, who spent his summers here.

Several nature paths begin from Langinkoski – if you walk north for 5km (3 miles), you'll pass Kyminlinna fortification, over Hovinkoski River through Kyminkartano (manor) to **Keisarin Kosket**. These "tsar's rapids" course around Munkkisaari Island

with its Orthodox chapel (Tsasouna). A pilgrimage of the faithful is made here every 14 August. The spot is also ideal for fishing and rapids-shooting. On the bank is Keisarin Kosket Lodge, an Orthodox monastery site from 1650 to 1850, with café, boats and cabins for hire; fishing licences are also sold (tel: 05-210 7400; www.keisarinkosket.fi for details).

In summer, **Kärkisaari**, just to the west of Kotka, makes for a lovely stop-over. The former youth hostel here has been turned into one of the most stylish bed-and-breakfast locations in the country (Villa Kärkisaari, Kärkisaarentie 60; tel: 05-260 4804; www.villakarkisaari.com). The food, including the tasty pastries, are well worth sampling, and there is a long swimming dock. On the adjacent peninsula is Santalahti beach, with caravan and cabin facilities.

Towards Russia

Kotka is only 70km (45 miles) from the nearest Russian city, Viipuri (Vyborg) and 270km (170 miles) from St Petersburg; the Kotka Tourist Board (tel: 05-234 4424; www.visitkotka.fi; Mon–Fri, also Sat in summer) can organise a number of trips to Russia, but remember to plan overnight trips in advance so that your visa will be ready.

Hamina ⑳ is the last of the large Finnish towns before you reach the border. Its concentric plan is part of a huge fortification, and its military nature is also preserved by the many young Finnish men based here for national service. Pastel-coloured wooden houses contrast prettily with red-brick barracks and magazines. Three old churches are to be found in Hamina, as well as several quaint museums. One of the large bastion sections has been turned into a covered concert venue; the vaulted fortress walls have excellent acoustics.

Further east lies Virolahti, a small town with a great collection of charming waterfront cabins at Hurpun Tila (www.hurpuntila.fi). Finally, there is **Vaalimaa**, the busiest border station on your way to Russia. A massive new shopping mall will open at Vaalimaa in 2010, selling products to Russians and Finns – more than 1 million people cross the border here annually. ❏

Old cannons on the Finno-Russian border are reminders of former tensions between the nations.

BELOW: the town hall of Hamina.

WESTERN FINLAND

The western area of Finland is known by many as the "essential triangle". It encompasses three major cities and various tributes to the industries and artists that have formed much of the modern Finnish nation

A round trip of some 500km (310 miles) from the capital Helsinki to the west of Finland takes in the three largest cities and is one of the best ways to get a feel for the country in a couple of weeks. Our route leads to Turku, the old capital at the heart of Swedish-speaking Finland, and then on to Tampere, the industrial capital, where water set the first 18th-century mills rolling.

Lakes, history and clean air

Along the way are most of the elements, past and present, that make Finland what it is today. In the south, there are coasts and lakesides, some lakes so vast that it is difficult to decide whether they are lake or sea. Beautiful old houses restored as museums and hotels lie along the route, as do historic castles with magnificent banqueting halls and dungeons, and statues that reflect Finland's history, sometimes warring, sometimes at peace. Further north, the lakes become more prevalent, and it may be tempting to leave the car and travel as local Finns once did, using waterways such as the Silverline route, which winds through the lake system between Tampere and Hämeenlinna. You can go north by the Poet's Way to Virrat, and swim, fish or sail on lake or sea.

This is a good opportunity to get to know something about Finland's arts and culture, remarkable in a country of only 5 million, and glimpse the Finns'

famed skill in design at glassworks and studios; here, visitors are welcomed and offered the opportunity to buy distinctive articles that could only be Finnish. Above all, between the cities lies the long Finnish road through forests and old villages, to make it a tour filled with flowers and fresh air.

Turku

Turku ❶ is the "other" face of Finland, the view from the southwest, closest to Scandinavia and the rest of Europe, not just in trade but also in culture. The

PRECEDING PAGES: misty headlands. **LEFT:** the *Sigyn* barque. **BELOW:** making lace.

*In Finland you
are never far from
nature's beauty.*

Aura River divides the modern city in two; the Baltic Sea, curling round the river mouth, has countless islands in an archipelago stretching southwest until it explodes into the collection of islands known as Åland, splayed about the Baltic Sea halfway between Finland and Sweden *(see page 231)*.

Turku is also a city of paradoxes. Known as Åbo in Swedish, it may feel like a capital, but it only ever held that title as the principal city and home of the viceroy in the Swedish-Finnish kingdom. It is Finland's oldest city and yet many of the buildings date only back to 1827, when the Great Fire destroyed a town then largely made of

wood. Islands, river and sea make Turku a summer paradise, yet it is also the birthplace of Finnish culture.

A brief history of Turku

The Swedes were the first known nation to arrive at the mouth of the Aura River when King Erik sailed in with an English bishop and an expeditionary force in 1157. This bishop, Henrik, later became the first Finnish patron saint. Even earlier, Finnish tribes from the southeast had settled and traded along the river valleys of southwest Finland, and sailors and merchants came and went to the first settlement, upriver at Koroinen.

The Swedes called their expanding own Åbo, and by 1300 it had become the spiritual centre of Finland. At this time, the solid lines of a castle began to rise near the mouth of the Aura River as the heart of royal power in Finland, where the Swedish governor lived and visiting dignitaries paid their respects. It was a castle often on the defensive, standing firm under a winter siege in the mid-14th century in one of the bloody struggles for the Swedish throne. In all, the castle was besieged six times. In the 16th century, Gustav Vasa survived another winter siege and proclaimed his young son (later Johan III) as the duke of Finland.

After Duke Johan returned a married man in 1552 with his wife, the Polish princess Katarina Jagellonica, Turku Castle entered its most colourful phase of royal glory. Katarina brought glamour with her Polish courtiers, her velvet and lace, and even her spoons, forks and knives, and introduced a splendid court life that was already common in most of Europe but had not yet reached Finland. In summer, the court relaxed on the island of Ruissalo, just off the coast, as Finns do today. But this gracious life did not last. After Gustav Vasa's death, feuds broke out between his three sons, and the eldest brother, Erik XIV, besieged the duke. The castle surrendered in three weeks and Johan and Katarina were bundled into captivity. Though later, as Johan III, Duke Johan gained his revenge and imprisoned Erik in Turku Castle, court life never again achieved such heights.

Turku Castle

Today, the massive facades, honey-coloured under the sun, grey in winter, of **Turku Castle** (A) (Turun linna; tel: 02-262 0300; May–Sept Tue–Sun 10am–6pm, Sept–mid-Jan Tue, Thur–Sun 10am–6pm, Wed noon–8pm; charge) look towards the modern town centre, some 3km (2 miles) away. The castle is one of the most impressive in all the Nordic countries and stands as a testament to the historical importance of the city, with a number of beautifully preserved halls, rooms, alleyways and corridors that together tell the story of medieval Turku. Many

If you are driving, pay special attention to these warning signs. Many traffic accidents are caused by wandering moose.

BELOW LEFT: Turku is on the banks of the River Aura.
BELOW: Turku Castle.

Turku is the former capital of Swedish-speaking Finland.

of its rooms have been restored in painstaking detail, including the austere room in which King Erik XIV was imprisoned for several weeks along with his wife Catharine Månsdotter, the only queen that Finland ever produced. The castle's old chapel has reclaimed its original role and the magnificent banqueting halls now regularly play host to civic celebrations.

Turku university

Turku was the first city in Finland to have a university, founded by the 17th-century governor general of Finland, Count Per Brahe. He travelled the length and breadth of his governorship and his name is commemorated in many towns and buildings. His greatest contribution to Turku, however, was **Åbo Akademi** ❸ which, after its ceremonial opening in 1640, made Turku the centre of culture and learning as well as religion. When Finland became a Russian Grand Duchy, the tsar ordered the Academy to be transferred to the new capital to become the University of Helsinki, but the old Academy building remains. In 1918,

independent Finland created a second Akademi as Turku's Swedish-language university, and also founded the University of Turku.

Exploring the city

After the Great Fire in 1827, market and town moved away from the cathedral to the west bank of the Aura, much of it designed and built to the plan of that industrious Fennophile German, Carl Ludwig Engel, who visualised a city of rectangular blocks intersected by broad streets, a plan still clear in modern Turku. The best start to a walking tour is among the bright stalls, piled with fruit and flowers, in **Market Square** ❸ (Kauppatori; market Mon–Fri 7am–6pm, Sat 7am–3pm). On one side, the Hotel Hamburger Börs is one of Finland's best, with busy bars, cafés and restaurants packing its ground floor. The hotel faces the green, cap-like dome of the Orthodox Church, another Engel design built in 1838 on the orders of Tsar Nicholas I. The yellow building to the southwest is the Swedish Theatre, yet another Engel construction.

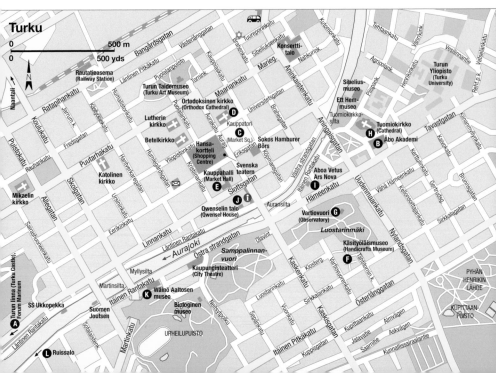

During the days of the Grand Duchy, the **Orthodox Cathedral D** (Ortodoksinen kirkko; tel: 02-277 5440; Mon, Tue and Thur 10am–1pm, Wed –6pm) served a Russian community, and its present congregation of 2,000 includes converts and several families who moved from Karelia during the World War II resettlement. Inside, it has all the rich beauty one would expect, the dome held up by ornate pillars. Paintings tell the story of St George and the Dragon, and Empress Alexandra (wife of the Roman Emperor Diocletian), to whom the church is dedicated. Continue on Aurakatu away from the market square and you arrive in Puolalanmäki.

Atop the hill is the imposing building that houses **Turku Art Museum** (Turun Taidemuseo; tel: 02-262 7100; Tue–Fri 11am–7pm, Sat–Sun 11am–pm; charge), with a collection of Finnish classics and exhibitions.

Handicrafts and sweets

A cluster of shops such as Pentik, Marikka and Sylvi Salonen, along Ylipistonkatu (Universitetsgatan) to the west, is a happy hunting ground for gifts and mementoes, with a selection of handicrafts, wood and chinaware and other typically Finnish goods. Between here and Eerikinkatu (Eriksgatan) is the **Hansa Shopping Centre** (Hansakortteli), enticingly weatherproof in a Finnish winter. Just across from Hansa, Mezzo is another indoor shopping complex with a variety of restaurants, cafés and shops.

More exciting is the 19th-century **Market Hall E** (Kauppahalli; Mon–Fri 7am–5.30pm, Sat 7am–3pm), across the street in Eerikinkatu. There is something about the smell of a market hall that lures you in, a mixture of cheese, meat, fish, sweets and a tang of exotic spices. The stalls stretch along the entire length, with tempting arrays of *munkki*, a sweet doughnut, and *pulla*, a cake-like bread. At Turun Tee ja Mauste you can breathe in the aroma of some 200 teas before you buy and pick up oddities such as ginger tea for Christmas or tea spiced with cloves – great for cold weather, the Finns say. Nearby, a stall sells typical wooden tulips and leaves, painted in bright

Paavo Nurmi (1897–1973) is considered the greatest long-distance runner of all time. He won a total of nine gold and three silver Olympic medals, and set 31 world records. He also carried the Olympic Torch in the 1952 Helsinki Games.

BELOW: the bustling university town is a good base from which to explore.

The clock tower of Turku Cathedral.

colours. Made by a sheltered workshop, they are half the usual cost.

Turning down Aurakatu towards the Auransilta (bridge) you pass the **tourist information office** (Apr–Sept Mon–Fri 8.30am–6pm and Sat–Sun 9am–4pm, Oct–Mar Mon–Fri 8.30am–6pm and Sat–Sun 10am–3pm). The bridge gives the first view of the numerous restaurant boats and the sleek white hull and complicated rigging of the *Suomen Joutsen*, the "Swan of Finland", which once plied the ocean between South America and Europe. Along the banks, people sit at open-air restaurants and, below the bridge, there is dancing on summer evenings.

Over the bridge, on the right-hand side, is a statue of long-distance runner Paavo Nurmi, Turku's most famous sportsman.

Step back in time

The entrance to one of Turku's most interesting areas is just a short walk from here. This is **Luostarinmäki** (Cloister Hill), the site of an early convent. There's a certain rough justice in the fact that the only part of the

wooden city to survive the Great Fi of 1827 was this hill, for it house those too poor to buy houses in th 18th-century city and they moved he to build their own community. Th escape has left an inheritance tha unlike most Nordic open-air museum stands where it was founded and is n a collection of relocated buildings.

The name **Handicrafts Museum** (Käsityöläismuseo; tel: 02-262 035 May–Sept and Dec–early Jan Tue–Su 10am–6pm; charge) is a slight misna mer because this old area is muc more; the woman spinning today i the dark interior of a wooden house a museum worker, but she is spinnin in the same way and in the same plac as the early inhabitants, and the 18t century costumes seem quite natura There are traditional sweets, every so of craft; a tin, copper and goldsmith' and a baker's which sometimes sel pretzels made in the traditional wa Seamstresses and tailors sew and th old way of life is revealed in the com munity houses where different familie lived in the same building, sharin their kitchen and their bathhouse, o

BELOW: take a step back in time to 18th-century Finland at Luostarinmäki.

y the truckle bed of a university stu-
ent who lived with a family, giving
ervice in return for his keep.

Coming down the hill, detour via
he Observatory on **Vartiovuori** Ⓖ,
nother Engel building, which has
een used as a museum and school
uilding. Nearby is an anti-aircraft gun
nemorial from World War II, when
rdinary Finns raised money for defen-
ve guns – Turku bought nine.

urku Cathedral

lso on the east side of the river is
urku Cathedral Ⓗ (Tuomiokirkko;
id-Apr to mid-Sept 9am–8pm, mid-
ept–mid-Apr 9am–7pm, subject to
ervices; free), the focal point of old
urku. Look down from the balcony
or the best view of the high arches of
e main aisle, with its side chapels.
he balcony is also where you'll find
e Cathedral Museum (charge), with
aluable collections opened to the
ublic in the 1980s after the most
cent restoration. Among the most
teresting chapels is the Kankainen
hapel, where the stained-glass win-
ow by Wladimir Swetschkoff shows
ueen Karin Månsdotter, wife of the
ckless Erik XIV, who was eventually
oisoned after his imprisonment.

Don't miss the statue of Mikael Agri-
la near the cathedral's south wall.
he architect of the Reformation in
nland, he was born on a farm in Pernå
st of Helsinki and took the name
gricola, meaning "farmer's son", when
e went to study in Rome. In the Cathe-
al Park, Count Per Brahe stands in a
assically proud pose, not far from Åbo
kademi, a block or two to the north.
he main buildings of the Swedish-
nguage university and the University
Turku are also nearby.

Modern art museum

ot far away stands the magnificent
ettig Palace, formerly a secretive resi-
nce of Hans von Rettig, tobacco
dustrialist, shipowner and one of the
chest men in Turku. The estate
s now been converted into one of

southern Finland's best museums.
Aboa Vetus Ars Nova ❶ (Itäinen Rantakatu 4–6; tel: 02-250 0552; early Jan–
Mar Tue–Sun 11am–7pm, Apr–early
Sept daily 11am–7pm, early Sept–late
Dec Tue–Sun 11am–7pm; guided tours
offered late June to Aug daily 11.30am;
charge) holds hundreds of compelling
works of modern art – the name is
Latin for "Old Turku, New Art". But it's
not just art that people come to find
here. When space for various building
extensions was being dug up in the
1990s, engineers stumbled upon the
remains of medieval alleyways and
stores from when the Finnish nation
was only a twinkle in the eyes of a few
Finns. These ruins are now visible
through the glass flooring in the
museum out by the garden, and there
are lots of activities for kids as well as
guided tours.

Along the river

In Turku you are never far from the
Aura River, which you can cross on one
of its five main bridges or by taking the
little ferry that still carries pedestrians
and cycles free of charge.

BELOW: the nave of
Turku Cathedral.

For a riverbank tour, the first stop is **Qwensel House** (Qwenselin talo; tel: 02-262 0322; May–Sept and Dec Tue–Sun 10am–6pm; charge), Turku's oldest wooden building, named after and built by Judge W.J. Qwensel, who bought the plot as long ago as 1695. Perhaps the best-kept secret in town, the backyard of this house has a café with 18th-century decor and recipes. From the waterside, low bushes trace the name TURKU/ÅBO, and Qwensel House now contains the **Pharmacy Museum** (Läntinen rantakatu 13; tel: 02-262 0280; May–Sept and Dec Tue–Sun 10am–6pm; charge), which keeps traditions alive by growing aromatic herbs in the garden. You can also see fine 18th-century furnishings, and old pharmaceutical items.

Maritime past

Walking past Myllysilta (Mill Bridge), in Borenpuisto Park, the dramatic statue entitled *Icy Sea* is dedicated to Turku's seamen. August Upman (inscribed on the pedestal) was a pioneer of winter navigation. Past the next bridge, Martinsilta, the SS *Ukkopekka*

was the last steamship to sail Finland coastal waters. Depending on how fa you care to walk, you can continue o this side as far as Turku Castle and th modern harbour areas that show ho important the sea still is to Turku, wit merchant tugs and tankers and the te minals of the Viking and Silja Lines.

On your way to the harbour at Li nankatu 74 is the **Forum Marinu** (www.forum-marinum.fi; tel: 02-282 95 exhibitions May–Sept daily 11am–7pr Oct–Apr Tue–Sun 11am–6pm; charg museum ships June–Aug daily 11am 7pm; charge). Turku has been a cent for shipbuilding since the Middle Age and many museum ships are her including the barque *Sigyn*, launche in Göteborg in 1887, and sailing as fa as the East Indies and South Americ Her last home port was the Ålan Islands and her last voyage from the in 1949. *Sigyn* is unique as the la barque-rigged ocean-going vessel.

Wäino Aaltonen

Heading back towards the centre yo come to the austere outlines of th **Wäinö Aaltonen Museum** (Wäin

altosen museo; Itäinen Rantakatu 38; el: 02-262 0850; Tue–Sun 11am–7pm; harge). Aaltonen was one of Finland's est known sculptors and artists, and a ational icon. He has famously culpted a number of likenesses of mous Finns, including Paavo Nurmi nd Jean Sibelius. The building con- ains much of his work, including the assive statues of *Peace*, hands raised, nd *Faith*, a mother and child. In a self- ortrait, this private man placed a text n front of his face to hide his feelings. utside the City Theatre is Aaltonen's tatue of Aleksis Kivi, one of the first uthors to write literature in Finnish.

The windmill on Samppalinnan- äki overlooking the river is the last of s kind in Turku. Here also, stopwatch hand, Paavo Nurmi trained against is own best times, and the polished ranite stone on the slopes is Finland's dependence memorial, unveiled in 977 on the 60th anniversary. On this ver walk, you will notice the water- uses by Auransilta Bridge and below artinsilta Bridge. A sightseeing cruise the best way to get a feel for this ater city.

Ruissalo Island

Boat services run several times daily to **Ruissalo Island** ❶, also reached in a few minutes by crossing a bridge. It is a green and leafy island, a place for botanists and birdwatchers as well as cyclists and walkers. Ruissalo is famous for its verdant oak groves (a woodland species only found in southern Fin- land) and its pretty "lace villas" (so called because of their latticed balco- nies and windows). The oldest exam- ples of the latter were built by wealthy merchants in the early 19th century. Choose one of several nature trails or rent a bicycle to explore the flora, fauna and beautiful villas on the island. Ruis- salo has the area's best beaches, includ- ing a nudist beach – something still rare in Finland, not because of any national prudery but because the Finns, with their isolated cabins on lonely lakesides, had not realised one might actually need permission to bathe without a swimsuit.

A good café and restaurant is Honka- pirtti, a Karelian-style pinewood build- ing built in 1942–3 by infantry soldiers near the front during the Continuation

Perched above a rocky coast in Naantali is Kultaranta, the summer residence of Finland's president. The extensive gardens, which supply the president's household with flowers and vegetables year round, are open to the public (contact the Naantali tourist board; tel: 02-435 9800, for further information).

BELOW: many tiny islands surround Ruissalo Island.

TIP

Viikinsaari island

The island of Viikinsaari, half an hour or so from Tampere by boat, is the perfect place to spend midsummer. The atmospheric restaurant on the island holds an outdoor barbecue, and Finns from all over the region come here to drink, dance and ring in the longest day of the year in style.

War. In summer, the island is home to Ruisrock, the world's oldest annual rock festival *(see page 101)*. There is also a spa hotel and a camping site, as well as the University Botanical Gardens on the island (daily; gardens free).

One of the most civilised ways to see the archipelago is a supper cruise aboard the SS *Ukkopekka*, which retains something of its steamship past and its original engine. As the passengers strive for window tables, the *Ukkopekka* moves smoothly down the river and out to sea. If the timing is right, a fisherman may sail out to the *Ukkopekka* with the fish he has caught and smoked that day.

Naantali and Moominworld

Naantali ❷, around 20 minutes west of Turku, is now a famous sailing harbour, packed with visiting boats. It is also a historic 200-year-old town, with old houses that are still lived in today. There is a beautiful greystone convent church, with a new organ that attracts famous organists, particularly during the June Music Festival when some 15,000 visitors crowd into the tiny town. At its start in the 1980s, the sceptics thought that little Naantali's festival "would die in 10 years". Now reaching into its third decade, it is proving them wrong. The harbour is also popular with artists, and galleries include the Purpura, which specialises in Finnish artists and supports an artist-in-residence scheme.

However, the city's main draw is **Moominworld** (tel: 02-511 1111; www. muumimaailma.fi; early June–late August daily 10am–6pm; charge), an outstanding theme park based on the beloved characters of Tove Jansson. It is perfect for a day out with the kids. The park is focused around the five-storey blueberry-hued Moomin House, and visitors can meet any number of Moomin characters and visit Moominmama's Kitchen, Hemulen's yellow house, Snufkin's Camp and Moominpappa's boat, among other favourite places from the books.

Glass village

For the most direct route to Tampere, leave the city on Road 40. This leads to **Aura ❸**, some 30km (20 miles) north

BELOW: something for everyone; Naantali is a very pretty spot...
BELOW RIGHT:
...and nearby is Moominworld.

here from Road 9 you have a fine ew of the Aurakoski (rapids). Road 9 ontinues northeast through rich rmland with a possible detour right : the Helsinki-Pori crossroads (Road) for a short drive to the Humppila lassworks, where at a glass-walled emonstration forge you can watch lassblowers at work. The Glass Village : Nuutajärvi, a little further north on e left of the road, was formed around inland's oldest glassworks from 1793, nd is also well worth a brief stop.

An alternative route, Road 41, slightly the west, goes through Oripää, a glid-g centre, where the Moorish-style uilding is the studio-home of sculptor iljo Syrjämaa, and from Vammala, the ad plies its way along the flat, fertile nd of the Loimijoki Valley. About 5km (15 miles) to the northeast is okia, a pleasant little town on the ores of Lake Pyhäjärvi that is the riginal site of the Nokia telecommuni-ations company. Boat cruises from ampere regularly stop at Nokia. Just orth of here are more magnificent pids at the start of the waterway sys-m that leads to Tampere.

Tampere

Officially Finland's second city, the citizens of Tampere may call their city the Manchester of Finland, but any-thing less like a classic industrial city is hard to imagine. It is one of the loveli-est places to visit in the country, not least for its waterways and lakes, which are easily explored in a day.

Tampere ❹ lies on a narrow neck of land between two lakes, great stretches of water so large that you feel you are close to a sea rather than way inland. Linking the lakes, the rushing waters of the Tammerkoski River first brought power, industry and riches to Tampere. Though it still provides some energy, the Tammerkoski is so clean nowadays that it attracts growing numbers of anglers, out for the season's trout. At weekends, the two lakes are bright with rainbow sails, while the shores are packed with picnickers.

Despite a changing pattern of indus-try, Tampere has managed to retain factories and workers' houses without allowing them to turn into slums, and the tall red-brick chimneys that do remain are symbols of both past and

Bronze statue by Wäinö Aaltonen on Hämeensilta Bridge, Tampere.

BELOW: on board a ferry leaving Turku for the Åland Islands.

Cruising through the Industrial Heartland

With its over-abundance of forests (two-thirds of the country is covered with mostly pine and birch trees), it's hardly surprising that Finland should find itself at the forefront of international paper production. It is still a thriving industry – more than 60 percent of the paper produced in Finland is exported around the world – and factories lining the waterways are a familiar sight. These days, though, recycled paper is often marketed as an attractive and ecological option. Textiles, shoe-making and wood production are other industries for which Tam-pere has been well known since the 19th century. Today, of course, it is mobile technology which dominates.

One excellent way to take in both Tampere's industrial heritage as well as its timeless natural surroundings is by going on a local lake cruise. In the summertime, various boats ply the beautiful Lake Pyhäjärvi, with cruises from Tampere to Virrat and to Hämeenlinna, the oldest town in Finland. A popular day trip is out to Viikinsaari, a wooded summer recreation area, where many locals venture to take in the sun and share a friendly beer. Another option is the guided water bus cruises to the shipyard of STX Europe Turku. The fascinating tour gives a sense of how massive cruise liners are built, as well as a sense of how important ship-building is to Finnish industry.

Tampere Orthodox Church, showing the Russian influence in Finland's second city.

present, for Tampere's factories are still high on the list of Finland's leading manufacturers and exporters.

There are some 200 lakes in and around the city. The two largest, Näsi-järvi to the north and Pyhäjärvi to the south, are the meeting point of two famous waterway routes. To the south, the Silverline threads its way though a labyrinth of lakes towards Hämeen-linna, passing Valkeakoski, another industrial town in a splendid rural setting, and stopping at the beautiful Aulanko Forest Park among other places (*see page 224*).

The romantically named Poet's Way boat, SS *Tarjanne*, steers north through narrow, winding waters to Ruovesi and Virrat. The whole journey takes nine hours and gives a two-day taste of Finland's lakes, with an overnight stay at either Virrat or Ruovesi. A little further north, Ahtäri has one of Finland's best native zoos. The national poet J.L. Runeberg began his best-known work, *Tales of Ensign Ståhl*, in Ritoniemi Mansion at Ruovesi and, near the village, Akseli Gallén-Kallela (*see page 86*) built his first "Kalela" studio-home.

Tampere's history

Tampere was officially founded in 177 by King Gustav III of Sweden-Finlan but, since the Middle Ages, the Pirkka area to the south of the centre ha been settled by farmers, attracted b the waterways which made transpo easy. From around the 13th centur when the Swedes granted them righ to collect taxes from the Lapp peopl they prospered richly. These earlie *tamperelaiset* (Tampere residents) a commemorated on the Hämeensil Bridge in a series of statues by Wäin Aaltonen. Also clear from the bridge the tall chimney of one of Tampere earliest industries, Frenckel, the pape makers, from 1783. The old mill is no a theatre with two stages.

Exploring the centre

The Tammerkoski has largely lost i working factories, and hotels, shoj ping centres and museums have take their place. The venerable and wel restored Grand Hotel Tammer, th Cumulus Koskikatu and Hotel Ilves a have splendid views of the Tammerk ski rapids, and, from the top of th

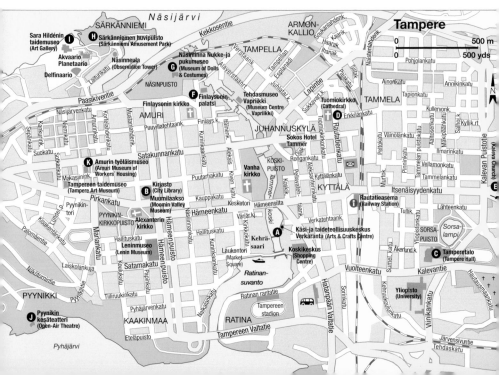

Ilves's 18 storeys, the panorama takes in the quay where the Silverline boats berth, the leisure craft, the red brick of the old factories and the magnificent stretches of lake. A minute or two away on the riverside, the **Verkaranta Arts and Crafts Centre** Ⓐ (tel: 03-225 1409; June–Aug Mon–Fri 10am–6pm, Sat–Sun noon–5pm, Sept–May Mon–Fri 10am–6pm, Sat–Sun 11am–4pm) sells good-quality craftwork. Above it on the town side is the tourist information office (tel: 03-5656 6800). Below the hotel, the Koskikeskus covered shopping centre has some 100 shops, and the market hall, for fresh produce, is at Hämeenkatu 19.

Old memories, new buildings

Across a footbridge over the rapids, one of the oldest factory areas stands on Kehräsaari (Spinning Island). In the independence (civil) War, the victorious White Army crossed the Tammerkoski here to capture Tampere. Today, its factories and boutiques are grouped around cobbled courtyards. Nearby, the only factory still working

on the river, Tako, makes carton paper. Keep an eye out, too, for the old factory chimney with a bomb shield on the top, a reminder that Tampere was bombed fiercely in the 1918 civil war, when it was an important "Red" stronghold, and again during World War II with eight heavy raids.

Tampere is also a centre for culture and education, but the culture is modern and the education scientific and technical. The architecture is also largely 20th-century, typified by the **City Library** Ⓑ (Kirjasto; Pirkankatu 2; Mon–Thur 10am–7pm, Fri 10am–6pm, Sat 10am–4pm), an astonishing building said to be based on the open wings and spread tail feathers of a wood grouse, though you might see it more as a series of mushrooms. In the mid-1980s the library and the Tampere City Building Office won several awards for its husband and wife architects, Reima and Raili Pietilä. Finns are great readers and borrow, on average, 20 books each per year. Adults as well as children are intrigued by the Moomin Valley Museum in the basement, where the original illustrations

Sugar snap peas are one of Finland's most popular homegrown vegetables and are sold in all city markets.

BELOW: aerial view of Tampere from Nasinneula Observation Tower.

Tampere's neo-Renaissance Finlayson Palace now serves as a restaurant.

of Tove Jansson's fantasy characters, the Moomins, are on display *(see page 105)*.

The **Tampere Hall** (Tampere-talo), is Tampere's pride, a spectacular blue-white event hall designed by Esa Piiroinen and Sakari Aartelo in 1990. Streams of light illuminate the main foyer's fountains, which commemorate the Tammerkoski rapids as the source of local prosperity. The main hall holds 2,000, while a smaller auditorium seats 500. If you arrive on a festival morning you can catch the sound of a choir or orchestra rehearsing on stage. Lit for an opera such as *Parsifal*, the large hall is magnificent, and Tampere denizens are happy to tell you that their hall is bigger than Helsinki's Finlandia, and the acoustics are much better. The hall is used for conferences and congresses and there is a café, the Café Soolo.

Tampere's churches

Lars Sonck was only 30 when he won a national competition with his design for the **Tampere Cathedral** (Tuomi-okirkko; June–Aug daily 10am–5pm, Sept–May daily 11am–3pm), which was then St John's Church, completed

BELOW: interior of St Michael's at Messukylä.

in 1907 at the height of the National Romantic movement. It stands in its own park at Tuomiokirkonkatu 3, a few blocks east of the river, and contains some of the best of Finnish art including Magnus Enckell's altar fresco of the Resurrection and his circular window that forms a cross and wreath of thorns. Hugo Simberg painted *The Wounded Angel*, a shattered form carried by two boys, and *The Garden of Death* – despite its name, not a gloomy picture. His note on the back of a working sketch reads: "A place where souls go before entering heaven." Around the gallery, his *Garland of Life* shows 12 boys carrying a green garland of roses, symbolising humanity's burden of life. This great church seats 2,000 and, softly lit, makes a beautiful setting for a Sunday evening concert.

The **Kaleva Church** (Kalevan kirkko; Liisanpuisto 1), east on the Kalevan Puistotie road, stands solid in the centre of a green park, like a silo rising out of a field. No wonder it's nicknamed "the silo of souls". Inside the stark appearance changes to dramatic, with a soaring light that pulls

our gaze upwards. A striking feature of this church, another Pietilä design from 1966, is the organ, its 3,000 pipes shaped like a "sail". Behind the altar the wooden statue is intended to be a reed – "a bruised reed He shall not break".

Tampere's oldest church is the 15th-century **St Michael's at Messukylä** (Kivikinkontie 2; June–July daily, May and Aug Wed–Sun; free), around 5km (2 miles) east along the Iidesjärvi (lake) on the old Lahti road. The oldest part is the vestry that once stood beside an even earlier wooden church. A moment of high excitement in 1959 revealed extensive wall paintings, now restored, from the 1630s. The church's most valuable wooden sculpture is believed to be that of the royal saint King Olav of Norway, whose tomb in Trondheim became a place of pilgrimage during the Middle Ages.

Industrial heritage

Tampere's rich industrial heritage illustrates how international the city was nearly two centuries ago. One of the most important industries, textiles, was founded by a Scotsman, James Finlayson. He arrived in 1820 from Russia to build a heavy engineering works at the north end of the Tammerkoski, with the first water-powered spinning mill. When he sold to Rauch and Nottbeck in 1836 it grew to become one of the biggest textile factories in the Nordic countries, but in those early days Mrs Finlayson was not too proud to sell the mill's products in the market. James Finlayson was an industrialist in the Quaker mould and Finlayson's became almost a town within a city, with its own police, health programme and hospital, factory school and a church: the yellow building with a wooden door near the factory complex. Visitors now find a completely refurbished area of bustling activity, with a microbrewery, a restaurant, a 10-screen cinema complex and museum devoted to the workers' movement.

After Finlayson returned to Scotland, the new owners continued the traditions and the name, and lived in a mansion house nearby, known as the **Finlayson Palace** Ⓕ (Finlaysonin palatsi; Kuninkaankatu 1) and built by Alexander von Nottbeck. It became a

Iittala products on sale in Tampere.

BELOW LEFT: fireworks above Tampere to celebrate Independence Day on 6 December.
BELOW: modern Tampere.

famous house, visited by Tsar Alexander II and his court, and there are portraits of both Alexander I and II on the central staircase, grand enough to feel you should be sweeping down it in full evening dress. The palace is now a club, with live music in the evenings. The restaurant serves food during the day and is also popular for art exhibitions and social functions. The surrounding park is open daily, admission free.

The other main company, Tampella, on the eastern side of the river, began as a foundry in 1850. This enormous edifice housed some of the EU meetings during Finland's presidency. It has now been renovated and renamed **Museum Centre Vapriikki** (from the Swedish word *fabrik*, or factory). The main museum (tel: 03-5656 6966; www.tampere.fi/vapriikki; Tue–Sun; charge) has exhibits on a wide range of subjects, including handicrafts, archaeology, the Industrial Revolution and the workers' movement. The Finnish Ice Hockey Museum is also housed here.

The greater part of Tampella has moved further out of town, with many of the old buildings converted into apartments, offices and similar use One former Tampella factory, on peninsula above Lake Näsijärvi, is no a spa hotel (Holiday Club Tampere which concentrates on healthy livin, and offers massage and other trea ments in a comfortable atmosphere.

Another Nottbeck home was **Näsi linna G**, an old mansion on a hill i Näsinpuisto Park overlooking the lak an easy walk from the Finlayson build ings. Don't miss Emil Wikström' Pohjanneito Fountain on your wa through. To illustrate how knowledg and skill are passed from generation t generation, on one side a grandmothe explains handiwork to a little girl, o the other a boy shows an old man ho water power has made work easier. O top is the Maid of the North from th *Kalevala* sitting on a rainbow, spinnin golden thread.

The Nottbeck house is now **Häm Museum** (Hämeen museo), which co tains the **The Museum of Dolls an Costumes** (Nukke-ja pukumuseo scheduled to open in early 2011. Th museum holds a private collection c several hundred dolls, including on from 12th-century Peru, as well as pu pet theatres and exhibits that illustrat the history of play and magic skills.

Tampere's amusements

From Näsinlinna, across the norther harbour entrance, is an even highe viewpoint: the Näsinneula Observatio Tower at the centre of **Särkänniem Amusement Park H** (Särkänniemer huvipuisto; www.sarkanniemi.fi), with it aquarium, dolphinarium, planetariur and children's zoo (tel: 0207-130 20(aquarium, planetarium and dolphina rium daily all year; amusement par daily early May–mid-Aug; times var so check website). The tower is th highest in Finland, and there is no be ter way to get an overview of Tampe than from the open-air platform ove 120 metres (400ft) up or from th revolving restaurant above it. Lookin immediately below, the funfair's rai ways, Ferris wheels, rollercoasters an

BELOW: Sara Hildén Art Museum, Tampere.

water park rides look like children's toys. The restaurant is good, but on the expensive side; it takes 50 minutes to complete a revolution and is open until midnight.

If your tastes run to modern art rather than funfairs, or if you like both, don't miss the **Sara Hildén Art Gallery ❶** (Sara Hildénin taidemuseo; tel: 03-3114 3512; May–Aug daily noon–7pm, Sept–Apr Tue–Sun; charge), in a beautiful building close by, which claims to have Tampere's best lake view. Sara Hildén was an art collector who specialised in Finnish and foreign art of the 1960s and 1970s, and there are also visiting exhibitions and concerts.

Between the lakes, the western part of the isthmus rises to form the Pyynikki Ridge, born 10,000 years ago during the last Ice Age round the old bowl of an ancient sea. It was once the home of the town's bishop, and its old viewing tower is a popular place for looking over both lakes and towards the **Pyynikki's Open-Air Theatre ❶** (Pyynikin kesäteatteri) down near Lake Pyhäjärvi. In a remarkable example of lateral thinking, the theatre auditorium revolves rather than the stage – truly theatre in the round, as the audience turns to face each new scene, with perhaps fairies from *A Midsummer Night's Dream* perched high in the trees. The theatre (mid-June–mid-Aug) is especially beautiful when the trees are drenched in white blossom.

Full circle

Further west is Pispala (Bishop's Village), now considered a very prestigious place to live. In fact, it was built in the late 19th century by factory workers. As a sign of progress, their children left and went to live in central Tampere, but now the grandchildren of the original builders are eager to return and restore. The **Amuri Museum of Workers' Housing ❸** (Amurin työläismuseo; Makasiininkatu 12; tel: 03-3146 6690; mid-May–mid-Sept Tue–Sun 10am–6pm; charge) shows how these houses would have looked up until 1970, when the city stopped old-style construction and began building terrace houses. There are 25 houses and two shops, all giving the impression that the owners might return at any

Tampere is a very bicycle-friendly city.

BELOW: recreated room at the Museum of Workers' Housing.

moment. Nearby, Café Amurin Helmi, decorated in the 1920s style, sells traditional biscuits for dipping, and the Amuri shop offers treacle-sugared sweets and caramel cones.

If you have time to spare, the unusual **Lenin Museum** (Hämeenpuisto 28; tel: 03-276 8100; Mon–Fri 9am–6pm, Sat–Sun 11am–4pm; charge) is also worth a visit. Exhibits document Lenin's stays in Finland after the failed 1905 revolution, including the occasion he met Stalin for the first time here in Tampere.

Whatever else you miss in this water city, do not miss a boat journey. GoTampere has details on trips out to various islands and beaches where you can birdwatch or relax under cool forest trees, and enjoy a picnic away from everyone else. Hard to believe that, strictly speaking, you are still in Finland's leading industrial city.

Back to Helsinki

The first stops along Road 3 from Tampere to Helsinki are Valkeakoski and Sääksmäki, yet more of those Finnish industrial centres that contrive to place themselves in beautiful surroundings. These happen to be set between two lakes. In the Middle Ages, **Valkeakoski ❺** was no more than a hamlet, later a mining village in the important parish of Sääksmäki; but even then, it harnessed its powerful rapids to grind corn and make paper. Later, the 19th-century National Romantic movement brought artists to Sääksmäki. For a feeling of Valkeakoski's industrial history, go to the wooden outdoor museum of **Kauppilanmäki** (tel: 040-563 601, June–Aug Tue, Thur–Sun noon–4pm, Wed noon–6pm; charge), typical of the early paper-mill workers' homes up to 1920. The workers' hall, with its union flags, was the centre of political thought as well as home to the community entertainment.

The old **Voipaala Manor** (Voipaalan kartano; May–Sept daily 11am–6pm, Oct–Apr Tue–Fri 11am–5pm, Sat–Sun noon–6pm) on Rapola Hill has become an art centre. The museum was once the studio of the sculptor Elias Ilkka, who owned the manor and the farm where the Valkeakoski Summer Theatre performs. Today exhibi

ons are held here. On the hill above
an ancient hill fort and a view of the
church of **Sääksmäki** ❻, a short walk
away. This early parish had an even
older church, but the present greystone building dates back to the 15th
century. A fire on April Fool's Day,
1929, destroyed much of the church,
but a 1932 restoration preserved some
wall paintings, as well as the altarpiece
and two wooden statues.

Art and glassware

Just over the bridge, detour right
towards Toijala and then right again to
Visavuori ❼ (Kirkkovainiontie 10, tel:
3-543 6528; June–Aug daily 10am–
pm, Jan–May and Sept–Nov Tue–Sun
10am–4pm, Dec Tue–Fri 10am–4pm;
charge), the studio home of one of Finland's best-known sculptors, Emil Wikström (1864–1942). Aged 29, he had
just won a competition to design the
frieze for Helsinki's House of Estates,
when he designed his house on the
peninsula overlooking the lake. Here
he worked in the wood-lined studio,
spending his nights observing the stars
in his rooftop observatory.

Of all Finland's well-known glass-
makers, **Iittala** ❽ (June–Aug daily
10am–5pm, Sept–May Sat–Sun 10am–
5pm) is probably the most famous,
with austere designs, beautiful functional glassware, and *objets d'art* such as
glass birds and fruit shapes so perfect
that you immediately want to hold
them – a practice not to be recommended in the museum.

Inside you will also find past and
present designs by such eminent Finns
as Alvar Aalto and Timo Sarpaneva,
designer of the "i-collection" which
became Iittala's trademark. Helped by
an expert glassblower who does most of
the work, you can try your talents on a
misshapen paperweight. Even better is
the Iittala shop where seconds – often
indistinguishable to the naked eye from
the real thing – are regularly less than
half the price of a perfect work.

Military hardware

There is no escape from modern history at the **Parola Tank Museum** ❾
(Panssarimuseo; tel: 040-5681 186; daily
May–Sept 10am–6pm, Oct–Mar until
4pm; charge), set up by the Association

*Gooseberries are part
of the summer's yield
in Finland.*

BELOW:
worker making an
Aalto vase in the
Iittala glass factory.

The old army camp ground near the Tank Museum, with the Lion of Parola statue, recalls Tsar Alexander II's signing of the Language Charter in 1863, in nearby Hämeenlinna, to give Finnish equal status with Swedish.

of Armoured Troops and Veterans, survivors of the Finnish campaigns during World War II. Some Winter War tanks go back to 1910, and the Continuation War terrace has some captured Soviet tanks, their hammer and sickle replaced by the swastika, after Finland found itself fighting on the same side as the Germans. For military historians this little-known museum is a fascinating tribute to the Finnish tank operators, but even the most casual visitor is intrigued by the armoured train in the woods above. To reach Parola, take Road 57, marked Hattula, off the main road, and then, just past the next crossroads, branch left again to Parola.

Ancient church and forest

Continue back on Road 57 to the **Hattulan Church of the Holy Cross** ❿ (Hattulan Pyhän Ristin kirkko; mid-May–mid Aug daily; free), one of Finland's best known and oldest churches. It was built beside the lake of Hattula in 1320, when Catholicism had only recently arrived in the region, following the Swedish construction of Häme Castle, about 6km (4 miles) further

south. Inside, your eyes are immediately drawn upwards by the delicat colours of the intricate 16th-centur frescoes which cover ceilings and wall They were later lime-washed and hiden until the mid-19th century, whe they were restored. Today, Hattula ha regained the atmosphere of a medieva church, and its most valuable statue a wooden St Olav, the 11th-centur Norwegian royal saint.

Aulanko Forest Park ⓫ (Aulango puisto), just off Road 3, is ideal for break. The forest had a fortress lon before the days of Christianity, but th man who made Aulanko what it today was Colonel Hugo Stander skjöld, in the 1930s the governor o Häme province. He had made his fo tune as an arms dealer in Russia an returned to build a new manor an beautify the forest park with ornamen tal lakes, follies and the observatio tower overlooking Aulankojärvi (lake The Bear Cave nearby has an appealin family group of bears carved by Rober Stigell. Jean Sibelius, born in Hämeen linna, is said to have commented o Aulanko: "I was thinking of thes

BELOW: altar detail at Hattulan Church.

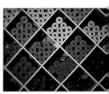

Map on
page 206

cenes from my childhood when I composed *Finlandia*". Aulanko is a stopping place for the Silverline boats and as a modern hotel, with golf courses and tennis courts. The outdoor theatre and lake excursions attract a quarter of a million visitors a year.

Castle and composer

Hämeenlinna ⓬ has two claims to fame: as the home of **Häme Castle** (tel: 3-675 6820; Jan–May Mon–Fri 10am–pm, Sat–Sun 11am–4pm, June–mid-Aug daily 10am–6pm, mid-Aug–mid-Dec Mon–Fri 10am–4pm, Sat–Sun 11am–pm; charge) and the birthplace of ean Sibelius.

In the 13th century, when Earl Birger ed the first Swedish foray into this ncient countryside, Swedish governors were ever-conscious of the proxmity to Russia and obsessed with the eed for defensive measures. Birger's rst task was to build a square-walled efensive camp with towers at its corers – still the heart of Häme Castle. Over the next 700 years, Häme was emodelled to suit the moods of various countries' rulers, and its red-bricked

walls now intertwine Swedish, Finnish and Russian history. The castle area also includes the **Prison Museum** and the **Artillery Museum**.

Hämeenlinna itself was granted town status in 1639 by Count Per Brahe, but it was already an important settlement on the Oxen Trail between Turku and Häme Castle. This centuries-old route has served soldier, merchant and traveller alike, though pack animals and carts have given way to motor cars and the track has become a modern road. With its busy centre and shady park, Hämeenlinna makes an excellent base for touring.

Sibelius was born in December 1865 in the little timberboard house of the town physician, Christian Gustaf Sibelius. The three Sibelius children were musical, and one room in the house, now the **Sibelius Home Museum** (Hallituskatu 11; tel: 03-621 2755; May–Sept Tue–Sun 10am–5pm; charge) shows Sibelius's upright piano from 20 years later and an old photograph of the young family trio performing at the Loviisa Spa Casino, where they gave summer concerts.

Silk threads in a rainbow of colours are part of the unique Silk Museum in the heart of Aulanko.

BELOW LEFT:
Häme Castle, Hämeenlinna.
BELOW:
armoured vehicles at the Parola Tank Museum.

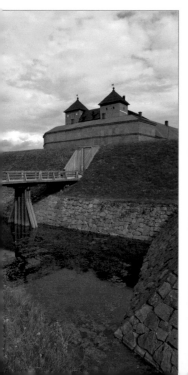

In Hyvinkää, in Rantapuisto Park, is Finland's largest statue, the gigantic yellow arches of the Triad Monument.

The dining room is now used for occasional recitals, and the house is full of memorabilia from the composer's childhood.

The **Finnish Glass Museum** (Suomen Lasimuseo; Tehtaankatu 23; tel: 020-758 4108; May–Aug daily, Sept–Dec and Feb–Apr Tue–Sun; charge) is the most popular place in **Riihimäki** ⓭, just off Road 3 some 35km (26 miles) south of Hämeenlinna. The building is an authentic glassworks from 1914, still active in the 1930s. The ground-floor exhibition traces the history of glassmaking, from the early days of Finnish independence, when the industry concentrated on mundane items such as window panes, to the 1930s, which saw both the beginning of glassmaking as a fine art and, later, its mass production.

Lake dwellers

Heading south through Hyvinkää to Järvenpää, you are only 45km (30 miles) from Helsinki. The area's lake attracted artists away from their city haunts to build studio-villas on the eastern side, just beyond **Järvenpää** ⓮.

The first of the late 19th-centur[y] artist-intellectuals were writer Juha[n] Aho and his artist wife, Venny Solda[n-]Brofeldt. Within a year they were fo[l-]lowed by artist Pekka Halonen, whos[e] work had already been inspired by th[e] beautiful **Lake Tuusulanjärvi** ⓯ an[d] by the farming life around him, as wa[s] another incomer, portrait painter Eer[o] Järnefelt, famous for his rural and fol[k] scenes. When Sibelius and his wif[e] Aino moved to the lake shores, th[e] Halonens' home, Halosenniemi (te[l:] 09-8718 3461; Tue–Sun), became [a] meeting point for convivial sauna[s,] recitals and the drinking of Halonen[s'] homemade rhubarb wine.

Ainola ⓰ (tel: 09-287 322; May[–] Sept Tue–Sun; charge) was the Sibeliu[s] home for 53 years. Designed by La[rs] Sonck, it is still furnished as it was i[n] Sibelius's time – the drawing roo[m] holds the composer's piano. Outside i[n] summer, the garden is quiet and peace[-] ful. Sibelius died at Ainola in 1957 a[t] the age of 91; his wife died in 196[9] aged 97. Underneath the apple tre[e] their grave is a square flat stone, wit[h] always a few floral tributes close by.

BELOW: inside Sibelius's lakeside home, Ainola.
RIGHT: Naantali harbour.

THE ÅLAND ISLANDS

Although separated from the mainland and
inhabited by Swedish-speakers, the Åland Islands
remain very much a part of the Finnish
landscape and heritage

T he Åland Islands (Ahvenanmaa in
Finnish) are a collection of
granite-bound skerries scattered
ut to the west of the Finnish coast.
Most people outside Scandinavia have
ever heard of them, though they are a
art of a unique, autonomous political
tructure that gives the 27,000 Swedish-
peakers here their own particular
dentity. They have had their own flag
ince 1954 and their own postage
tamps since 1984.

Geography and culture

n 1917 the islands demarcated the west-
rn limit of the Grand Duchy of Russia
hat Finland then was, and the Russians
egan sending reinforcements to the
slands. But, while Finland was celebrat-
ng independence from Russia in
918–19, Ålanders were petitioning to
ecome part of Sweden. Although the
eague of Nations assigned the islands
s a demilitarised, semi-autonomous
ntity to Finland (with Swedish as the
fficial language), today's Ålanders
old few grudges. Like mainland Finns,
landers take tremendous pride in a
innish athlete or team beating the
wedish competition. But they do not
hink of themselves as ordinary Finns.
landers have inhabited their islands
or thousands of years, and have a
trong sense of cultural identity and
ride in their traditions. The fact that
hey never became a part of Sweden
eems, if anything, to have nurtured
ven greater pride in their uniqueness.

From June to August, the archipelago is a place of breeze-ruffled inlets
edged with tiny, sun-kissed beaches of
glacier-worn granite and fishing villages
that huddle at the edges of rocky promontories. Winters here are sodden and
windy and rarely cold enough for any
real snow. Although the islands attract
fleets of oversized sailing and motor
yachts, and with them crowds of well-
to-do boat owners, the sentiment here
is never elitist – merely restful.

The Ålanders have scraped a living
from the soil and extracted it from the

Main attractions
MARIEHAMN
ECKERÖ
GETA
KASTELHOLM
FÖGLÖ
DEGERBY
KÖKAR

PRECEDING PAGES:
summer on the
Åland Islands.
LEFT: Åland district
coat of arms.
BELOW: the island
of Sund.

sea for centuries. In the days before motorised sailing, it took six weeks to ply the rough waters to Helsinki, where Ålanders traded sealskins and oil. They also profited from local apples, herring and loaves of sweet black bread known as *svartbröd*, which goes especially well with herring.

Today, Ålanders earn their living in a slightly less gruelling fashion. Fifteen percent are directly employed in tourism and another 15 percent in tourist-related services. Seal hunting has dropped out of the picture, but farming, fishing and construction remain fundamental to the local economy. One unique Åland product you'll see is the Finnish potato crisp, made from island-grown spuds.

The grand-scale shipbuilding that once took place here has largely died out, but a large part of Finland's merchant navy is still owned by Åland shippers, and Ålanders have recently revived their traditional boatbuilding skills with three ocean-going, wooden sailing ships that you may be lucky enough to see in Mariehamn. The Finland-Sweden ferries provide hun-

dreds of jobs – locals have worked in the marine industry since old Åland grain ships once plied worldwide routes as far as the Antipodes.

Ålanders also continue to follow old customs. Many of these centre on weddings: until very recently, brides from certain islands wore black and a few brides still wear the traditional high crown of birch leaves and wild flowers. A proper Åland wedding can go on for days. The Ålands also regularly host the international Island Games, a mini Olympics with participants from British islands such as the Isle of Man, the Shetland and Orkney islands – and some from as far afield as the Falklands.

Mariehamn and around

An enjoyable way to visit the Åland Islands is by taking the Viking Line ship from Turku *(see page 205)* to Mariehamn, which provides a scenic cruise through the thousands of islands and skerries. The main ring of islands includes Åland, Föglö, Kökar, Sottunga, Kumlinge and Brändö.

Mariehamn ❶ is the capital of the main island, Åland, and has 11,100

TIP

You can easily make your way around the Åland archipelago by renting a bicycle in Mariehamn from Ro-No RENT (tel: 018-12821; www.visitaland.com/rono). Bikes can be taken on all ferries for free, and on buses for a small fee.

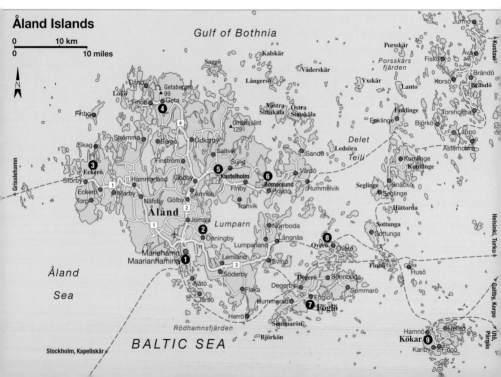

nhabitants; the original town on this ite was called Ytterna, and some of its ld buildings can still be seen in south Mariehamn.

Near the west harbour is the **Maritime Museum** (tel: 018-19930; Sept–Apr 10am–4pm, May–June and Aug 9am–5pm, July 9am–7pm; charge), an xcellent museum designed in the mage of a ship; it has plenty of exhibts on the seafaring history of Åland's eoples – the islands once maintained he largest number of wooden ships in he world. Moored out behind the museum is the four-masted museum hip *Pommern* (tel: 018-531 421; May–ept daily; charge) – built in Glasgow n 1904 and since restored to its origial state – which together with a visit o the nearby Maritime Museum will ive you the lowdown on the archielago's seagoing history.

On the cultural side is the **Ålands Museum**, located at Stadshusparken tel: 018-25000; June–Aug daily 10am–pm, Sept–May Tue and Thur 10am–pm, Wed and Fri 10am–4pm, Sat–Sun oon–4pm; charge), a museum and art allery with exhibitions on prehistoric

and Ice and Bronze Age Åland life. From more recent times are displays on folk customs and archaeological finds from the islands' many medieval churches.

The **Lilla Holmen Bird Reserve**, below the east harbour, is an island park filled with roaming peacocks and roosters, mixed in with Angora rabbits and guinea pigs (caged). There is also a café and short strip of beach. A more interesting excursion is hiking or cycling out to the Ramsholmen Nature Reserve on the nearby island of Jomala.

Onningby and Eckerö

Mariehamn is the only town-sized settlement on the islands, but there are dozens of villages, many dating back centuries, such as **Onningby ➋** at Jomala, much favoured by painters, including the acclaimed Finnish artist Victor Westerholm, who had a summer house here. The smallest islands are either wholly uninhabited, or inhabited perhaps only by a single family.

On the main island, the countryside stretches out for miles in all directions from Mariehamn, alternating between

A decorative maypole celebrates the start of spring on the Åland Islands.

BELOW LEFT: making hand-crafted boats. **BELOW:** traditional wooden houses, both in Mariehamn.

TIP

Spread across the islands is accommodation in campsites, cottages or guest-houses, as well as some picturesque rural farmhouses. For more information, contact the Åland Islands' Tourist Information at Storagatan 8 (tel: 018-24000; www.visitaland.com).

wide open fields and sea vistas to dense, aromatic forests crowded with pines and birches. The scenery is particularly beautiful along the straits that cut into Eckerö ❸, straits which resemble rivers at their narrower points. Eckerö Harbour is set off by the cherry-red boathouses clustered along its bays and promontories. Due to its western exposure, you can watch the midnight sun in Eckerö from its evening dip towards the sea until its early dawn rising.

Several museums in Eckerö are worth a visit. The large Russian-era **Post House** (Posthus) has two small museums, both open daily in summer, which detail the dangerous voyages made by postmen delivering mail between here and Sweden in previous centuries. In mid-June the **Postrodden** or mailboat race leaves from Eckerö, a re-enactment of the once arduous journey to Stockholm to deliver post. Participants sail over in 18th-century costume, and stay at the old postal workers' hotel at Storby.

At the attractive fishing harbour, the **Hunting and Fishing Museum** (Jakt och Fiskemuseum; tel: 018-38299;

May–mid-Sept daily 10am–5pm charge) has interesting exhibitions on the subject, and a shop selling local handicrafts.

Eckerö is closest to the Swedish mainland (Grisslehamn) and so is a popular car ferry departure point. The journey takes two hours.

Moving across the north to **Geta** ❹ you'll find a tremendous landscape of shelves of granite laced with natural grottoes dug out aeons ago by glaciers and then eroded by the sea. There is a small café at the end of the Geta road; the grotto path is to the right. The teetering piles of stones that line the path are said to be remains from age-old bread ovens.

East Åland

Saltvik, Sund, Lumparland and Lemland on the east side of the islands are farming areas. With its numerous forest-fringed inlets and natural protection from the open sea, Lumparland Sound is a fine spot to fish or picnic, or arrange a cottage stay.

In Åland's northeast are the historic Kastelholm and Bomarsund fortresses. **Kastelholm** ❺ in Tosarby Sund (tel: 018-432 150; May, Sept daily 10am–4pm; June, Aug 10am–5pm, July 10am–6pm; charge) was once the administrative centre of the islands, and dates from the 1300s. The Russians began fortifying it in 1829; ultimately the site was destroyed by fire, but it is now under extensive restoration. Adjacent are the Cultural History Museum and Jan Karlsgården Open-Air Museum (May-Aug daily; charge). Five km (3 miles) to the north of Kastelholm is the 13th-century granite church of Sund.

About 13km (8 miles) east of Kastelholm is **Bomarsund** ❻, which was built by the Russians as a huge fortified area, surrounded by a stone wall and then knocked out by British and French firepower during the Crimean War. The 1856 Peace of Paris that followed included Tsar Alexander's declaration that the islands would have no more military reinforcement.

BELOW: medieval church in Eckerö.

Ålanders are, even today, exempt from national service in Finland.

Bird island

Southeast of Åland lies the second-most populated island, **Föglö ❼**. The ferry takes about 30 minutes from Svinö (a bus from Mariehamn to Svinö takes about 40 minutes) and lands at the enchanting port town of **Degerby**, once a popular vodka smugglers' destination as well as an important customs post. In the eastern part of the island is a natural bird reserve, inspiration for the three golden birds on Föglö's coat of arms.

Degerby's cross-shaped Maria Magdalena Church used to be a key landmark for sailors crossing the north Baltic. It dates from the 12th century and was renovated at great expense in 1859. On the altar is a precious silver crucifix from the 1500s (excavated in the 1960s), preserved in a lucite casing. The church's sacristy holds an extraordinary collection of priests' robes.

The Maria Magdalena cemetery has many headstones carrying the name Perón; any Föglö resident named Perón is related to the family of the late Argentinian president. One version of the unlikely story explaining this link claims that an Argentinian seaman became involved in work at the Degerby customs station, found a Degerby wife, and never left.

Föglö has wonderful possibilities for touring by bike, with its empty roads and lack of steep terrain. From Degerby you can ride to **Overö ❽**, the northernmost island in the Föglö group, in just over an hour, using a series of car bridges that stretch to the last strait before Overö. To cross this, you must go on board the cable ferry, which, like the inter-island ferries, is considered an extension of the road system so is free.

Unless you decide to rent a private cottage along the Föglö Straits, the only choice for accommodation will be the charming **Enigheten Guesthouse** at Degerby, a preserved farmhouse manor run by volunteers (tel: 018-50310; www.enigheten.ax).

Archaeological treasures

Kökar ❾ is a bare island and most of its vistas look towards the open sea. By the rocky coast at Hamnö is a fascinating medieval church, founded by Franciscan fathers and renovated in 1784. The soil around the church has yielded rich archaeological treasures, including ancient Estonian coins and the church's original baptismal font, now located near the altar. Other finds are displayed in the stone chapel in the churchyard.

The **Kökar Museum** (tel: 0457-524 4077; mid-June–mid-Aug noon–5pm daily; charge) has a collection of old photos whose written commentary has been hand-corrected by locals who perhaps recognise a wrongly identified grandparent. There are also farm tools, costumes and narratives about the Germans' failed attempts to shoot down Kökar's beacon tower in World War II.

The amenities here include only two food shops, one café, one bank and two taxis. However, Havspaviljongen in Hälsö has cottage accommodation, miniature golf, bicycle hire and a restaurant with a great view over the Kökar archipelago (tel: 018-55800). ❑

Nowhere is very far on the Åland Islands.

BELOW: bucolic summer scene on a lake jetty.

Apostolit hautsit Maarian majälä laudalla ja Maarian hostaanette taiwaasta

THE WEST COAST

Sprinkled with islands, the beautiful Gulf of Bothnia preserves its rich maritime heritage and retains a harmonious blend of Finnish and Swedish culture and language

The west coast of Finland is a fascinating mixture of past and present. There are plenty of reminders of days gone by: old wooden houses; museums that focus on the great days of sailing ships and the export of tar; and monuments to fierce battles when Sweden and Russia tussled over the body of Finland, caught fast between its powerful neighbours. The present is represented by modern industry which, fortunately, is usually well clear of historic town centres. The interland is either flat or gently undulating, largely an area of farms and forest with a sprinkling of lakes – in other words, typically Finnish.

As this is the part of Finland which is closest to Sweden, Swedish was the language of many communities during the centuries when Finland was dominated by the Swedes – especially in the southern part of the coast. Even today, many still speak Swedish as a first language, and some towns are even better known by their Swedish name than their Finnish name.

An industrial heritage

The first main town north of Turku (see page 205) on Road 8 is **Uusikaupunki ❶** (Nystad in Swedish), typical of this coastline. At the end of the 19th century, it boasted Finland's second-largest sailing fleet. An earlier high point came on 30 August 1721, when the Peace Treaty of Nystad ended the "Great Hate", a particularly bloody period in Russo-Swedish hostilities. The town's fortunes declined with the arrival of the steamship, and the decline of the tar industry, but revived with the advent of new industries in the 1960s. The Saab-Valmet car assembly plant offers tours and a motor museum exhibits rally-winning vehicles. The harbour is now used only by pleasure boats plying the archipelago, and the old salt warehouses are now antiques shops and restaurants.

Nevertheless, maritime memories remain. The **Cultural History Museum**

Main attractions
UUSIKAUPUNKI
RAUMA
PORI
VAASA
NYKARLEBY
OULU
KEMI
TORNIO

PRECEDING PAGES: Aspo Island. **LEFT:** inside Rauma church. **BELOW:** street view of Rauma.

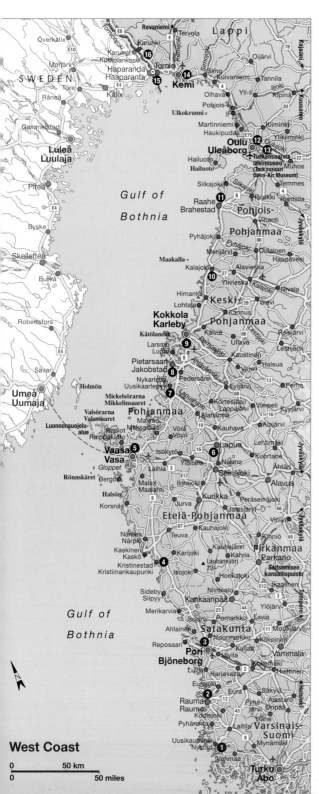

West Coast

```
0        50 km
0              50 miles
```

(Kulttuuruhistoriallinen museo Ylinenkatu 11; tel: 02-8451 5399 June–Aug Mon–Fri 10am–5pm, Wed until 8pm, Sat–Sun noon–3pm, Sept–May Tue–Fri noon–5pm; charge) is in the house of F.W. Wahlberg, a former ship-owner and tobacco manufacturer. Vallimäki Hill has a pilot's cottage, in use from 1857 to 1967, which is now a small museum. The church, completed in 1629, received a vaulted roof in the 1730s and the 1775 steeple also served as a fire watchtower. Myllymäki Park is a reminder that many retired sailors became millers in a region whose countryside was once dotted with windmills; four windmills and a tower remain.

World Heritage Site

Rauma ❷ (Raumo in Swedish) is one of six Finnish towns founded in the Middle Ages and today is the largest medieval town in Scandinavia, listed as a Unesco World Heritage site. The 600 or so wooden buildings, painted in traditional pastel shades, are still private homes. Although the dwellings and shops are 18th- and 19th-century, the pattern of narrow streets dates back to the 16th century.

Like most west-coast towns, Rauma expanded and prospered in the days of sailing ships, and the **Marela Museum** at Kauppiaankatu 24 (tel: 02-834 3528; mid-June–Aug daily 10am–5pm, rest of year Tue–Sun 10am–5pm; charge) is the home of a former merchant and master shipper, Abraham Marelin. Much of the interior – panelling, stoves and doors – is original, and the museum has an interesting display of period costumes. Kirsti's, an early 20th-century sailor's home, provides another maritime connection, continued by the Rauma Museum in the Old Town Hall.

The museum's other main attraction is lace; bobbin lace-making has been associated with Rauma since the mid-18th century. Nobody knows how lace came to the town, but by the 1850s it was a major industry, and almost every woman in the town

killed lace-maker. The bubble burst when lace bonnets went out of fashion, but since the 1950s there has been something of a revival of interest, with a lace week in summer, and some locals have acquired the old skill. Lace is sold in specialist shops.

Pori and jazz

Pori ❸ (Björneborg in Swedish), 47km (30 miles) north of Rauma, was founded by Duke Johan of Finland in 1558, as a port at the mouth of the Kokemäenjoki River. Since then the sea has receded and the land has risen, a phenomenon common to the Gulf of Bothnia coastline; so today Pori is marooned some 10km (6 miles) from the sea. In the intervening years, the town burnt down nine times – something of a record even for Finland. The last conflagration, in 1852, led to the stylish rebuilding of the present centre. With a population of 77,000, it is, above all, an industrial centre and port, accessed through a series of canals and inlets that lead from the city centre out to the sea.

Post-1852 buildings include the Jenélius Palace, now the Town Hall,

built in the style of a Venetian palace. The Pori Theatre, completed in 1884, is one of the most beautiful in Finland. More offbeat is the strange **Juselius Mausoleum** (tel: 02-623 8746; May–Aug daily noon–3pm, Sept–Apr Sun noon–2pm; free) at Käppärä Cemetery, built by a Pori businessman in memory of his young daughter. Its interior is one of Akseli Gallén-Kallela's masterpieces *(see page 86)*, restored by the artist's son in the 1930s.

The **Satakunta Museum** (Satakunnan museo; Hallituskatu 11; tel: 02-621 1078; www.pori.fi/smu; Tue–Sun 11am–6pm, Wed until 8pm; charge), dating from 1888, is Finland's largest cultural history museum, with over 60,000 items on display, plus an archive of 110,000 photographs and 10,000 books. The museum has a particularly fascinating section on Pori itself. The **Pori Art Museum** (Porin taidemuseo; Eteläranta; tel: 02-621 1080; www.poriart museum.fi; Tue–Sun 11am–6pm, Wed until 8pm; charge), in a skilfully converted warehouse, is also worth a visit.

Kirjurinluoto Island in the river has a park with a summer theatre hosting

The clock tower of Rauma's Town Hall. Built in 1776, the building now houses the Rauma Museum.

BELOW: old and new on the Pori riverbank.

A former ship-owner's home preserved as a Maritime Museum at Kristinestad shows the importance of local naval life.

BELOW: farming life at Brage Open-Air Museum in Vaasa.

the great annual **Pori Jazz Festival** (www.porijazz.fi). Of all Finland's summer festivals *(see page 101)*, Pori Jazz is both one of the best known and one of the earliest, with modest beginnings in 1966. It now lures in jazz musicians from all over Europe and beyond, and, for a hectic week in July, this old town is alive with jazz day and night. An audience of between 40,000–60,000 bumps up the town's population by more than half.

The 20-km (12-mile) peninsula leading from Pori to Reposaari (island) has a long sandy beach on the side away from the port and shipyard, Yyteri. It is one of Finland's best resorts, with a big hotel and congress centre. A golf course illustrates the huge surge of interest in the game in Finland.

Beside the sea

Kristinestad ❹ (Kristiinankaupunki in Finnish) was founded by the enthusiastic Swedish governor, Count Per Brahe, in 1649. A master of tact and diplomacy, he gave the town the name of both his wife and Queen Kristina of Sweden-Finland. This Swedish influence is still noticeable, and even today almost 60 percent of the population is Swedish-speaking and uses the town's Swedish name.

Despite its illustrious beginnings, Kristinestad remained quiet until the 19th century, when it became the home port of one of the country's largest merchant fleets and a shipbuilding centre. The importance of this is shown clearly in the **Merimuseo** (Kauppatori 1; tel: 06-221 2859; May–mid-Aug Tue–Sun 10am–5pm; charge), set in the house of former ship-owner S.A. Wendelin, and displaying his maritime memorabilia. But, as elsewhere, the ship-owners were caught out by the switch from sail to steam. The building of a railway in 1912 failed to halt the decline, and many citizens emigrated to the United States.

Kristinestad is now a modest sort of place beside the water with an interesting townscape, including an impressive Town Hall by E.B. Lohrmann dated 1856. During Swedish rule, every traveller into the town had to pay customs duty and the wooden customs house (Staketgatan) built in 1720 is

ow the tourist information office. nother customs house, at the northrn end, is even older – dating from 680 – while the oldest street is the trangely named Kattpiskargränden Cat Whipper's Lane). Ulrika Eleonoa's Church (1700), named after nother queen of Sweden-Finland, was estored and reconsecrated in 1965. It s typical of a coastal church, with umerous votive ships, donated by sailrs, hanging from the ceiling.

The **Lebell Merchant House** (Lebllin Kauppiaantalo; Rantakatu 51; tel: 6-221 2159; June–Aug daily 11am– pm; charge) is worth seeing. Lebell vas a Polish aristocrat and soldier who narried the mayor's daughter and took er name. He lived in the Lebell family ome, which was gradually extended, vith the result that its 10 rooms now epresent a variety of styles spanning he 18th and early 19th centuries.

aasa and Ostrobothnia

aasa ❺ (Vasa in Swedish) is an obvius division between north and south, t the heart of the region of Ostrobothia. Its origins lie in Old Vaasa, estab-

lished in the 14th century when the present site was below sea level. It has had a history of devastation by wars and fire, the last of which in 1852 left little but smouldering ruins.

Today, Vaasa (population 56,000) is a handsome ensemble of wide, attractively laid-out streets and a large market square, a mixture of Art Nouveau and modern architecture. Axel Setterberg designed the Orthodox church, which is surrounded by late 19thcentury buildings of the Russian Grand Duchy, and the Court of Appeal (1862). The Town Hall (1883) is the work of Magnus Isaeus and is equally imposing. For the best view of the town, clamber up the 200 steps in the tower behind the police station headquarters.

Vaasa is well endowed with museums reflecting the region's life, the most important being the **Ostrobothnian Museum** (Pohjanmaan museo; Museokatu 3; tel: 06-325 3800; http:// museo.vaasa.fi; Tue–Fri 10am–5pm, Wed until 8pm, Sat–Sun noon–5pm; charge) which covers local history and art. The **Brage Open-Air Museum**

The market square, Vaasa.

BELOW LEFT: Vaasa's coastline. **BELOW:** flat, quiet roads make cycling popular.

The Jaeger monument by Lauri Leppänen in Vaasa.

(Bragen ulkomuseo; Hietalahden puisto; tel: 06-312 7166; late-June–mid-Aug Tue–Fri 11am–5pm, Sat–Sun noon–4pm; rest of year Tue–Sun noon–4pm; charge), shows how Ostrobothnian farmers lived at the end of the 19th century, and a strong culture is clear in several other art museums and three professional theatres. The **Motor Museum** (Auto-ja Moottorimuseo; Varastokatu 8, opposite the bus station; tel: 050-369 3734; June–Aug Tue–Fri 1–5pm, Sat–Sun noon–4pm; charge), has a private collection of vintage vehicles, such as the glossy black 1939 American Pontiac, all lovingly restored.

This area is also rich in political history. In the civil war of 1918 the whole area around Vaasa was a stronghold of the "White Guard" (right-wing government troops with German military support). Nearby **Lapua** ❻, on Road 16 inland from Vaasa, was the birthplace of the anti-Communist Lapua movement, which reached its zenith in 1930, when 12,000 people from all over Finland poured into Helsinki on the "Peasants' March" and forced the Finn-

ish government to outlaw Communist newspapers and public displays of Communist sentiment and sympathy.

From an adjoining island, Vaskiluoto, linked by a causeway, ferries leave on three routes to Sweden, and this is also where you will find **Wasalandia** (www.wasalandia.fi; late May–early Aug daily from 11am, closing times vary; charge), the town's colourful amusement park, which has a good variety of rides. Nearby is the "spa paradise" Tropiclandia, with water slides, waterfalls, Jacuzzis and different kinds of sauna (tel: 020-796 1300).

Offshore islands, which necessitate a short ferry crossing, add to the charms of Vaasa, as does the collection of old farm buildings at Stundars, 16km (10 miles) from the town. North of Vaasa, the flat, farming country recalls parts of Sweden, with the Swedish influence being especially clear in the architecture.

Travelling north

St Birgitta's Church at **Nykarleby** ❼ (Uusikaarlepyy), built in 1708, is one of the most beautiful in the Ostro-

ne of the most beautiful in Finland. completed in 1686, it is dedicated to the Swedish Queen Eleonora. Alatornio church, on the outskirts, is a vast edifice, the largest in northern Finland, and ble to hold a congregation of 1,400. It a splendid example of Jaakko Rijf's eoclassical style. Tsar Alexander I rdered the building of an Orthodox nurch in 1825. After Finnish independance in 1917, the building lay empty ntil 1987, when it was restored, reconccrated and reopened to serve the 150 rthodox Christians who live locally.

The fine **Aine Art Museum** (Aineen idemuseo; Torikatu 2; tel: 050-594 868; Tue–Thur 11am–6pm, Fri–Sun 1am–3pm; charge) houses the Aine uvataide Foundation art collection nd a historical museum of western apland. On a clear day, the best place o get a view of the town is from the bservation platform on top of the ater tower.

iolf and fishing

ornio Golf Club on the Finnish-wedish border is perhaps the oddest n Europe, geographically speaking.

During a round of 18 holes, you play nine in Sweden and nine in Finland – and there's a one-hour time difference between the two. It opens in June when conditions allow and the season lasts until October, or when the snow arrives. It is a rare delight to play a night round in summer, thanks to the midnight sun. After the ninth hole in Finland – just after midnight – you will cross the border and continue in Sweden – yesterday.

If you travel 9 miles (15km) north of Tornio off Road E78, you will come to **Kukkolankoski** , the longest (3,500 metres/yds) free-flowing rapids in Finland. At the highest point the fall is 18.8 metres (45ft). The rapids have been famous for fish since the Middle Ages. Today, as they balance precariously on a crude boardwalk over the fast-flowing river, fishermen still use the old technique of a long-handled net. At the nearby Café Myllypirtti (tel: 0400-694 356; June–Sept) freshly grilled and skewered white fish is the main item on the menu, an authentic taste to end the 1,000-km (600-mile) drive north along the coast. ❏

Furry mascot at Kemi's spectacular Snow Castle (Lumilinna).

BELOW:
a restaurant dug out of the snow at Lumilinna.

ENJOYING THE FINNISH SUMMER

Summer is the best time in Finland, and many Finns who live abroad return annually for the long evenings, warm weather and cool lakes

On Friday afternoons in summer nearly all Helsinki denizens leave the city in the weekly rush hour. But once in the heartland of the country, the traffic eventually thins out as cars turn off at intervals onto what might seem to outsiders like invisible dirt tracks. Thousands of these roads lead to yet more thousands of summer cottages. Here, Finns live their parallel lives.

Life at the Summer Cottage

Daily life at a *mökki* (summer cottage) is a mixture of bohemian, Chekhovian and Finnish lifestyle aesthetics. Families visit relatives and friends; food is eaten leisurely and coffee (and beer) drunk over the long days, and everyone spends time in the sauna before jumping into the lake. Cottage gardens yield salad vegetables and new potatoes, but the nearby *kyläkauppa* (village shop) is a steady source of bottled drinks and ready-made food. So important is the influx of summer visitors in small villages that in summer months sales (and population) may triple.

But Finns rarely stay at the cottage every day: aside from summer sports, such as fishing, cycling, swimming and sailing, summer festivals are always on the agenda (*see page 100*). Nearly every town and village in Finland has tried the same formula – pick a theme and build its reputation as a "must-do" event.

A summer in Finland is a totally different experience from winter snow; it is Finnish comfortable living at its best.

LEFT: the simple canoe has a variety of uses: ideal for leisurely fishing trips that may take half a day, or for simply crossing from one edge of the lake to the other.

ABOVE: for those who can't escape to the country, city parks provide space to soak up the summer sun.

RIGHT: stretching out on the sand with friends, with nothing to do but get a sun tan and think about the next swim.

PAYING FOR A ROOM WITH A VIEW

Many Finns rent rather than own their *mökki* – a lakeside location is preferred but it is not cheap, and buying a nice house near water is impossible for the majority of Finns. Many cottages are inherited. "If I sold this cottage, I could easily move to a big house in Tampere," says one divorced woman in her late thirties. "But I would never forgive myself for selling this," she says, very fond of her lakeside property with two tiny islands.

Less than an hour's drive from big towns such as Tampere, Finns may enjoy unrestricted freedom, with no noise and no pollution. Finnish law stipulates that no new houses be built on the lakeshore, so most cottages are hidden and the lake view remains unmarred by unscrupulous investors.

However, wealthy urbanites masquerading as jovial country people do not always impress the locals – the cultural gap between town and country is ever-widening.

E: the countryside in summer offers a sense of space and ⸱m that can't be found in the city, as well as the chance to fill ⸱ungs with clean, fresh air.

⸱: what could be ⸱han an evening sail, ⸱ng the breeze and ⸱ing the colours of ⸱tting sun?

⸱w: vast tracts of ⸱ provide berries and ⸱rooms for summer ⸱ng, as well as great ⸱tunities for trekking.

ABOVE: a good *mökki* should be rustic, yet equipped with modern amenities. The simple life is very attractive to city dwellers, but electricity is a must.

LEFT: summer breaks may involve energetic activities, or they can be leisurely affairs. A gentle woodland walk with the family may be all that is needed after a hard week in the office.

LAKE

Finland's central region of lakes, surrounded by lush pine forests, matches the image most people have of the country, and a tour of the waterways will not disappoint

f you could flood the whole of Scotland and dot it with some 33,000 islands and peninsulas, you would have the equivalent of the Saimaa Lake area alone. Add on the Päijänne system and you could cover Wales as well.

The Great Lakes of Saimaa and Päijänne in central Finland are among the best known and most popular places to visit in the country and are the target for thousands of visitors who long only to be in, on, or beside them. But despite the number of visitors, this watery landscape never appears crowded, because there is so much of it — lakes large and small, smooth curving bays with yellow-grey beaches or jagged and broken shores, rushing torrents squeezed between high banks or flooding over hidden rocks, and rivers linking the different waters.

Canals, seals and sunbathing

Where the land intervenes, Finnish engineers turned their skills as long ago as the 19th century to building canals to connect the stretches of water. Today, boats can journey the length and breadth of both lake systems, calling at the small, strategically placed towns, and the even smaller villages, or stopping along the endless lakesides.

Sometimes, the land is flat beside the water or crunched up into ridges where rocks and trees point upwards. This varied landscape owes its beauty to the Ice Age, when glaciers carved out the shape

of lake and ridges, the most famous being at Punkaharju, an 8km (5-mile) chain of ridges which winds between the lakes. Far inland, Saimaa has its own resident species of seal, the Saimaa marble seal, whose ancestors were trapped in the lake system long ago when the glaciers cut off the route to the sea.

There are two perfect ways to get to know the Great Lakes: from the water by passenger steamer or smaller craft, or by doing as the Finns do and renting a lakeside cabin, to fish, swim, canoe, sauna or simply sunbathe.

Main attractions
LAPPEENRANTA
IMATRA
PUNKAHARJU
SAVONLINNA
VALAMON LUOSTARI
KUOPIO
LAHTI
JYVÄSKYLÄ

PRECEDING PAGES: classic Lakeland.
LEFT: Olavinlinna, Savonlinna.
BELOW: water-skiing is a popular lake sport.

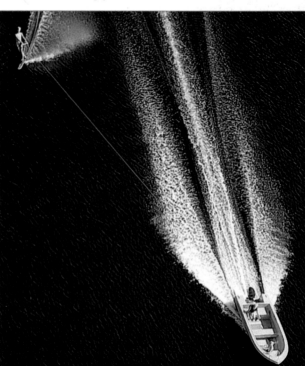

...maa system

as well as package tours
to St Petersburg.

...a waterway was the historic
...e between the kingdom of
...nland and tsarist Russia, at
...nging hands with dizzying
... Subsequently it became part
...tier with the Soviet Empire.
... and geopolitical effects of
...ing borders are recurring
themes as you travel the area.

It would be hard to visualise landscapes more fragmented or more liquid
than the Saimaa waterway. A series of
large and lesser lakes are linked by rivers, straits and canals, and framed by an
amazing complexity of headlands,
ridges, bays, islands and skerries, to

form Europe's largest inland waterwa
system. Up to a quarter of the Saima
region's total area of 70,000 sq kr
(27,000 sq miles) is covered by water.

Saimaa's waters provided natura
highways for goods and people lon
before railways and, especially, road
probed into its remoter reaches. To
large extent, they still do. No lakesid
home is without its rowing boat, usu
ally with outboard engine. Tugboa
hauling their floating timber trains, u
to 500 metres (1,600ft) long, from fo
est to factory, are common sights.

Embryonic tourism dates from th
19th century, as the well-to-do of tsari
St Petersburg boarded the then nev

angled railway to explore the Grand Duchy of Finland on the fringes of their empire. They went to take the waters in the handful of newly created spas, to marvel at such natural wonders s the foaming cascades of Imatra and to hunt and fish in the richly stocked orests and lakes.

The best approach to the lakes region rom the south is via industrial **Kouvola ❶**, about 140km (85 miles) northast of Helsinki and a junction of road nd rail routes into Saimaa. Although ot the most interesting town in Finand, Kouvola's Kaunisnurmi quarters, ormerly a railway staff colony, house uaint handicraft shops and several nuseums. Kouvola is also a jumpingff point to the unspoilt lake regions f Iitti and Jaala, northwest of Kouvola. aala's Unesco-listed World Heritage te **Verla** is a perfectly preserved cardoard factory, dating from the 1880s nd in operation until 1964.

From Kouvola road and rail routes ad north into the heart of the lakes egion. Yet to capture the spirit of aimaa, we suggest heading east on oad 6. About 80km (50 miles) on, nd close to the Russian border, you each Lappeenranta, South Karelia's ain town.

inn-Russian control

ike almost every Finnish community, **appeenranta ❷** combines work and lay. There is a great deal of industry nd some excellent holiday facilities – or most kinds of watersports, for xample. Its spa amenities have underone a recent renaissance too, though eir origins lie in the Tsarist 1820s. he town is the southern terminus for aimaa's venerable lake fleet.

In the past Lappeenranta was a ajor military town, heavily fortified y the Swedes in the 18th century, only be rebuilt by the Russians after they estroyed it. The Linnoitus (fortress) is e oldest and most interesting area, here you will find Finland's oldest rthodox Church (1785), the **South arelia Museum** (tel: 05-616 2255;

June–Aug daily 10am–6pm, Sept–May Tue–Sun 11am–5pm; charge), with a fascinating exhibit on the old city of Vyborg (now in Russia), and the **Cavalry Museum** (Ratsuväkimuseo; tel: 05-616 2261; June–Aug Mon–Fri 10am–6pm, Sat–Sun 11am–5pm; charge), detailing the history and distinctive red uniforms of Finland's proud soldiers. There are also a number of handicraft workshops and a great deal of military hardware.

These days Lappeenranta is just a few miles from the Russian border, but back in the days of the Grand Duchy and the first decades of the Republic, Finnish territory extended east beyond Vyborg (Viipuri) and included substantial portions of huge Lake Ladoga. In 1856, when the Saimaa Canal was completed, Saimaa was linked with the Gulf of Finland through entirely Finnish territory – indeed, it was the advent of the canal that encouraged the development of a string of inland ports, Lappeenranta among them.

Victorian travellers hailed the canal as one of the greatest engineering feats of the 19th century; soon after leaving

The 19th century recreated in Lappeenranta.

BELOW: view over Lappeenranta and harbour at dusk.

A flea market is held in Lappeenranta's main square on Sunday mornings.

BELOW: reindeer in autumn. **BELOW RIGHT:** wooden church in Kerimäki.

Lappeenranta, Road 6 crosses its watery slit or, rather, that of its successor. Post-World War II reparations transferred over half of its length to the Soviets, after which it lay disused and in growing disrepair until the 1960s. After lengthy negotiations and the privilege of paying for its restoration, the Finns regained use of the canal, which reopened in 1968.

Niagara of Finland

Despite the overwhelming predominance of lake and forest, parts of Saimaa's southern shores are undeniably industrial. Just a few miles beyond Lappeenranta, **Imatra ❸** lies in the midst of the most concentrated industrial area of Finland. It also has some claim as a famed beauty spot, and was described by one early 20th-century British visitor, with shameless exaggeration, as the "Niagara of Finland". Nevertheless, the very fine rapids of **Imatrankoski** were responsible for the presence of the grand old (restored) Imatran Valtionhotelli, built to cater to the sightseers who flocked here, including many distinguished, wealthy and high-born guests.

It was the eventual taming of the surging waters which triggered off the industrial boom. Today the town is leafy and laconic. The remaining splendour of the rapids can still be seen on certain summer evenings, sometimes dramatised by Sibelius's music and special light shows; check with the local tourist office (tel: 05-235 2330).

About 50km (30 miles) on from Imatra, Road 6 passes within a few hundred metres of the Russian border; multilingual frontier-zone notices and watchtowers did not quickly succumb to the best efforts of glasnost. Soon after, around Parikkala, the road turns north away from the border. Switching to Road 14, you soon come to one of Finland's best-loved beauty spots.

Punkaharju

Punkaharju ❹ is one of countless ridges bequeathed to Finland by the last Ice Age. In places it is just wide enough to carry the road; elsewhere it widens to carry magnificent pine and birch woods framing the ever-changing permutations of lake and sky, island and skerry, bedrock granite and the

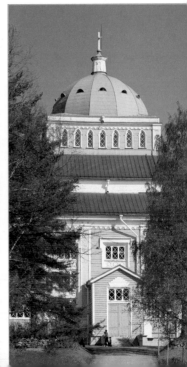

green gold" forests. The light is ever-changing too, to combine all the main elements of essential Finnish scenery.

In addition to the narrow ridge, the unkaharju Islands include a large esearch forest (Tutkimuspuisto) and a rotected nature reserve, associated ith the superb Forestry Museum, **usto** (tel: 015-345 100; May–Sept aily 10am–5pm, until 7pm June–Aug, ct–Apr Tue–Sun 10am–5pm; charge). n architectural achievement in its wn right, Lusto has a complete exhibition on Finland's forests and anything associated with them – design, ilderness trekking, forestry industry nd research. Bicycles may also be ired here.

Tucked away amongst Punkaharju's dges are well-equipped holiday entres and the **Summerland Leisure entre** (Kesämaa Leisure Centre; tel: 15-739 611; June–mid-Aug daily; harge) for family fun. One attraction the area that definitely should not e missed is the Art Centre of **Retretti** el: 015-775 2200; June–Aug daily)am–6pm; charge). Part of the centre housed in caverns blasted out of the

rock to provide 800 sq metres (8,600 sq ft) of exhibition space and an atmospheric underground area. Artificial pools and waterfalls also provide stunning settings for changing exhibitions of Finnish art and design. An underground concert hall can cater for over 1,000 spectators. Olavi Lanu is the sculptor responsible for the striking human and other shapes that populate Retretti's surrounding pine forests. The annual Retretti art exhibition, featuring four usually quite different, internationally acclaimed artists, is something of a media event in Finland.

In summer, a regular lake steamer sails between Punkaharju/Retretti and Savonlinna: the trip is a delightful mini-odyssey through the islands, taking more than two hours compared with a 20-minute spin along the highway. Road travellers, however, should make a short detour on Road 71 to **Kerimäki ⑤**, a typically scattered Finnish rural community harbouring the world's largest wooden church,

The drama of the rapids at Imatrankoski is sometimes heightened by light shows and recordings of Sibelius's music.

BELOW: Lusto, a museum on forestry.

Savonlinna is a useful port for backpackers touring the country.

BELOW: Olavinlinna is the dramatic setting for the Savonlinna Opera Festival.

built in 1848 with a congregation capacity of 3,500 people – larger than the town's population – and a 25-metre (82-ft) cupola (tel: 015-578 9123; June–Aug daily; free). Classical music concerts are staged here in summer.

Savonlinna

Savonlinna ❻ – the name means "Savo fortress" – sprawls over a series of interlinked islands. It is the most charming of Finland's main lakeland towns and makes the best base for a stay in the Saimaa region. It has the spectacular medieval castle of Olavinlinna, as well as spa facilities, excellent lake sports amenities, varied sightseeing and a great deal of culture. Castle and culture combine particularly successfully in the annual International Opera Festival, one of Finland's leading events, which takes place throughout July *(see box below right and page 315)*. Tickets and accommodation for the festival should be booked well ahead (tel: 020-744 3447).

The main venue for this operatic extravaganza, **Olavinlinna** (tel: 015-531 164; June–mid-Aug daily 10am–

6pm, rest of year Mon–Fri 10am–4pm Sat–Sun 11am–4pm) occupies an isle a short walk from the town centre With its massive granite walls, rampart and shooting galleries topped by thre great round towers (surviving from th original five), its Knights Hall and grim dungeon, it has everything you'd eve want in a medieval castle. Originall built by the Danish-born noblema Erik Axelsson Tott in 1475, it wa intended to be a main defence agains the Russians, but so frequently did th eastern border shift that Olavinlinn often lay too far from the battlefield.

The town of Savonlinna itself grew out of a small trading centre by the ca tle, its growth greatly hampered b wars and fires. The arrival of steam an the opening of the Saimaa canal pro vided the necessary stimulus, becaus the town's situation made it a natura junction for lake traffic that in du course spread to the four points of th Saimaa compass.

The days have long gone when th venerable Saimaa fleet was powered b wood-burning engines, but a numbe of the attractive double-decked woode

essels, now converted to diesel, continue to ply Saimaa's waters. One mpressive sight in Savonlinna is the morning departure and evening return f these romantic vessels to the passenger harbour, right by the open-air market on Kauppatori in the centre of own. Another, near the castle, is the museum ship *Salama*, a steam schooner uilt in 1874, shipwrecked in 1898 and ised from the lake in 1971. The *alama* is one of three converted old hips that form the inland navigation ction of the **Savonlinna Provincial Museum** (Savonlinnan maakuntamuso), on Riihisaari (tel: 015-571 4717; ily daily, Aug–June Tue–Sun; charge).

he northern route

ravelling from Savonlinna to Kuopio y lake steamer is a full day's journey, opposed to a few hours by road. If ou have the time it is a great way to nmerse yourself fully in the region's enery – from forest and meadow rough reed bed or granite shore, mber-built farms and summer cotges huddled along the lakefronts, to lands emerging suddenly from head-

lands – and watch the reflections tossed from huge sky to broad lake and back again in endlessly varying light and colour tones.

Road travellers have a choice of continuing west from Savonlinna on Roads 14 and 5 to Mikkeli and thence further west still into the Päijänne lake system *(see page 265)*, or staying with Saimaa to its northern limits beyond Kuopio. **Mikkeli ❼**, a provincial capital, is a pleasant market community and also a historic army town. Mannerheim's headquarters during World War II are now a museum, the **Päämajamuseo** (Päämajakuja 1–3; tel: 015-194 2424; May–Aug daily 10am–5pm, Sept–Apr Fri–Sun 10am–5pm; charge). Exhibits include a copy of London's *Daily Telegraph* from 18 December 1939, with the headline: "Finns smash two Soviet Divisions."

Also open in Mikkeli is a wartime **Communications Centre** (Viestikeskus Lokki), located inside the Naisvuori Hill (tel: 015-194 2429; May–Aug daily 10am–5pm; charge). In summer, you can buy a joint ticket by the name of *Kulkulupa* ("access permit")

The Päämajamuseo preserves General Mannerheim's headquarters as they were during World War II.

BELOW: opera performance at Olavinlinna.

The Opera Finnished

The intact medieval Olavinlinna in Savonlinna is possibly the most splendid setting to hear opera in Europe, whether for *Aïda* in Italian, *Faust* in French or *The Magic Flute* in Finnish.

During the summer season, tickets for the most popular performances – regularly featuring world-class singers performing well-known librettos – often sell out months in advance. Opera-goers from all over the continent often come dressed to impress, the wisest of them armed with blankets, for Finnish summer nights are predictably cool. After the performance, with daylight fading at last, Olavinlinna is softly illuminated to provide a memorably romantic backdrop as you stroll back past the town's elegant restaurants and cafés, many still open and welcoming.

The market hall at Kuopio.

BELOW: lakeland house in the mist.

giving access to five attractions.

Some 5km (3 miles) northeast of Mikkeli, the **Visulahti Family Leisure Centre** (tel: 015-18281; www.visulahti.fi; June–early Aug daily) is set in a park populated by life-size model dinosaurs, an automobile exhibition and waxworks.

If you are travelling directly from Savonlinna to Kuopio, the recommended route to is to leave Road 14 about 35km (20 miles) west of the former and follow Road 464 via Rantasalmi, a particularly attractive and watery route. This joins Road 5 a little south of Varkaus. Varkaus itself is industrial, although music specialists should note its **Museum of Mechanical Music** (Mekaanisen Musiikin museo; Pelimanninkatu 8; tel: 017-558 0643; July daily 10am–6pm, rest of year Tue–Sat 11am–6pm, Sun 10am–5pm; charge), unique in the Nordic countries. The little town of **Joroinen** ❽, 15km (10 miles) to the south, is very typical of a smaller Finnish community. In contrast with its own modernity are the fine old farms and manor houses dotted about these fertile

landscapes, some used as settings for the music festival which is arranged here each summer.

Significant monastery

Road 5 is the direct way to Kuopio, 75km (45 miles) north of Varkaus, while to the west Road 23 leads to the pleasant rural community of Piesämäki on Saimaa's western fringe. Northeastwards from Varkaus, the same road leads to Joensuu in North Karelia *(see page 273)*, passing close to two major religious houses: the Orthodox monastery **Valamon luostari** and the **Convent of Lintula**. On all three counts of history, culture and scenery these merit a visit, a recommended possibility being the monastery cruises that depart from Kuopio in the summer months.

The clue to the monastery's history lies in its name. Valamo is the large island on Lake Ladoga on which an Orthodox religious foundation was established in the Middle Ages, attracting a growing number of pilgrims over the centuries, though latterly its fortunes declined. During the Winter War of 1939–40, the surviving handful of elderly monks were forced to leave and eventually accorded the present site Uusi ("New") Valamo (tel: 017-57 111; www.valamo.fi), originally an old manor house and outbuildings. One of these outbuildings was adapted as the monks' first place of worship, embellished by the precious 18th-century icons and other sacred objects which they had brought with them.

Valamon luostari has since experienced something of a renaissance. An injection of younger blood ensures its continuance; there is a fine new church completed in 1977, a cafeteria, a wine shop, souvenir shop and a modern hotel to cater for the growing number of visitors and pilgrims. The **Convent of Lintula** (Lintulan luostari; tel: 017 563 106), a few kilometres away, has a similar but shorter history. The pioneer inhabitants of both contribute to the upkeep by working the land in the

delightful lakeside settings, although you may find the rather humbler features of Lintula more conducive to spiritual reflection.

Kuopio to Iisalmi

Kuopio ⑩ is a thoroughly pleasant town and one of Finland's liveliest, with a crowded summer calendar that includes the International Dance and Music Festival in June (see page 100). Its daily market is one of the most varied outside Helsinki and hard to miss as it fills most of Kuopio's central *Tori* (Market Place). Here you can try freshly baked *kalakukko* (fish and pork in a rye crust), traditional local fare that is definitely an acquired taste; in season you may be tempted by the varied edible fungi or succulent mounds of berries straight from the forests. There is a smaller market on summer evenings at the passenger harbour (east side of the town).

Like many Finnish country towns that developed in the 18th and 19th centuries, central Kuopio follows a gridiron pattern of parallel streets more familiar to Americans than Europeans.

This was designed to provide plenty of firebreaks between the then predominantly wooden buildings, though, alas, it failed in its purpose all too often. Most of those that survived the regular conflagrations have been replaced by modern buildings, but the **Kuopion kortellimuseo** (Old Kuopio Museum; Kirkkokatu 22; tel: 017-182 625; mid-May–Aug Tue–Sun 10am–5pm, rest of year Tue–Fri 10am–3pm, Sat–Sun 10am–4pm; charge), a few blocks south of the market place, preserves a number of original dwellings complete with authentic furniture, warehouses, and even gardens dating from the 18th century to the 1930s – a quiet oasis showing how much of small-town Finland used to look.

A little to the east of the marketplace, the **Kuopion museo** at Kauppakatu 23 (tel: 017-182 603; Tue–Fri 10am–5pm, Wed until 7pm, Sat–Sun 11am–5pm; charge) houses excellent regional collections of a cultural and natural history order in a castle-like building that is a typical example of Finnish early 20th-century National Romantic style.

TIP

The famed "lumberjack evenings" at Kuopio's Rauhalahti spa – home to the world's largest woodsmoke sauna – is a memorable rural affair. For around €30 you can eat your fill at a Finnish barbecue and observe (or participate with) Finns of all ages dancing the night away.

BELOW LEFT: the annual wine festival in Kuopio.
BELOW: boats in Kuopio's harbour.

Admiring the lake views from the Puijo Tower.

BELOW: the daunting ski jump in Lahti.

Among several famous Finns associated with Kuopio, statesman Johan Vilhelm Snellman worked and married here in the 1840s. The conjugal home at Snellmaninkatu 19 is also a small, but less detailed, museum of the period (mid-May–Aug Wed and Sat 10am–5pm; free).

On the edge of the town centre, the **Ortodoksinen kirkkomuseo** (Karjalankatu 1; tel: 0206-100 266; www. ortodoksinenkirkkomuseo.fi; Tue–Sun 10am–6pm, Wed until 8pm; charge) is unique in Western Europe, housing collections of icons (many from the 18th century, some from the 10th century) and sacred objects brought here from Valamo and Konevitsa in Karelia and a few from Petsamo in the far north, all territories ceded to the Soviet Union.

A little further on is Puijo hill, topped by **Puijon torni** (tel: 017-255 5255; daily 10am–9pm; charge), over 75 metres (250ft) high. The vistas from the tower's viewing platforms and revolving restaurant (open throughout the year) are beautiful, with lakes and forests merging into purple distances. Try to time your visit for an hour or two before sundown – in good weather the colours are out of this world.

By the time you reach **Iisalmi ❶** 80km (50 miles) north of Kuopio c Road 5, you are almost exactly halfwa between Helsinki and the Arctic Ci cle, and you are still – just – in th Saimaa region. Should you launch canoe from Iisalmi's lakeshore, would be either level paddling or hea ing gently downhill all the way to th Gulf of Finland – which is over 400kr (250 miles) away.

Iisalmi is a pleasant small provinci town, birthplace of writer Juhani Ah in 1861 (the family home is a museur on the outskirts of town), and site c one of Finland's innumerable battl against the Russians (1808; the Finr won this one, even though they wei reputedly outnumbered seven to one

Evakkokeskus, a Karelian-Orthodc Cultural Centre at Kyllikinkatu 8 (te 017-816 441; mid-June–mid-Aug dail mid-Aug–mid-June Mon–Fri; charge displays valuable relics recovered fror territory now in Russia, along with 8 models of churches and chapels sinc destroyed there. You can dine at Kuapp

(June–July daily), "the smallest restaurant in the world", or, if it's full, at Olutmestari, the nearby beer hall with an attractive terrace in summer. Iisalmi's Olvi brewery has a museum upstairs.

The Päijänne system

In the southwest of the lake region, Päijänne is Finland's longest and deepest lake – extending for 119km (74 miles) as the crow flies, though many times that if you follow its wondrously intricate shoreline. At opposite ends of the lake system are two of Finland's more substantial towns, Lahti and Jyväskylä. The watery topography between the two defeated the railway engineers, but they are linked to the west of Päijänne by one of Europe's main highways, E24, and to the east of it by a network of slower, more attractive routes. Alternatively, in summer there is the leisurely 10½-hour waterborne route.

Further removed from troublesome historical border areas than many regions of Finland, this area has been subjected less to conflict and change. Tourism also reached it later, though it has made up for it since, capitalising on the lovely well-watered, deeply wooded landscapes.

Lahti ⑫ lies 103km (64 miles) north of Helsinki on Road 4 (E75). It straddles part of one of Finland's more distinctive topographical features, the extensive ridge system called Salpausselkä, which is regularly the setting for major world skiing championships. Here, too, is the **Lahden Urheilukeskus**, the town's sports centre, with some of Finland's best winter sports facilities, including three ski jumps (50-, 70- and 90-metre). It is the venue for the annual Finlandia Ski Race and the Ski Games (see page 320).

From the viewing platform on top of the highest ski jump, the town spreads at your feet. Beyond, the gleaming sheets of Vesijärvi (lake) are linked, by the Vääksy Canal a few miles to the north, to the much more extensive waters of Päijänne. Lahti is a modern place, one of its few older buildings being the Kaupungintalo (Town Hall, 1912), designed, as were so many Finnish public buildings of the period, by Eliel Saarinen.

TIP

Lahti famously has one of the best places in Europe to hear excellent classical music – the **Sibelius Hall**. Sibelius himself was actually from Järvenpää and only visited Lahti twice in his life.

BELOW: a cruise boat at Lahti.

Three blocks to the north is the market, a lively morning spot, and two blocks beyond that, at Kirkkokatu 4, the highly individualistic **Church of the Cross** (Ristinkirkko). This was the last church in Finland designed by Alvar Aalto, powerful in its simplicity and a fine main venue for the Lahti Organ Festival every summer.

The **Lahden Historiallinen museo** (tel: 02-814 4536; Mon–Fri 10am–5pm, Sat–Sun 11am–5pm) in Lahti Manor, an exotic late 19th-century building at Lahdenkatu 4 (tel: 03-814 4536; daily; charge), has good regional ethnographical and cultural history sections, as well as art and furniture collections.

A short distance northwest is the area known as **Tiirismaa**, home to south Finland's highest hill (reaching a very modest 223 metres/730ft), some of her oldest rocks and the snow centre **Messilä** (Messiläntie 308; tel: 03-86011) combining a beautiful manor house, restaurants, hotel, log cabins and a camping site. Downhill skiing, snowboarding or cross-country skiing are your winter options, whereas during the summer you can choose from golf or horse riding. Sixteen kilometres (10 miles) further on, the 15th-century greystone **Hollola Church** (May–Aug 10am–6pm) has some good wooden sculptures and is among the largest and finest of about 80 churches surviving from that period in Finland. Close by are a good rural museum (June–Aug Tue–Sun noon–6pm) and some excellent coffee houses.

Fishing and birdwatching

From Lahti it's only 35km (21 miles) northeast on Road 75 to the pleasant little town of **Heinola** , on the way passing Suomen urheiluopisto, the top Finnish Sports Institute at Vierumäki. Taking the popular summer lake route it is an astonishing – and lovely – 4½ hours by steamer, 3½ hours by hydrofoil. A glance at the map reveals the contortions needed for lake traffic plying this route, first negotiating the Vääksy canal north into Päijänne, and later squeezing southeast through narrow straits into the wider waters that lead to Heinola.

There are more narrow straits at Heinola, where the scurrying waters o

Jyrängönkoski (rapids) provide good sport for local canoeists and for fishermen casting for lake and rainbow trout. You can also try for the latter, with rather more likelihood of success, from the teeming tanks of Siltasaari Fishing Centre by the rapids where, for a few euros, you can rent a rod and have your catch smoked to eat on the spot or take away.

Heinola blossomed into yet another spa town in tsarist times. There are a number of wooden buildings dating from the turn of the 20th century, including a Chinese pavilion on the ridge-top park, now a restaurant, redolent of a more leisurely age. Not far away, the pond of Kirkkolampi is a focal point of the well-arranged **bird sanctuary and hospital** (*lintutarha*) with four aviaries (daily; free). The town's main church, an octagonal wooden building from the early 19th century, has a separate bell tower designed by the prolific architect, C.L. Engel.

Lake and forest views

From Heinola, Road 5 continues northeast to Mikkeli in western Saimaa. From here you could branch north onto Road 13 for Jyväskylä, but there is a slower and more attractive way. For this, leave Lahti north on Road 24 and after 25km (15 miles), soon after crossing the Vääksy canal at Asikkala, branch right onto minor Road 314. This carries you along the several miles of Pulkkilanharju (ridge), another relic from the last Ice Age which vies with that of Punkaharju for narrowness and magnificence of lake and forest views.

Continue on a series of asphalted but lesser roads via Sysmä and Luhanka, twisting along or across the complex succession of headlands, bays, capes and interlinked islands that make up Päijänne's contorted eastern shore. At **Luhanka ⑭**, the **Peltola Cotters Museum** (Mäkitupalaismuseo; tel: 014-877 108; June–mid-Aug Tue–Sun 10am–5pm) throws light on the unenviable lot of the 19th-century "cotters" – smallholders who effectively mort-

gaged their working lives to wealthy landowners in return for a scrap of land whose lease could be revoked at the owner's will.

To rejoin Road 9 (E63) at Korpilahti for the final leg to Jyväskylä you can now use an enormous bridge across Kärkistensalmi, one of Päijänne's many narrow straits. Road 24 provides a more direct main road link all the way from Lahti to Jyväskylä in 174km (107 miles). A particular beauty spot inside a national park, a little way off this route is the long, slender island of **Kelvenne ⑮**, about 60km (37 miles) north of Lahti, with its lakes, lagoons and curious geological formations. You can reach it from Kullasvuori camping area at Padasjoki. Road 24 also bypasses Jämsä and joins Road 9 to the south of the town, thereby avoiding the industrial district of Jämsänkoski.

Architecture and cultural identity

Jyväskylä ⑯ (pop. 75,000) has contributed much, as an educational centre, to the country's cultural development: at a time when the Finnish

Cotton grass grows abundantly in the lake region.

BELOW: the 15th-century Hollola Church.

language was still regarded by the Swedish-speaking ruling classes as the "peasants' language", the first Finnish-language secondary school opened here in 1858, and a teachers' training college opened a few years later. It now also has a lively university whose campus is the work of Alvar Aalto. Indeed, it was in Jyväskylä that this renowned architect embarked on his career, and there are no fewer than 30 major buildings by him around the area, as well as the **Alvar Aalto museo** (Alvar Aallon katu 7; tel: 014-624 809; Tue–Sun 11am–6pm; charge), which has exhibits on his architecture and furniture designs.

As with many Finnish towns whose older buildings have been largely lost, Jyväskylä, a popular congress centre, is predominantly modern. From the observation platform of the water tower on the ridge running through the town you can gaze across to the lakes. There are sports facilities on the same ridge and at Laajavuori, a winter and summer sports centre on the northwest outskirts of town. Jyväskylä caters for most sports, but is best

known as the venue for the 1,000 Lake Rally in August, which draws 400,000 spectators to watch Finland's premier motor racing event. In June, the Jyväskylä Arts Festival chooses a different theme each year, examining its every aspect in seminars, exhibitions, concerts and theatre performances.

For a glimpse into the region's past go to the excellent **Keski-Suomen museo** (tel: 014-624 930; Tue–Sun 11am–6pm; charge), next to the Alvar Aalto Museum. Or, with a little more time, head 32km (20 miles) west on Road 23 to **Petäjävesi**. Built of logs in 1765, the Petäjävesi Lutheran church (tel: 040-582 2461; June–Aug daily 10am–6pm) here is listed by Unesco as a World Heritage site. It is a stunning example of an architectural tradition unique to eastern Scandinavia, combining Renaissance structure and Gothic vaulting.

Another attractive 18th-century wooden church is at **Keuruu** (June–Aug daily 10am–5pm), a further 28km (17 miles) away. Road 23 continues west to Virrat at the northern end of the Poet's Way route (see page 216).

North of Jyväskylä, Road 4 (E4/75) continues through yet more forested, lake-strewn landscapes harbouring a growing scattering of holiday and leisure centres. After 35km (21 miles) Road 13 forks left to Saarijärvi, focal point of a pleasant holiday area. Just before this, turn south on Road 630, then shortly east to **Summassaari** ⑰ (tel: 030-608 5100; June–mid-Aug Tue–Sun, July daily 10am–6pm; charge) where a Stone Age village has been reconstructed. A short distance beyond Saarijärvi in **Kolkanlahti** ⑱ is the elegant 19th-century house, now a museum, **Säätyläiskotimuseo** (tel: 014-459 841; mid-June–late Aug Wed–Sun noon–6pm; charge), where Finland's national poet, J.L. Runeberg worked as a tutor in the 1820s.

Back on Road 4 (E4/75), before long you bypass Äänekoski, of no particular interest, as the highway leads ever northwards towards the Arctic Circle. ❑

Canoeing and Kayaking

Thousands of lakes, rivers and streams mean that canoeing and kayaking are the ideal way to see the Finnish countryside.

One of the main events in the Finnish sports calendar is the Finlandia Canoe Relay each June. This unique seven-day event – the longest canoe/kayak relay in the world – usually heads through the Saimaa system, and is divided into approximately 30 stages, each stage varying from 10 to 50km (6 to 30 miles). With 187,888 lakes (at the last count) and innumerable rivers to choose from, it is surprising that canoeing has only become popular in Finland in recent years. There is now, however, a growing range of packages which allow you to canoe well-paddled routes of varying lengths.

A particularly popular series of waterways forms an overall 350km (217-mile) circuit, beginning and ending at Heinola. This needs 10–15 days but can also be fragmented into more manageable two- to five-day sections. Another, along 320km (200 miles) of the Ounasjoki River in Lapland from Enontekiö to Rovaniemi, features sections of true Arctic wilderness; the rapids are mainly Grade I, but it's possible to portage round the most daunting of these. Yet another follows a 285km (200-mile) lake-and-river route taken by the old tar boats from Kuhmo to Oulu.

Paddling round the lake region

If you're attracted to the idea of pioneering across the lakes, the possibilities are legion. Any road map which covers the country on a scale of 1:200 000 will be sufficient for general planning, but absolutely essential for more detail are the special inland waters charts, for example the 1:40 000/1:50 000 scale Saimaa map.

It's not until you are in your canoe, however, that the logistical problems of navigation become clear. From a low-riding canoe, one island of rock and pinewood looks very like another. Across wide expanses of water there are few helpful landmarks, so be sure to pack two essentials: a compass and a pair of binoculars.

Other than getting lost, the greatest inconvenience you are likely to encounter is wind squalls. As these can blow up quickly and whip water up into turbulence, head for shelter at the first sign.

Camping may prove more difficult than you might expect in seemingly empty landscapes. Most of the lake shorelines are either rocky or fringed by reed beds. Finding enough space between trees can be a problem even for the smallest tent, and any clearings you come across may belong to a cottage or farm. The national right to pitch your tent anywhere (*ihmisoikeus*) has become a contentious issue these days due to abuse by some campers, so you should make sure you ask for permission to camp whenever possible (but, of course, this being the Finnish countryside, there is often no one around to ask). It is one of the joys of canoeing in Finland that you may travel for days without any sign of humanity other than a tugboat hauling its train of timber, or a fisherman.

For information on the best places to rent canoes in the Lakeland region, *see page 319.* ❑

ABOVE: lone kayaker.
RIGHT: the best way to explore the lakes.

KARELIA AND KUUSAMO

The ancient rural communities of eastern Finland are considered the cultural heartland of the country: the region of myths and legends immortalised in the epic poem the *Kalevala*

astern Finland, which stretches broadly to the country's eastern frontier, is an expansive region here the landscape shifts from the eat Finnish Lakelands area to Lappi, Lapland. Few people live in this wild rritory, but the character of Karelia id its distinctive Orthodox churches ve charm, tradition and colour.

Finland's most famous and perhaps ost photographed scenery stretches low the lofty summit of the Koli eights above Lake Pielinen; this area fers very good winter skiing, snow-oeing and sledging, as well as white-ater rafting, hiking and fishing in the mmer months. The "Bard and Bor-r Way" takes the traveller to the fron-r sights, including battlegrounds om World War II.

estival centres

ensuu ❶ at the mouth of the River elisjoki is the "capital" of North Kare-a. It has a relaxed and welcoming air, r the majority of the inhabitants are arelians, people who have a well-rned reputation for good humour id ready wit, traits particularly in evi-nce at the town's busy markets.

The **Pohjois-Karjalan museo** Museum of North Karelia; tel: 013-267 22; Mon–Fri 10am–5pm, Sat–Sun am–3pm; charge) exhibits articles om prehistory, history and the folk lture of this part of Karelia. The useum is housed in a new tourist ntre, Carelicum, opposite the market

square at Koskikatu 5, which also has a tourist information office (tel: 013-248 5319), a café and other cultural venues. There is also the **Taidemuseo** (Kirk-kokatu 23; tel: 013-267 5388; Tue–Sun 11am–4pm, Wed until 8pm; charge), with an icon collection and Finnish paintings from the 19th and 20th cen-turies. The **University Botanical Gar-dens** (Yliopiston kasvitieteellinen puutarha; Heinäpurontie 70; tel: 013-251 2630; Wed–Mon; charge) feature a range of plant species and a butterfly section. In many places in Joensuu, you

PRECEDING PAGES: season of mists... **LEFT:** whitewater rafting at Kainuu. **BELOW:** main square of Joensuu.

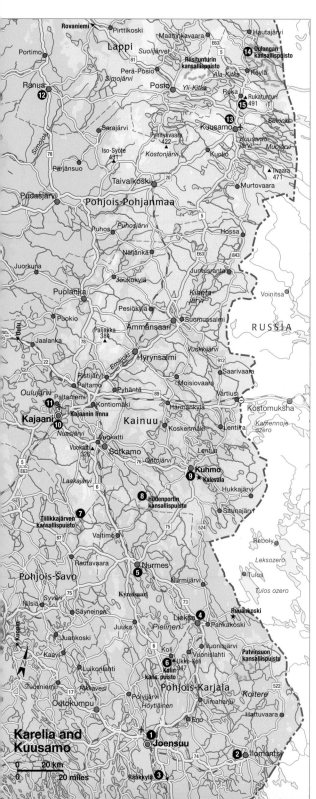

will find restaurants serving Karelia
specialities, such as Puukello (tel: 01.
123 272), on the island of Ilosaari at th
rapids, which offers Karelian roasts an
pies with salted fish.

Before turning north, go as far east a
you can in Finland to **Ilomantsi** ❷. Tak
Road 6 south out of Joensuu and the
Road 74 east for the 70-km (50-mile
drive. Ilomantsi was the scene of heav
fighting in World War II, and in the vi
lage of Hattuvaara to the northeast th
Warrior's House (Taistelijan talo; te
013-830 111; May–Sept daily 9am–8pn
marks the spot where fighting ended i
1944. On a more peaceful note, Ilomant
has been a stronghold of the Orthodo
Church since the 14th century. Easter
the most impressive festival, but the are
is full of old rites and rituals.

For more light-hearted music an
colour, it would be hard to beat the vi
lage of **Rääkkylä** ❸, about 50km (3
miles) south of Joensuu on a secondar
road along the southern end of Lak
Pyhäselkä. Two local sisters founde
the renowned Finnish folk group Vär
tinä, which has achieved internation
acclaim, winning the national fol
music championship and many othe
awards. There are often interestin
local musical events. Some of th
young musicians who play here ar
masters of the most Karelian of instru
ments, the *kantele*, a stringed contrap
tion similar to a zither.

The Lieksa region

Heading north from Joensuu, tak
Route 6 north out of the town. Whe
the road divides, take the right for
eastward (Route 73), which leads alon
the eastern shore of Lake Pielinen t
Lieksa ❹. The roads through thes
backwoods are tarred and well mair
tained but narrow and sometime
differ little from the minor roads an
lanes that lead off into the forest. Bu
usually driving is quiet and simpl
with the main routes numbered an
villages signposted.

At Vuonisjärvi, 29km (18 miles) t
the south, is **Paateri** – the studio c

Eva Ryynänen, a well-known wood sculptor who has decorated the area with her work, including a spectacular wooden wilderness church (mid-May–mid-Sept daily; charge).

The **Ruuankoski rapids** are a sight not to be missed from Lieksa. For some 3km (21 miles) the Ruunaa plunges through six sets of foaming rapids and drops around 15 metres (50ft) on the way. Equipped with lifejacket and waterproofs, shooting the rapids is safe under the careful supervision of a proficient guide. The **Ruunaa hiking area**, looking right onto the Russian border and inhabited by wild forest reindeer, is an ideal place for white-water rafting and canoeing trips.

In Lieksa, the **Pielinen Outdoor Museum** (Pielisen museo; tel: 013-689 4151; mid-May–mid-Sept daily 10am–5pm, mid-Sept–mid-May Tue–Fri 10am–3pm; charge) showcases numerous buildings from different ages which document the settlement of the surrounding area – the oldest is from the 17th century. The town's attractive church was built in 1982 by husband and wife team Raili and Reima Pietilä.

Lieksa may not be the most prepossessing of towns, but it is an important centre for visitors to this part of Finland's wilderness, which stretches as far as the Russian border. Capercaillie, elk, bear, reindeer and even wolves roam these dense pine forests. The best way to get an idea of its sheer size is from the viewing platform of the town's 47-metre (150ft) tall water tower.

"Never go hiking on your own," is the oft-repeated warning of this region, and inexperienced walkers in particular should take guided tours, which can be arranged for individuals or groups. Most walks involve camping, and the local shops in Lieksa can provide all the equipment and maps that are needed. Expeditions include the "Bears' Walk" along the Russian border; one of the attractions en route is in an exhibition of bear skulls and stuffed animals by Väinö Heikkinen, a famous bear hunter, at **Kaksinkantaja** three days into the hike (June–Aug daily 10am–5pm; charge).

Exhibits at the Museum of North Karelia, Joensuu.

BELOW: a typical Karelian house.

Karelians

When Finns have gone to war, it has almost always concerned Karelia; this region is said to be the soul of Finland.

The Karelians were one of the earliest communities in Finland, evident in Bronze and Iron Age discoveries, though their true origins are lost in myth and legend. The *Kalevala*, that great epic saga of ancient life in the far north, is really about the Karelians. This long poem, which in the 19th century became the cornerstone of the struggle for national culture, tells how, with magic and sword, the northern heroes fought for survival against the powers of evil. It recounts weddings, funerals, rituals, bear hunts and journeys into the mysterious Otherworld, and finally the heroes' joy as they celebrate in song the salvation of the land of Kalevala from its enemies.

This is a vivid and romantic part of the country, one that has long been an inspiration for Finnish artists, writers and musicians. A Karelian theme runs through a great deal of the music of Jean Sibelius: his *Karelian Suite* reaches sublime heights of elegy and patriotism. In his earlier years, Sibelius was

deeply inspired by Karelian folk music, and later on he returned to spend his honeymoon here.

The Karelians emerge into recorded history as a people living in the area of forest and lakes stretching from the present-day southeastern Finnish-Russian border to the White Sea. Slash and burn was their way of converting the impenetrable woodland into productive fields, and they used the ash as a fertiliser. With these techniques came the production of grain and the need to dry it through steam heat, adapted first for grain-drying and then for relaxation. Thus, the sauna was born.

From the Middle Ages the Karelians began to be affected by Russian influences, although in no sense did they become "russified". The most obvious aspect, the Orthodox religion, is a feature of the Karelian people, although it is accorded the title Greek Orthodox rather than Russian. There are 60,000 adherents and many churches in southeast Finland today.

The terrible Winter War of 1939–40 was fought to save Karelian land and has become the Finns' great *cause célèbre*, but it was only one war out of some 200 which were fought for Finnish Karelia. After the war, the Karelian Isthmus was lost, along with all of East Karelia, now settled by Russians. Many of these areas have since been all but abandoned by the Russian state, with many former Karelian villages dilapidated. Some 400,000 Karelians were resettled to many other parts of Finland, where they continue to live today: few have moved back.

It is a fact that Karelia today exists only as a fragment of its former self. The fractioned border has all but cut it out of the Finnish body politic and its people have dispersed. A line roughly parallel to the border from Lieksa down to the Isthmus now delineates modern Finnish Karelia. Yet even in this small region something distinctive remains. It may be the grandeur of the forest, it may be the distinctive taste of their cuisine, or the lively and talkative nature of the people (in contrast to the more taciturn nature of most other Finns). The Karelian dialect, as distinct from Finnish, however, has declined – although less so on the Russian side of the border. ❑

ABOVE: a Karelian folk musician playing the balalaika.
LEFT: Sibelius was influenced by Karelian music.

Trout, landlocked salmon (a relic of the Ice Age), and coarse fish such as bream all swim in the unpolluted waters of Lake Pielinen and the Pudaskoski River. Join a guided fishing expedition if you would like to try your hand at catching them. A package will include the services of a guide, transport, accommodation and licences. Otherwise, you can buy a fishing licence from any local post office, or a regional fishing licence from a tourist office. The region is also well known for being a whitewater rafting destination. These adrenaline-filled trips usually depart from the centre of Lieksa. You can learn more and book tours at Lieksa's main tourist office, on the town's main street, Pielisentie (tel: 013-248 5312; Mon–Fri, June–Aug also Sat).

The national landscape

From Lieksa, Road 73 leads towards Nurmes ❺, taking about an hour, and keeping close to the shores of Lake Pielinen. First mentioned in documents in 1556, Nurmes only became a city as recently as 1974. Nicknamed "the town of the birch", it sits on a ridge between two lakes at the northern end of the Pielinen lake system; it is a beautiful town, with wooden houses built in authentic early Karelian style.

Bomba House (tel: 013-687 250; www.bomba.fi) is a traditional Karelian house at Ritoniemi, about 2km (1¼ miles) from the town, surrounded by a recently built "Karelian village" which provides visitors not only with comfortable accommodation but also with delicious meals comprising local specialities. Bomba House's menu includes an assortment of local pies, warm smoked lamb, hearty meat casseroles, cold smoked whitefish, fried wild mushrooms and baked cheese with Arctic bramble jam – all designed to get the taste buds working overtime.

It would be a pity to miss Finland's most gracious way to travel, and Nurmes is a great place to experience it – leave the car and take a leisurely steam-boat ride down Lake Pielinen to a famous beauty spot, the **Koli** Hills. The lake

scenery is wonderful, and you may meet Finland's largest inland waterway ferry as well as numerous other boats, big and small.

The Koli Hills rise halfway down the western side of the lake, the highest, **Old Man Koli** ❻ (Ukko-Koli), reaching 347 metres (1,100ft). Scramble up to the top (there are steps), and spread out below you is a view that has inspired some of the greatest artists, including Albert Edelfelt and Eero Järnefelt, whose paintings immortalised Koli around the turn of the 20th century and did much to stimulate the national awakening of the time (see page 85). Sibelius, too, wove the Koli Hills into his symphonies and, looking down, it is not hard to understand why this countryside is always called Finland's "national landscape". The legend goes that Sibelius loved the area so much that he had a grand piano carried to the top of this hill to celebrate his marriage.

The wilderness way north

Finland's wilderness way north has three of the country's glories – sauna,

TIP

One fascinating experience in Kuusamo is winter rally driving at Juha Kankkunen Race Track (see page 320), where you get to experience the thrill of steering a world-class race car around a snow-powdered track.

BELOW: Orthodox Archbishop Paavali blesses the opening of Bomba House near Nurmes.

TIP

Many formerly Finnish villages that now reside on the Russian side of the border still speak Karelian, a dialect closely related to Finnish, but not mutually intelligible. The Karelian language and the history of the region is filled with proverbs, adages and aphorisms rife with lore of the Karelian people. One particular proverb, *Kundele korvilla ela perziel* ("Listen with your ears, not your backside") was used to encourage people to get off their seats and get to work in the fields.

BELOW: salmon leaping upstream.

salmon and scenery, the last embodied in its national parks although not confined to them. You will meet these three great assets at almost every turn in Finland, but never so frequently and in such abundance as in the region that starts north of Nurmes, roughly along the line of the Oulu waterway – lake and river – that almost bisects Finland, and stretches north to Rovaniemi (*see page 289*) and Lapland proper.

To many, however, the biggest attractions in this area are the traditional **saunas**. There is purportedly one sauna for every 2.5 people in Finland, and visitors will find them everywhere – in hotels, private homes, on board ships, at motels, holiday villages and forest camps. Finns are terribly proud of the sauna, the one word which the Finnish language has offered to the rest of the world, and nothing better complements the end of a long northern day in the open air to refresh and revitalise body and soul (*see page 192*).

On the stove or in the stream there is only one really classic fish in this area and that is the Atlantic salmon. Though Finland has no sea border with the Atlantic, thanks to the Ice Age, this region retains an Atlantic legacy in the salmon that swim in the large natural landlocked lakes and in the smaller waters well stocked with the species.

A natural world

Northern Karelia is known for its national parks, where nature is left as untouched as possible but some amenities are provided for visitors; marked trails, campsites and cabins are set in the larger parks, with hotel accommodation just outside the park proper. With so much unspoilt territory, it may hardly seem necessary for Finland to designate national parks, but it has a total of 25, and some of the best of them are found along the wilderness way north.

From the east of the country, the natural route into the area is from Nurmes on Road 75 to Kuhmo, or via Road 6 north, either turning right onto Road 76 just before Sotkamo to reach Kuhmo or continuing left on Road 6 for Kajaani on Oulujärvi (lake) to the west. From the west coast, the natural route would be

rom Oulu (see page 246) along the waterway connecting the Oulu River, ake, Kajaani and Kuhmo.

Heading north from Nurmes on Road 6, turn left onto Road 5850 owards Rautavaara, and after some 0km (32 miles) you come to the emote national park **Tiilikkajärven ansallispuisto ➐**, near Rautavaara. It vas established to conserve the uninabited area of Lake Tiilikka and the urrounding bogs.

Another national park, the **Hiidenortin kansallispuisto ➑**, is southeast f Sotkamo and also best reached from Road 6. Turn right onto Road 5824, nd some 25km (16 miles) on you ome to the park on the left. This is a ugged area, with the narrow Hiidenortti Gorge, a large rift valley with ock sides dropping some 20 metres 70ft) to the floor of the gorge. Both he park and the neighbouring Peurarvi hiking and fishing area have desgnated trails, marked with orange aint, and campsites. At Peurajärvi, ermits are sold that allow anglers to atch just one salmon each. Although ou could wriggle through a compli-

cated series of minor roads on the Sotkamo route from here, unless you are feeling very adventurous, it is probably a lot easier to go back to Road 18.

Both in and outside the parks, the further north you go, the more likely you are to find reindeer. These semi-domesticated animals are the main source of income for many people living in these parts, and it is very important to take special care on roads – reindeer may be around at any time of the year.

The Finnish frontier

Kuhmo ➒ is a frontier town surrounded by dense forests in the wilderness area of Kainuu. The largest municipal area in Finland, Kainuu covers 5,458 sq km (2,100 sq miles). Close to the Russian border and remote and empty though the area is, Kuhmo has established an international reputation through the annual Kuhmo Chamber Music Festival, first held in 1970 (see page 100). Fifty km (30 miles) southeast in Saunajärvi is the Winter War

The Kuhmo region is famous for its herds of rare forest reindeer.

BELOW: the lynx is one of the wild animals that dwells in the Karelian forests.

While trekking might not be the first thing that comes to mind when thinking about Finland, the fact is that the country holds thousands of miles of trails, walkways and manicured paths perfect for hiking.

BELOW: dense birch forest.
BELOW RIGHT: Karelia abounds with berries in summer, such as these bilberries.

Memorial marking Finland's desperate 100-day struggle in 1940 against overwhelming odds. Travel agents in Kuhmo arrange trips across the border to Russian Karelian villages, but visas are required and can take several days to arrange.

At one time this entire area was devoted to making tar, by a lengthy process of cutting, leaving and then burning forest trees to extract the sticky liquid that formed the basic ingredient. Once it was in barrels, peasants loaded their small boats for the slow journey down through lake and river to the port of Oulu where, in a rare symbiosis, shipbuilders bought it for their own craft and entrepreneurs shipped it abroad. In the 19th century Finland was the biggest exporter of tar in the world.

A fascinating recreated **Kalevala Village** in a wooded park on the outskirts of Kuhmo displays numerous local folk traditions (tel: 08-652 0114; June–mid-Aug daily 10am–5pm; charge). The aim is to give modern-

day visitors some idea of Finnish culture as it was immortalised by the folklorist Elias Lönnrot and artists such as Akseli Gallén-Kallela. The result is a "living" demonstration of the daily culture of ancient times as portrayed in Finland's epic poem, the *Kalevala (see page 103)*.

The village also serves as the scene for numerous events based on other folk literature, including plays, celebrations and performances by theatre groups. Guided tours teach visitors about primitive hunting and fishing skills and how tar was made in the Finnish wilds. The village has models of ingenious traps to catch birds and animals, including bears, and examples of how the old fishing families and peasants lived. The large Hotel Kalevala serves a tasty buffet lunch during the holiday season (tel: 08-655 4100; www.hotellikalevala.fi).

North of Kuhmo, near the village of Lentiira is Lentiiran Lomakylä, one of the most welcoming and comfortable holiday village chalet complexes by the lake. With a wood-fired sauna and cold beer included, this must surely b

Finnish tourist hospitality at its very best (tel: 08-650 141; www.lentiira.com).

Political past

A long straight road through some of Finland's darkest forests leads west out of Kuhmo to Sotkamo and then onwards to **Kajaani** ⑩, the area's principal town, on the eastern edge of Oulujärvi (lake) and once the collecting point for barrels of tar ready for their journey to the coast.

Kajaani was founded in 1651 by the Swedish governor general Count Per Brahe in the shelter of an existing fortress designed as a bastion against Russia. In 1716 the fortress fell and the whole town was razed during the disastrous war between Sweden and Russia. The town still has the ruins of the 1604 castle. The Town Hall is yet another designed by the well-travelled German architect K.L. Engel, who was responsible for so much of early Helsinki's architecture (see page 164). The old tar boat canal and the lock keeper's house by the Kajaani River are still visible. Famous residents have included Elias Lönnrot, who at one time lived in

Kajaani, and the town is also known as the home of Finland's longest-serving president, Urho Kekkonen.

The Tsar's Stable in nearby **Paltaniemi** ⑪ is a relic of a visit by Tsar Alexander I. Also in Paltaniemi is the birthplace of the poet Eino Leino, and the city has a Cultural and Congress Centre. Heading some 20km (12 miles) from the centre, you reach Ruuhijarvi Wilderness Village, which offers peaceful fishing grounds and old hunting lodges which are open all year.

The road from Kajaani to the coast at Oulu hugs the shores of Lake Oulu, plunging first into thickly wooded hill country. Before entering Oulu (see page 246), the route passes through Muhos, which has the second-oldest church in Finland, dating from 1634. Oulu continues the tradition of tar-making, and the lakeland town still lights tar pits on Midsummer's Eve.

Distances are long in this scantily populated area. Across the breadth of the country along Road 20 from Oulu and **Kuusamo**, a regional hub close to the Russian border, is some 360km (225 miles). Before Kuusamo, if you

TIP

Hunting has been a way of life for most Finns for centuries. Worldly though they might be, many remain ardent supporters of the right to hunt – rights their forefathers took full advantage of to survive. Today, while hunting may not be the pastime of Helsinki urbanites, rural folk often own guns, and tradition holds that many take part in local and regional hunting events. As with fishing, hunting is heavily regulated, so if you partake, be sure to have the appropriate licence.

BELOW: tundra takes over the landscape near the Arctic Circle.

TIP

Spread about the Koillismaa region fronting the Russian border are hundreds of miles of trails that are perfect for either cross-country skiing, snowshoeing or husky sledding. A number of tour companies run invigorating wintertime adventure trips in and around Oulanka National Park. See page 320 for more information.

BELOW:
hunting and fishing are two sports often combined.

feel like a detour, turn left at Pudasjärvi and take Road 78 for 90km (55 miles) to **Ranua** ⑫, which claims the world's northernmost zoo, featuring polar bears (the only ones in Finland), brown bears, lynx, wolf and the wolverine – one of the most endangered animals in the Nordic countries.

Rushing water and wind

Kuusamo ⑬ lies in the midst of marvellous wilderness country, with tundra as far as you can see in any direction, areas of forest, racing rivers with water foaming through gorges and canyons, some bare, others a dense dark green. The main sound in these parts is a mixture of rushing water and wind high in the pines. There are dozens of rapids, some suitable for canoeing, others for fishing. The Oulankajoki and Iijoki (rivers) are excellent for family canoeing trips, but the Kitkajoki calls for experienced canoeists only.

There are literally thousands of excellent fishing spots in both rivers and lakes. The "Russian" brown trout rise in the rivers from Lake Paanajärvi in greater numbers each year thanks to

efficient tending of the fishing grounds. This is also berry country, with blueberries, raspberries, lingonberries and cloudberries filling the landscape of the Arctic tundra with colour. The only snag is the number of mosquitoes: they multiply rapidly in the northern summer, so take plenty of protection.

In both summer and winter, this vast unspoilt area is given over to recreation. In the middle, Karhuntassu Tourist Centre (tel: 020-564 6804) has been specially built to provide information on every kind of activity, plus accommodation and most other aspects of the region, and there are other more distant centres. In winter, the area is excellent for skiing, and the skidoo or snowmobile comes into its own. Snowmobiling is both an exhilarating and a practical way to get around this snowbound landscape, though many consider this modern convenience outweighed by its noise and fumes.

There are two national parks near here. The largest, **Oulangan kansallispuisto** ⑭, to the north stretches over an largely untouched region of 270 sq km (105 sq miles), bordering the Oulanka River. It is a landscape of ravines and rushing torrents, sand banks and flowering meadows. Karhunkierros (The Bear's Trail), the most famous walking route in Finland, stretches some 80km (50 miles) through the pine forests and quiet river banks of Oulanka canyon to the **Ruka tunturi Fells** ⑮. A few kilometres will give the flavour of the trail, but to cover the whole route, staying at campsites or forest cabins en route, takes several days. In winter the area is given over to winter sports, with some 28 ski pistes. A smaller national park, Riisitunturi, lies to the southwest of Oulanka, another untouched wilderness of spruce dominated by hills and bogs.

Almost imperceptibly on the way north, the landscape and culture have changed from the traditions of Karelia to the traditional lifestyles of the Sami people. From here on, it is all clear: the land is Lappi.

Elk and Wolf Hunting

The large numbers of elk and wolf – the "big game" of the Finnish forests and tundra – continue to attract skilled hunters.

L urking in the northern forests and tundra of Finland are two of the largest European mammals, the elk and the wolf. The fact that both survive in large numbers has meant a great deal of sport for local hunters, in season.

The great bull elk of Finland, standing 1.8 metres (6ft) high at the shoulder, gazes through the northern forest. Crowned by massive horns, this impressive animal (which is the same species as the North American moose) is not the sluggish, lumbering giant it appears to be. Silent as night, wary, elusive, fast and with highly developed senses, this titan of the tundra and one-time cohabitant of the mammoth tests the limits of hunting skills to the utmost.

The justification for shooting elk is the paramount need to protect both food and the young timber that is so important to Finland's economy. The elk breeds so well in modern Finland that an annual cull of around 50,000 animals is necessary. Hunters, however, have no place in pest control. It is the thrill of the chase that brings the elk hunter with his .300 calibre rifle and his pack of dogs to the forest in October for the short elk-hunting season.

The challenging conditions of the sub-Arctic tundra make the pursuit of the elk arduous and competitive. With dense trees and thick brush, trained dogs are needed to aid the hunter in his quest. A dog can hold an elk at bay simply because it is disinclined to move.

If the quarry moves, the dogs will hunt it by following its scent. The signal for the hunter is the renewed barking of the dog, because this means the elk is standing still and the approach can begin. Now comes the most critical time of the hunt, for if an elk is tolerant of a dog, it is most decidedly intolerant of man. The ground is covered in material which, to quote a well known old advertising slogan, "snaps, crackles and pops". The hunter must proceed with light footsteps, and may have to crawl on his belly for the final approach. It is sudden

RIGHT: wolves are common in northern Finland.

movement that attracts attention, and a day's effort may be ruined by one false move.

Hunting the Russian Wolf

While culling may be the justification behind elk hunting, it is the *raison d'être* for wolf hunting. Wolves still prowl the border area of Finland and Russia. Once in Finland, wolves kill domestic reindeer, protected by a close season in the east and year-round in the south.

Hunting wolves is a difficult affair, but the Finns use an ingenious method of encirclement – one also found in parts of Eastern Europe. From large spools strapped to their backs, the men lay a line of string with red flashes through the woods. It can take up to two days to set the lines but some curious instinct tells a wolf not to cross them; it is the opposite of the blood-red rag to a bull. The helpers then drive the wolves to where the hunters are waiting. The guns now have some advantage, though the cunning and speed of wolves often saves them from the bullet – only a small number of wolves are successfully shot each year.

You can venture out on hunting tours with guides in several areas of Finland, with elk hunting – lasting three or four days – being the most popular. Hunting usually means living in a hut or cabin. After many hours in the open, nothing is more welcome than the ritual of the sauna to replenish body and soul.   ❑

LAPLAND

Usually associated with Christmas and bleak Arctic landscapes, Lapland is also a thriving region of quaint farming and fishing communities

D eep in the Finnish Arctic, Lapland is one of the most magical parts of the world, filled with juxtaposition and wonder – gorgeous coniferous forests fronting barren tundral wastelands, fast-flowing rivers and rapids alongside tranquil campsites, man-made glass-roof igloo hotels for viewing the outstanding Northern Lights and Sami nomads proudly melding their traditional lives with mobiles and snowmobiles. It is without a doubt the one place in Finland that most captures the imagination and inspires the senses.

Two main roads wend their way northwards through the province of Lapland (Lappi). Road 4, sometimes called the Arctic Road, links Kemi with Rovaniemi before continuing through ever more sparsely inhabited landscapes to empty into Norway at Utsjoki. The other is Road 21 (E8), which follows the Tornio Valley upstream from Tornio on the coast, continuing beside various tributaries that form the border with Sweden, eventually to cross into Norway near Kilpisjärvi. This is the river route of the Arctic Canoe Race, and the road that accompanies it is also sometimes known as the "Way of the Four Winds", after the four points of the Sami traditional male headgear. Bridges and ferries provide links with Sweden.

Arctic landscape

These two routes extend across Finnish Lapland for 540km (330 miles) and 457km (284 miles) respectively. Both cover a great deal of Arctic countryside, but from neither will you glean anything but the faintest hint of what Lapland is all about. For that you must depart from the main routes – preferably from the minor ones too – and set out on foot or in a canoe or, in winter, on a pair of skis. Yet you don't need to venture very far, for there are silent spaces within a few hundred metres of the most modern hotel, that feel caught in another epoch entirely. The vital need for proper clothing and equip-

Main attractions
ROVANIEMI
SODANKYLÄ
TANKAVAARA
IVALO
INARI
UTSJOKI
ENONTEKIÖ
KILPISJÄRVI

PRECEDING PAGES: herd of reindeer. **LEFT:** spectators at Inari's reindeer races. **BELOW:** Laplander's hut.

Lapland

0 — 50 km
0 — 50 miles

ment, however, can't be over-stressed: climatic changes occur with ferocious suddenness and, for all its magnificence, the Arctic wilderness can be a ruthless place where Mother Nature reigns supreme.

As you progress northwards the trees become more spindly, the forests more sparse, the settlements fewer, the hills more numerous – until you reach the sweeping undulations of the bare-topped fells of northern and north-western Lapland. Up above the ever-descending tree line, vegetation begins to creep and crawl – dwarf juniper and willow and miniature birch clinging to the fellsides among the mosses and the lichens, the minuscule campions and tiny saxifrages. In summer it is vital to bring along plenty of mosquito repellent.

In 1944 the German army followed a scorched-earth policy as it retreated north into Norway. As a result, any old buildings that survive are largely away from the main roads. But despite the monumental changes wrought on the province by the second half of the 20th century (*see page 117*), at least some elements of an age-old way of life endure.

Rovaniemi

From the coast at Kemi, Road 4 follows the Kemijoki Valley, where a rash of timber-based industries has spawned a succession of communities. You reach Rovaniemi ❶ within 115km (70 miles). This, the administrative capital of Lapland, all but nudges the Arctic Circle and is the launching point for most trips into the province. The town, well placed at the confluence of the Ounasjoki and Kemijoki rivers, has been completely rebuilt since World War II, nearly quadrupling its population (now about 34,500) in the process. In early summer timber is still floated down the Ounasjoki from the forests of central Lapland for processing into paper and other commercial products.

The reconstruction plan for Rovaniemi was devised by Alvar Aalto,

who also designed the fine Lappia Hall complex on Hallituskatu, containing a theatre and congress facilities and, next to it, the Library. The beautiful **Arctic Centre** (Arktikum), half-buried underground and thus offering a sensation of midnight sun through the glass ceiling, has exhibits illustrating Arctic history and culture (tel: 016-322 3260; www.arktikum.fi; June–Aug daily 9am–7pm, Dec daily 9am–6pm, rest of year Tue–Sun 10am–6pm; charge).

Also in the Arktikum building, the Lapland Provincial Museum gives visitors a good introduction to Lapland's flora and fauna, Sami traditions and Rovaniemi's history, but you will get a better feel of bygone living from the 19th-century farm buildings at the **Rovaniemi Local History Museum** (tel: 016-348 1095; June–Aug Tue–Sat noon–6pm; charge) south on Road 78. **Rovaniemi Art Museum** (Lapinkävi-jäntie 4; tel: 016-322 2822; Tue–Sun noon–5pm; charge) has a collection of modern Finnish art. Not far from Lappia Hall, the main Lutheran church features a modern altar fresco, *The Source of Life*, by Lennart Segerstråle.

Sami textiles reflect local lifestyles, such as their dependence on reindeer.

BELOW:
the Arktikum provides a fascinating insight into the Arctic.

The city is also home to a number of interesting events: the Arctic Lapland Rally in late January, the Reindeer Race in late March and the Snowmobile Races in early April. Rising up from the confluence of the Ounasjoki and Kemijoki to the southeast of town are the wooded slopes of **Ounasvaara** ❷, now a well-developed skiing area and site of annual international winter games. It's also a favourite gathering place on Midsummer Night.

Land of Santa Claus

Eight km (5 miles) from Rovaniemi on Road 4, soon after the turn-off for the airport, the **Santa Claus Workshop Village** ❸ (Joulupukin Pajakylä; tel: 016-356 2096; www.santaclausvillage.info; daily) straddles the Arctic Circle (Napapiiri). Its post office annually handles hundreds of thousands of letters from children worldwide, and there is a collection of souvenir shops, a puppet theatre, art exhibitions, a glass factory, a few reindeer and, of course, Santa Claus (*see page 140*).

Santa Park (tel: 016-333 0000; www. santapark.com; late Nov–early Jan daily

10am–6pm; June–Aug Tue–Sat, 10am–6pm; charge) was recently opened in a man-made cave inside the Syväsenvaara Hill some 2km (1¼ miles) south of the Arctic Circle. A miniature train transports visitors to the site, which was originally planned in cooperation with British theme park designers but which has since changed its concept into a more traditional idea of Christmas.

A number of fell areas east of Road 4 in southern Lapland have been developed for winter and summer tourism. One of the best is centred on Pyhätunturi, about 135km (84 miles) northeast of Rovaniemi. Another, just north of it, is Luostotunturi, south of Sodankylä. At the **Scandic Hotel**, Luosto (tel: 016-624 400; www.scandichotels.com), you can stay overnight in a cosy log cabin with an Arctic-style built-in bed and blazing fire. There are popular hiking and skiing routes between these two centres.

By this point you will have noticed the landscapes – predominantly forested – becoming progressively emptier. However, there are reindeer aplenty and the occasional elk, so do drive slowly; keep your eyes open and

BELOW: Santa Claus is Lapland's most famous export.

ur camera handy – legend has it that hite reindeer bring good luck.

Sodankylä ❹, on Road 4 some 0km (80 miles) from Rovaniemi, is e first substantial settlement along is route, a long-established commuty reputed to be the coldest in Finnd. It is the home of the Midnight n Film Festival held each June. Next its 19th-century stone church, its ooden predecessor is Lapland's oldest urch, dating from 1689. Road 5 comes to Sodankylä from the southeast and inor byways wander off east and west link tiny scattered communities.

old country

orthwards, there's little to detain you r the next 100km (60 miles) or so til, a few miles beyond Vuotso, you ach **Tankavaara ❺**. Gold panning has en practised in various parts of Lapnd for well over a century, and at nkavaara there is an entertaining **Kulkylä** (Gold Village; tel: 016-626 171; w.tankavaara.fi); its Kultamuseo (Gold ospectors' Museum; June–mid-Aug ily 9am–6pm, mid-Aug–Sept daily m–5pm) not only chronicles man's

historical endeavours to discover gold, but for a modest fee provides tuition and allows you to pan for gold yourself for an hour, a day, or several days, in an authentic wilderness setting. At nearby **Kultala ❻** (*kulta* is the Finnish word for gold), in trackless wilderness to the northwest, on the banks of the Ivalojoki you can also observe a gold-washing station dating from 1870.

About 40km (25 miles) further north there is a great deal more self-catering accommodation, together with modern hotels, spas and sports facilities, centred on Laanila and **Saariselkä ❼**, a winter sports centre immensely popular with the elite of Helsinki's business life. To the east of Saariselkä are the forests and slopes of a huge area of primeval fell extending to the Russian border, an excellent area for skiing with

You can have a go at gold panning in Gold Village, Lapland.

BELOW: the colours of summer in Lapland.

Mosquitoes, midges, blackflies, horseflies and other biting insects are the curse of any visit to Finland's northern regions for around eight weeks, starting in mid-June. Four species (Culiseta, Aedis communis, A. Punctor and A. Pionips) cause the most irritation. It is only the females that bite. Most people are surprised to learn that malaria only disappeared from Finland in the 1950s.

BELOW RIGHT:
drying reindeer
meat.

plenty of wilderness huts. Much of this region is designated as a national park named after Urho Kekkonen, Finland's longest-serving president.

Ivalo and Inari

In another 23km (14 miles) you pass the turn-off for Ivalo airport, Finland's northernmost. **Ivalo ❽** itself straggles along the east bank of the Ivalojoki. It's the largest community in northern Lapland, with all the usual facilities, though Sami culture is much less in evidence here than in Inari *(see below)*. There is, however, an attractive little wooden Orthodox church tucked away in the woods, serving the Skolt Sami, a branch of the Sami people who formerly lived in territory ceded to the Soviet Union in 1944. They have different costumes, language and traditions to Finnish Sami, and some now breed sheep in addition to (or occasionally instead of) reindeer. A number of Skolt Sami families live in Nellim, about 45km (29 miles) northeast of Ivalo near the Russian border.

Ivalo's Lutheran church stands near the bridge which carries Road 4 over

the Ivalojoki; then it's a further 39k (27 miles) to **Inari ❾** – much of it delightful route along the contorte shores of Lake Inari. Inari village mak an excellent base for wilderness explo tion; you can lodge at the love boutique rooms in Villa Lanca (tel: 04 748 0984; www.villalanca.com). Thoug smaller and rather more scattered tha Ivalo, this is nevertheless the administ tive centre for a vast area, and a trad tional meeting place for colourful costumed Sami people during we dings and other festivities, especial the Church festivals of Lady Day an Easter. If you're in the market for trad tional handicrafts, pay a visit to **San Duodji** (tel: 016-671 254; www.samidu dji.com), located just opposite the tou ist office at Inarintie 51.

The focus of many Sami festivities the simple modern church set by t lake's shoreline. **Lake Inari** is Finlanc third-largest, covering 1,300 sq k (808 sq miles) and is dotted with abo 3,000 islands, some of them considere sacred according to Sami tradition. It a wild, lonely, beautiful lake, the then of numerous haunting songs and ma

Sledging

The easiest way to traverse Lapland's vast and largely flat (or gently undulating) landscape has always been on skis or sledges; the latter less exhausting for longer distances. There are many different types of sledging, but the most popular and readily associated with northern Finland is the dog sledge. Four or six husky dogs, hardy beasts naturally acclimatised to snow and ice, are harnessed to the front of a sledge, with passengers standing on the back runners. Unlike horses, however, the huskies are not readily controllable, so keeping the sledge stationary – or bringing it to a halt – is achieved by means of a hook wedged deep in the snow. Once the hook is withdrawn, the dogs immediately lurch forward.

Reindeer sledging, as epitomised by images of Santa and his sleigh each Christmas, is another method of getting around, with the advantage that these animals can cover longer distances (and are better at coping with deep snow cover), although they are slower than the dogs.

Many centres in Lapland now offer the chance of sledging excursions for tourists – contact tourist information offices in main towns for more details. It is essential that the right equipment is worn: thermals, waterproofs, hats and goggles are necessary to combat the dampness and icy bitterness of the snow.

-gends. Boat trips and sightseeing
-ights are available during the summer
- holy Ukko Island (particularly
-vered by the local Sami).

Inari's excellent **SIIDA** (Sami
-luseum and the Northern Lapland
-lature Centre; tel: 016-665 212; May–
-ept daily 9am–8pm, Oct–Apr Tue–Sun
-)am–5pm; charge) chronicles how the
-fe of the Sami has changed (and how
- hasn't) over the years. There is also an
-pen-air museum, as well as exhibits on
-rly Skolt Sami culture and modern
-ami life. The SIIDA building also
-ouses the Ylä-Lapin luontokeskus
-Nature Centre for Upper Lapland),
-hich sells fishing permits and assists
- hiking plans for those wishing to
-xplore the wilderness. From the
-useum a marked trail covering a
- turn journey of some 15km (9 miles)
-ads to a remote 18th-century wooden
-urch at Pielppajärvi, one of Lapland's
-ldest surviving buildings. It's a beauti-
-l spot that is also accessible by boat.

Be sure, however, to leave enough
-me for shopping at Inari's many fine
-andicraft shops, which include a silver-
-nith's shop, knife-maker Petteri Laiti's

studio and Sami Duodji, which sells
Sami handicrafts, literature and music.

Towards Norway

The minor Road 955 from Inari leads
40km (25 miles) southwest to **Menesjärvi**, a Sami settlement from which
one can continue by road then by
river boat or on foot up the wild and
beautiful **Lemmenjoki Valley** ❿
("warm river") to a remote gold prospectors' camp. It is best to see this isolated and extensive national park area
of canyon and forest with a hired
guide. From Menesjärvi, Road 955
continues across Lapland to join
Road 79 north of Kittilä.

Around Inari and north of it, the
road passes a number of attractive holiday centres, mostly of the self-catering
variety. After 26km (16 miles) you
come to Kaamanen from which a
minor road branches northeast 100km
(60 miles) to **Sevettijärvi** ⓫, the modern main settlement for the Skolt Sami.
An interesting time to visit is during
the Easter Orthodox festival. While
there, visit the Sami graveyard, with its
unusual turf-covered graves.

*Hiking on the fells
requires proper
clothing and equip-
ment, but the scenery
makes it worthwhile.*

BELOW LEFT: wintry
Lapland scene.
BELOW: women in
traditional Sami
costume.

There are no wild polar bears in Finland, but you can see them in captivity at Ranua Zoo in Karelia (see page 282).

BELOW: football Lapland-style.

Just a couple of kilometres north of Kaamanen you have a choice of routes to the Norwegian border: to go north on Route 4 to the town of Utsjoki, 94km (58 miles) away, or bear northwest along Road 92 to the border 66km (41 miles) away at Karigasniemi.

Whichever direction you head, the landscapes get hillier, wilder and even emptier as you progress. You will also pass the coniferous tree line, beyond which only the hardier dwarf birch survive on the lower fell slopes, their gnarled and weathered forms looking curiously biblical in this barren Arctic countryside.

The route to Utsjoki is more beautiful, passing a series of lakes close to the eastern fringes of the Kevo Nature Park, where Turku University runs a sub-Arctic research station. Utsjoki ⑫ itself is an important Sami community – good for fishing and hiking – close to Finland's northernmost point. Its church (1860) is one of the few p... World War II churches still standing Lapland. The village and road foll... the Utsjoki downstream to join w... the Tenojoki, a famed salmon river.

Both Utsjoki and Karigasniemi ... dominated by "holy" fells known *Ailigas*, the one dominating Karig... niemi reaching over 620 met... (2,000ft). From these border poi... you can join the Norwegian road s... tem for a variety of routes, eventua... returning into western Lapland Kilpisjärvi or Enontekiö.

Western Lapland

Your route through western Laplan... likely to begin at Tornio on the Gulf Bothnia about 80km (50 miles) sou... of the Arctic Circle (*see page 248*). T... earlier stretches of the Way of the Fo... Winds or Road 21 (E8) follow t... Tornionjoki River and the Swed... border, and present a very differe... face of Lapland from the Arctic Ro... The countryside here is much mo... populated than you'd imagine, a... served by Finland's northernmost r... way branch as far as Kolari.

In its southern stages the road passes through a string of small communities mainly based, in these marginally milder and more fertile conditions, on agriculture and dairy farming. The Tornionjoki is also a good salmon river; at **Kukkola** ⓭ look out for the Kukkolankoski rapids.

About 70km (43 miles) north of Tornio, beyond Ylitornio, is the 242-metre (794ft) **Aavasaksa Hill** ⓮, the most southerly point from which the midnight sun can be seen, attracting considerable throngs for Midsummer Eve festivities. A few miles nearer Juoksenki, you cross the Arctic Circle. The scenery now gets wilder as you pass between Pello and Kolari. A little south of the latter Tornionjoki is replaced by a tributary, the Muonionjoki, at the Finnish–Swedish border.

Fell country

About 10km (7 miles) north of Kolari, a worthwhile detour by minor Road 940 to the right leads to **Akäslompolo** ⓯. This well-equipped tourist resort and skiing centre is set along the shores of a small lake amidst magnificent for-ested hills and bare-topped fells; the highest of these is Ylläs, at 718 metres (2,355ft), which is served by chair lifts. A marked trail follows the chain of fells stretching northwards from here, eventually leading, in about 150km (90 miles), to the beginning of the Pallas-Yllästunturi National Park. The park contains a number of glorious trails, and there is overnight shelter available in untended wilderness huts – these are even marked on the 1:200,000 road maps.

From Akäslompolo you can continue north along minor roads and in 31km (19 miles) turn left onto Road 79. This is the main road from Rovaniemi, providing an alternative approach to western Lapland. After a further 10km (7 miles) Road 957 to the right is highly recommended as the best approach to Enontekiö. A further branch left off this route leads from Road 79 to the lonely hotel complex of Pallastunturi, magnificently cradled in the lap of five of the 14 fells which make up the Pallastunturi group (the highest being Taivaskero at 807 metres/2,647ft).

Signposts won't let you forget quite how far north you've travelled.

BELOW: sparkling meltwaters at Windelhed.

From here the choice of fell walks includes the long-distance 60-km (37-mile) trail north from Yllästunturi across the fells to Enontekiö. Road 957 brings you to the upper Ounasjoki Valley via the small community of Raattama to **Ketomella** , where there's a car ferry across the river, offering a view of a number of venerable old farm buildings. Along the entire route you get lovely views of first the Pallas, then the Ounas fells. At the junction at Peltovuoma you turn west for Enontekiö and, eventually, Palojoensuu, back on Road 21.

Enontekiö

Enontekiö ⓱, also known as Hetta, is the attractively situated administrative centre of this extensive, sparsely populated area. The village sprawls along the northern shore of Ounasjärvi (lake), looking across to the great rounded shoulders of the Ounastunturi fells – the highest of which is Outtakka at 723 metres (2,372ft). Once completely isolated, it's now accessible by air and road from all directions, with a road link north into Norway.

Most of Enontekiö's buildings are modern, including the pretty wooden church whose altar mosaic depicts Sami people and reindeer. There's a good range of accommodation available, from campsites to top-class hotels, all set up for the avid fishermen, hikers and canoeists for whom this makes an excellent holiday centre. It is also a main centre for the Sami of western Lapland, most of whom live in lone farmsteads or tiny communities in and around the area. Here, too, the Sami festival of Marianpäivä is held in early March – the largest of its kind in the Nordic countries.

From Palojoensuu, Road 21 continues northwest along along the Swedish border following the Muonionjoki and Könkämäeno valleys. The scenery becomes ever wilder and more barren especially once you cross the tree line.

At **Järämä**, 10km (6 miles) further from the tiny settlement of Markkina, German soldiers built fortifications during the Lapland War of 1944. Many of these bunkers have been restored and are now open to the public.

Lakes and mountains

A little south and north of **Ropinsalmi** ⓲ there are good views respectively of Pättikkäkoski and Saukkokoski, two of the more testing rapids on the Muonionjoki River. The mountains reach ever greater heights; Finland's highest Halti, soars up to 1,328 metres (4,357ft) on the Norwegian border.

More accessible and distinctive is **Saana** ⓳, 1,029 metres (3,376ft) above the village and the resort of Kilpisjärvi **Kilpisjärvi** is an excellent launching pad for wilderness enthusiasts. There is a lake of the same name whose western shore forms the border with Sweden, and a marked trail which takes about a day leads to the boundary stone marking the triple junction of Finland-Sweden-Norway. The Mallan luonnonpuisto, a nature reserve to the north of the lake, requires a permit for entry, but once you are within it there is a pleasant 15-km (9-mile) trek. ❑

✹INSIGHT GUIDES TRAVEL TIPS
FINLAND

TRANSPORT

GETTING THERE AND GETTING AROUND

GETTING THERE

By Air

Finnair is the national carrier of Finland and operates international and national routes. Both Finnair (www.finnair.com) and British Airways (www.ba.com) connect London and Helsinki with daily flights. Finnair (and many other airlines, including Lufthansa and Scandinavian Airlines) fly direct between Helsinki and most European capitals. Finnair also links with several North American cities including New York. You may be able to find value-for-money package fares and charter flights from New York or London, but they are rare; try the internet sites of the airlines for offers.

From Helsinki, Finnair and Blue 1 (www.blue1.com) fly numerous domestic routes to more than 20 cities, including several to north Finland airports, and have cross-country flights between some of them. Budget airline easyJet (www.easyjet.com) flies between Stansted and Helsinki. Ryanair (www.ryanair.com) flies between Tampere and London, Riga or Frankfurt.

By Sea

You can travel to Finland by boat from Sweden, Estonia and Germany. **Viking Line** and **Silja-Tallink** run daily routes between Stockholm and Helsinki. These ferries are luxurious with restaurants, saunas, swimming pools, tax-free shops and children's playrooms. The all-night discos on these ships are legendary, often opening at 8pm and continuing to play loud dance music (but not necessarily serve alcohol all night) until the ship arrives at its eventual desintation. There are several links from Germany to Finland: Finnlines sails from Helsinki to Travemünde, while Tallink Silja Line's refurbished GTS Finnjet boat sails between Rostock–Tallinn–St Petersburg from the end of April to mid-September – a route that you can conveniently join in Tallinn.

There are plenty of services to choose from for a trip between Helsinki and Tallinn. For a fast trip Tallink Silja Line's SuperSeaCat and Linda Line's hydrofoil take the trip in 1½ hours during the ice-free period. These fast boats are dependent on weather conditions, whereas Viking and Eckerö Lines' bigger boats manage also in rough weather.

It's less expensive to travel by ferry from Stockholm to Turku or Naantali in western Finland and then overland to Helsinki rather than by direct ship to Helsinki. Viking provides very cheap bus tickets for the overland trip; the ferry ticket is also cheaper as the voyage is shorter. One can also travel to Finland's Åland Islands by boat from Stockholm or Turku – Viking and Tallink Silja Line has a daily service to Mariehamn. Also, RG Line operates boats between Vaasa and Umeå.

Eckeröline
Tel: 0600-04300
www.eckeroline.fi
Linda Line
Tel: 0600-066 8970
www.lindaline.fi
RG Line
Tel: 0207-716 810 (Finland)
090-185 200 (Sweden)
www.rgline.com

Sailing around the Baltic

Visas are required for travel to Russia. Most Finnish travel agents can organise these for non-Finns, but be sure to allow at least one week for processing. Most Western nationalities may enter Estonia, Latvia and Lithuania without a visa, and daytrips to Tallinn (Estonia) are extremely popular and recommended. There may be over 20 departures on an average summer day, and discounts are not unusual. Look especially at the front page of the main Finnish newspaper *Helsingin Sanomat*, which frequently advertises such discounts, especially in the warmer months. Tickets are available at harbours on Katajanokka, Olympialaituri and

Länsisatama, Helsinki and, of course, online.
Kristina Cruises
Tel: 05-21144
www.kristinacruises.com
Offer a summer St Petersburg trip, lasting 3–4 days, with lodging on board and guides for the city. The cruise includes a group visa for EU citizens, but once in St Petersburg passengers must remain with the guided tours. For independent travel you must produce your own visa. For information in the UK on sea or other options for travel to the former Soviet Union, contact:
Voyages Jules Verne
Tel: 020-7616 1000
www.vjv.co.uk

Tallink Silja Line
Tel: 0600-174 552
www.tallinksilja.com
Viking Line
Tel: 09-12351
www.vikingline.fi

By Rail

It's a long haul to Finland from just about any other country by rail, because you inevitably finish the long rail trip north with a 15-hour journey by boat and train from Stockholm to Helsinki. From Britain, the handiest route is Sealink from Harwich to the Hook of Holland, overland to Copenhagen, then the connecting train to Stockholm and boat/boat and train to Helsinki. Total travel time is about 45 hours. Rail travel to the far north of Finland requires completion by bus as Finnish rail lines only run as far as Rovaniemi and Kemijärvi (in winter to Kolari).

GETTING AROUND

On Arrival

Finland's main international airport, Helsinki-Vantaa, is connected by Finnair bus and local bus to Helsinki; fares are usually slightly more on the Finnair bus, but neither costs more than €6. Travel time is approximately 35 minutes. There is also a "shared" taxi stand at the airport. Expect to pay around €35 for a taxi to any destination in the city centre.

Public Transport

By Air

Finnair and Blue 1 both operate domestic flight services. Fares are relatively inexpensive, and in the summertime they can drop tremendously. It is a good idea to fly if, for example, you want to get to Lapland from the south but don't want to spend days driving there, or taking the overnight train. Discounts are available for groups, families and senior citizens.

By Rail

The Finnish Rail (Valtion Rautatie) operates an excellent network of trains throughout much of the country. Most trains are very comfortable, punctual and speedy; a series of recently introduced Pendolino trains has reduced the duration of certain journeys. The largest selection of train services is in the southern

ABOVE: Finland has a very efficient rail service.

part of the country, with superb ties between Helsinki and Karelia, the lake region and the southern coast. Further north, direct connections are a bit more spartan, sometimes requiring at least one change of trains; if you are travelling to Vaasa, for example, from Helsinki, you will need to make a connection in Seinäjoki.

Though few areas of Lapland have been laid with railway tracks – in part to preserve the unspoilt nature of its Arctic wilderness – there is a direct overnight connection between Helsinki and Rovaniemi. Solid bus connections in the far north make up for the lack of trains.

In late 2010, the Finnish rail service Valtion Rautatie will launch several daily departures of a new high-speed direct train between Helsinki and St Petersburg that will cut the current duration of the journey in half, to approximately 3 hours. Finnrail passes are available for 3-day, 5-day and 10-day periods; first-class passes are also available, though these passes do not cover travel to Russia. In summer, a special Lomapassi (Holiday Pass) costs €145 and entitles you to 3 travel days in a month. More information on family tickets, group tickets and other types of discounts is available online at www.vr.fi or contact:
Finnish Railways
Viihonkatu 13, 00101 Helsinki
Tel: 030 710

By Boat

If there is one aspect of topography that defines Finland's great outdoors, it is the body of water known as the lake. The country has over 180,000 of them, from tiny ponds to massive, sea-sized reservoirs. Throughout

the year, the lake is a focal point for transport for Finns – by ski or skidoo when frozen over in wintertime, or by ferry, passenger boat or canoe in the summer. Ferries and passenger boats in Finland also play a large role where international destinations are concerned (see page 300). From June to August there is regular boat service along Finland's waterways and – naturally – the Lake region is the best point of departure for such exploration of the country.

There are several Lakeland ferry routes particularly worth pursuing, including the **Silverline** and **Poet's Way**, which begin in Tampere and cover much of the western lakes. Further east are numerous tours along the country's largest lake, **Saimaa**, with daily departures from Lappeenranta, Kuopio, Savonlinna and Punkaharju.

Canoeing is another, slightly more leisurely way, to explore Finnish waters, especially in the **Päijänne** region. There are great canoeing experiences to be had around Nurmes, while trips along the Saramojoki River from the village of Saramo are good for beginning and intermediate-level canoers. Lieksa is another ideal departure point for canoe trips, with routes beginning either at Jonkeri or Aittokoski. Otherwise, in Nurmijärvi, try the fairly leisurely paddling route that follows the Lieskajoki to Pankasaari. Many other operators run trips on the lakes; for more information, contact the central or regional tourist boards (see page 326).

In the harbour capital of Helsinki, boats are generally an important mode of transportation for leisure-time activities only – especially exploring the islands around the

ABOVE: traffic congestion is not usually a problem in Finland.

perimeter of the city. Helsinki's only real commuter island is Suomenlinna, with ferries travelling back and forth roughly every half-hour (schedule depends on season). Most of these ferries are part of the public transport network of Helsinki. Other Helsinki islands closer to the coast are connected by road.

Päijänne Cruises Hildén
Tel: 014-263 447
www.paijanne-risteilythilden.fi
Roll Risteilyt
Tel: 017-266 2466
www.roll.fi
Silverline and Poet's Way
Tel: 0400-236 800
www.runoilijantie.fi

By Bus and Coach

Finland is greatly dependent on buses for transporting the bulk of its passenger traffic. There are coach services on 90 percent of Finland's public roads (40,000 long-distance departures a day) which also cover the areas that trains don't, particularly in the north and in smaller areas throughout the country where rail coverage is erratic. The head office for long-distance bus traffic is **Matkahuolto**, Lauttasaarentie 8, 00200 Helsinki, tel: 09-682 701. Timetable enquiries can be made at the **National Timetable Service**, tel: 020-04000 (€1.50 per call plus local telephone charges) or online at www.matkahuolto.fi.

There is no penalty for buying a ticket on the coach, but you cannot get group discounts (for three adults or more on trips over 80km/50 miles) from the coach ticket-seller. Senior citizens and full-time students (university and lower) are also eligible

for discounts, but must purchase a coach card entitling them to this discount – at least 30 percent. Bring a photo, ID and international ISIC student card where relevant. Accompanied children under four travel free.

Visitors can reserve long-distance coach seats (for a small fee) by calling Matkahuolto or visiting the main bus station in the Kamppi shopping centre at the top of Simonkatu in Helsinki.

Driving

Finland's roads are not too clogged with traffic, although they do get very busy between the capital and the countryside on Fridays and Sundays during the summer. There are few multi-lane motorways. Most are two-lane only.

Pay close attention to road signs showing elk and reindeer zones. These animals really do wander onto the roads in Finland and collisions with them can be very serious. Use caution at all hours, but especially at dusk when elk are most active. For winter driving from November to March, studded tyres should ideally be used and are strongly recommended throughout December and January at all times.

Foreign cars entering Finland should have a sticker on the back demarcating the country in which they are registered. In most cases, your own insurance with a green card will suffice in Finland, but check ahead to be sure. If you are driving a foreign car and are involved in an accident, contact the **Finnish Motor Insurers' Bureau**.

For more information about driving in Finland contact:
Finnish Motor Insurance Bureau
Bulevardi 28, 00120 Helsinki
Tel: 09-680 401
www.vakes.fi/lvk/english
Finnish Road Administration
PO Box 33, 00521 Helsinki
Tel: 020-42211
www.tiehallinto.fi
The Central Organisation For Traffic Safety In Finland
Sitratie 7, PB 29, 00421 Helsinki
Tel: 020-728 2300
www.liikenneturva.fi

Rules of the Road

Driving rules, regulations and norms in Finland are relatively straightforward. Drive on the right, overtake on the left. All cars must use their lights outside built-up areas. Elsewhere, lights must be used at dusk or at night or in bad weather (UK cars must sweep their lights right). Wearing of seat belts is also compulsory.

Traffic approaching from the right has right of way. Exceptions are on roads marked by a triangle sign; if this is facing you, you must give right of way; similarly, if you are on a very major thoroughfare it is likely that the feed-in streets will have triangles, giving you the right of way. On roundabouts (rotaries), the first vehicle to reach the roundabout has right of way.

Speed limits are signposted, and range from 30kmph (18mph) in school zones to 100kmph (62mph) on motorways.

Never ever risk driving while drunk in Finland. The limit is very low (0.5 percent blood alcohol) and the fines very steep; imprisonment is also not unheard of in a number of cases. Taxis are available throughout the country, even in the backwaters; be safe, do as the Finns do and use them if you've been drinking.

Taxis

Taxis operate throughout the country, with fares starting at around €3. In Helsinki, taxi stands are located throughout the city centre, including outside the Central Railway Station, around Senate Square, along Esplanade Park and at the ferry terminals.

In the centres of other large cities, as well as most major airports, bus and railway stations, you'll find taxi stands. Otherwise local telephone books list the number of the nearest company (under *Taksi* in the White

Pages). Finding the closest one is worthwhile, especially in Helsinki, as taxis charge from embarkation point (plus an order fee). You can also hail a cab on the street, but this is not always a surefire way to get a taxi in many places. In Helsinki, the phone number to pre-book a taxi is 0100 0700. Otherwise, call 0100 0700 if you want one immediately (ie within 5 or 10 minutes). This call costs €1.15 + €0.08/10 seconds. Be aware, too, that the cost of an advance order itself is €6; this will be added to the fare shown on the meter. It is much cheaper to hail a cab on the street (the yellow light on the roof will be illuminated if it's available for hire), though this isn't always as easy as it sounds. If you are heading to the airport, the Yellow Taxi operates taxi runs on a shared basis, which brings the price down. To order a place in one, call tel: 0600-555 555.

For information on stands and phone numbers for ordering in other Finnish cities, contact:
Finnish Taxi Assocation
(Suomen Taksiliitto),
Nuijamiestentie 7, 00400 Helsinki
Tel: 020-775 6800
www.taksiliitto.fi

Bicycles

Finland is one of the best places in Europe to cycle, with thousands of well-engineered and well-indicated cycle paths and a gently rolling landscape with few real hills. Similarly, the number of outfits renting cycles has grown over the past decade and cycles are now fairly easily hired in many towns. Your best bet is the local tourist office or YHA youth hostel. Bicycles can be taken on many Finnish trains for a nominal fee; in some areas they can also be carried on buses – this is most commonly done on the buses in Åland.

Be aware that the roads tend to be worse in the more remote regions of the far north, so you will want to be certain you have spares with you. In the capital, one major hire point is Greenbike (Bulevardi 32; tel: 050-550 1020; www.greenbike.fi). In the Åland archipelago, a very popular summer cycling destination, there is a Ro-No rental outlet on both harbours of Mariehamn (see page 232).

The Finnish Youth Hostel Association also offers planned route tours at good-value prices. These generally leave from Helsinki, and cost upwards of €280 including accommodation and rental for 7 days. Also ask the Finnish Tourist Board (see page 326) about other firms that run cycling tours in the country.
Finnish Youth Hostel Association
Yrjönkatu 38B, 00100 Helsinki
Tel: 09-565 7150
www.srmnet.org

Hitchhiking

Hitching a ride is less common than it used to be as a means of getting about in Finland. This means you may have to wait a long time to get picked up, particularly at weekends and in the furthest reaches of Lapland where traffic can be pretty thin. Hitchhiking is prohibited on Finland's motorways; the smaller secondary routes are a better option anyway. As with anywhere in the world, however, safety can never be guaranteed on the road, and this mode of transport is on the whole not to be recommended.

Snowmobiles

The snowmobile has evolved as a defining aspect of Sami society in the north of Finland. For Samis, snowmobiles are most definitely a core means of transportation for plying the fells, valleys, mountains, plateaus, iced-over lakes, tundra and permafrost of Lapland. The vehicle is now as integrated as the ski or the showshoe for Arctic Finns.

For visitors, however, it is largely a means of recreation and thrill-seeking, with hundreds of skidoo-able trails. Numerous tour companies organise snowmobile/skidoo trips around all areas of Lapland. See page 326 for details of tour operators.

Getting around Helsinki

Helsinki is so small and efficient that there is no better way to get around than your own two feet. Still, if you want to travel by public transport, trams are by far the best way of getting around. Purchase a **Helsinki Card** at the Tourist Office on Pohjoisesplanadi (also available from hotels and R-kiosks) for 1, 2 or 3 days; with this you get free entry to museums and unlimited transport by bus, tram, metro, commuter trains and the Suomenlinna ferry in Helsinki, as well as assorted discounts at restaurants and concerts.

The 3T and 3B trams double as a sightseeing route, covering a figure-eight around most of Helsinki. Catch either of them from in front of the railway station.

Alternatively, you can get Helsinki City Transport's (HKL) Tourist Ticket for 1, 3 or 5 days. This also entitles you to unlimited use of public transport and can be purchased from a number of outlets: from

HKL customer service points below ground at the railway station, vending machines at metro stations, and from Kauppatori Market Square or from the tourist office.

Bus drivers and conductors on commuter trains will only sell single-ride tickets and 1-day tourist tickets. There is also a 24-hour group ticket for families. Although it is cheaper to buy your tickets in advance, you can buy tickets from the driver on trams and buses.

Route maps are available in the tourist office, at the HKL service point and posted at nearly every stop. Note that there is an extra fare charged on regional journeys (to Espoo and Vantaa) and a night fare applies from 2–4.30am on all the buses. Most buses and trams run from 6am until 1am, but ask the tourist office about night buses in Helsinki and to Espoo and Vantaa.

When travelling on the metro, you purchase your single ticket from the vending machine before entering the platform. Single tickets allow you to make any number of changes within one hour of purchase. An exception is a special tram ticket which is €0.20 cheaper and only valid on the tram journey.

Helsinki operates a single metro line that runs east–west, serving local commuters in and out of town. It is fast and clean, with trains running at either 5- or 10-minute intervals, but the service shuts down at 11.20pm so is not suitable for late-night travel.

It can be very useful if you are trying to get across to some of the more remote parts of the city. For example, the Kaapelitehdas in the west of the city is connected by metro, as are some of the outer parts of Kallio and, further on, some of the suburbs now settled by recent immigrants to Finland.

Still, as the city is so easy to navigate on foot and by tram, there will be little reason for you to use the metro.

A CCOMMODATION

HOTELS, BED AND BREAKFAST AND HOSTELS

Choosing a Hotel

You can depend on Finnish accommodation being clean and in good shape, but prices remain high. If you have patience, however, there are bargains to be hunted out. Big discounts (up to 60 percent) are available in most hotels at weekends, and in summer when they lose their business and conference trade.

Budget accommodation includes youth and family hostels, guesthouse accommodation, family villages, farmhouses, camping and various forms of self-catering. During the summer holidays – usually beginning 1 June – some student residences become summer hostels. The local tourist boards and booking centres will provide up-to-date prices, including details of weekend and summer discounts.

General information is available from the **Finnish Tourist Board** in your home country, or the head office in Helsinki (see page 326).

Helsinki has its own hotel booking centre at the railway station: **Hotel Booking Centre**, Railway Station, 00100 Helsinki, tel: 09-2288 1400; www.helsinkiexpert.fi.

Chain Hotels

In addition to foreign chain hotels, Finland has many large hotel chains of its own. These include Sokos Hotels and Cumulus, which on the whole offer fairly comfortable standard services in most big towns, though many of their rooms often lack character. Some other chains, such as Radisson Blu (formerly Radisson SAS), offer somewhat more comfortable services. On the whole, such hotels

will provide extremely clean rooms with most modern amenities, as well as standard (chain) restaurants – with identical menus – all around the country. Some of the best known are:
Best Western Finland
Nuijamiestentie 10, 00320 Helsinki
Tel: 09-6226 4900
Restel Hotel Group (Cumulus)
Hämeentie 19, PO Box 72,
00501 Helsinki
Tel: 09-73352
Sokos Hotels (SOK)
Fleminginkatu 34, PO Box 60,
00511 Helsinki
Tel: 020-123 4600
www.sokoshotels.fi
To get discounts, enrol in the Finncheque scheme, in which some 110 hotels participate. By spending around €41 on a Finncheque, you get a night's free accommodation and breakfast in these hotels. The system is a cooperation between a number of hotel chains; further details from the Tourist Board (see page 326).

BELOW: Hotel Kämp.

Camping, Farmstays, Bed and Breakfast

Farmstays are not terribly common in Finland but they do exist in certain parts of the country. Bed and breakfasts and rural inns are much more common, and are usually run as small family entities. Often you will find tiny huts and cabins in the middle of national parks that are rented out by their owners. Campsites in Finland are plentiful, and you can almost always be guaranteed that they will have a sauna somewhere on their grounds – possibly near a lake or riverbank. Additionally, many campsites offer inexpensive accommodation in wooden cabins, which may or may not have kitchens.

Hostels

Finland has a widespread network of over a hundred youth and family hostels, which vary from small farmhouses to manors, camping and special centres. They usually have family rooms (2–4 guests) or dormitories (5–10 guests). About half of these hostels are open year-round, the remainder in summer only.

Details of hostels and the Finnish Youth Hostel cheque system are available from the **Finnish Youth Hostel Association**, Yrjönkatu 38B 15, 00100 Helsinki, tel: 09-565 7150, www.srmnet.org.

Hotel Listings

Hotels are listed in alphabetical order by region, with the most expensive first.

HELSINKI

Expensive

Hotel GLO
Kluuvikatu 4, 00100 Helsinki
Tel: 09-5840 9540
www.palacekamp.fi
This amazing and unique luxury lifestyle hotel right off Alexanterinkatu features modern rooms with everything under the sun. Concierge lets you order anything you want to your room: gym equipment, bright light lamps – even spa treatments. €€€

Hotel Haven
Unioninkatu 17, 00130 Helsinki
Tel: 09-681 930
www.hotelhaven.fi
Helsinki's new darling of upscale hotels is a gorgeous affair of luxury and refinement right at the harbour. Rooms look onto the Uspenski Cathedral, and offer Egyptian cotton linens and Elemis bath products. €€€€

Hotel Kämp
Pohjoisesplanadi 29, 00100 Helsinki
Tel: 09-576 111
www.hotelkamp.fi
Opened in 1887, this central neoclassical five-star boasts 189 Belle Epoque rooms and suites with marble bathrooms, polished stonework and lavish furnishings that all

BELOW: Hotel Haikko Manor, Porvoo.

evoke a very decadent glamour. €€€€

Rivoli Hotel Jardin
Kasarmikatu 40, 00130 Helsinki
Tel: 09-681 500
www.rivoli.fi
An intimate, charming hotel with 54 tastefully furnished rooms with all the amenities. City centre location. Breakfast buffet included. Sauna, open-air terrace. €€€

Scandic Grand Marina
Katajanokanlaituri 7,
00160 Helsinki
Tel: 09-16661
www.scandichotels.com
Designed in 1911 by noted Finnish architect Lars Sonck, this Katajanokka hotel offers nearly 500 exquisitely decorated and well-equipped rooms, plus extensive conference facilities, numerous restaurants and a heated garage. €€€€

Moderate

Hotel Anna
Annankatu 1, 00120 Helsinki
Tel: 09-616 621
www.hotelanna.com
This quiet, comfortable hotel has 64 comortable rooms set in a quiet shopping quarter in the city centre. €€

Hotel Katajanokka
Vyökatu 1, 00160 Helsinki
Tel: 09-686 450
www.bwkatajanokka.fi
This Best Western Premier hotel is unique to Helsinki, being the only hotel set in a former prison. The layout is preserved and rooms are done up in designer furnishings and linens. €€

Klaus K
Bulevardi 2, 00120 Helsinki
Tel: 020-770 4700
www.klauskhotel.com
Top-of-the-class Klaus K's opening several years ago put Helsinki on the map of world cities with amazing boutique hotels. This one features gorgeous rooms with every amenity and amazingly affordable prices. €€

Radisson Blu Royal
Runeberginkatu 2, 00100 Helsinki
Tel: 020-123 4700
www.radissonblu.com
Recently renovated rooms and sunny open dining and bar areas. Just next to the Kamppi shopping centre and bus station. €€

Sokos Hotel Torni
Yrjönkatu 26, 00100 Helsinki
Tel: 020-123 4604
www.sokoshotels.fi
With 13 floors, Torni is a classic and stately hotel set into Helsinki's tallest building. Rooms are either original Art Deco or functional in decor; try for those overlooking the courtyard. €€

Inexpensive

Academica
Hietaniemenkatu 14, 00100 Helsinki
Tel: 09-1311 4334
www.hostelacademica.fi
Hostel of the Year in 2008, this basic summer-only hostel has small, modern rooms with their own shower and kitchenette. Family rooms and extra beds also available. Residential but central location. €

Helsinki

Eurohostel
Linnankatu 9, 00160 Helsinki
Tel: 09-622 0470
www.eurohostel.fi
Next to the Katajanokka ferry terminal, this no-frills hostel has 135 rooms with shared facilities, as well as launderettes, sauna and café. Convenient for those travelling by ship, and just 10 minutes from the centre. €

Omena Hotelli
Eerikinkatu 24 and Lönnrotinkatu 13, 00100 Helsinki
Tel: 060-018 018
www.omena.com
Two great new hotels with no reception staff – everything, from booking to checking in – is done by automated computer. Rooms are very modern, with deep, dark woods and designer bedsheets. €

Stadium Hostel
Olympic Stadium, Pohjoinen Stadiontie 3B, 00250 Helsinki
Tel: 09-477 8480
www.stadionhostel.com
This massive hostel is 3km (2 miles) north of the city centre, with free internet for guests. Easy access by bus and tram. €

PRICE CATEGORIES

Price categories are for a double room in high season:
€ = under €75
€€ = €75–150
€€€ = €150–225
€€€€ = over €225

ACCOMMODATION

EATING OUT

ACTIVITIES

A – Z

LANGUAGE

SOUTHERN FINLAND

Ekenäs

Stadshotellet
Norra Strandgatan 1, 10600 Ekenäs
Tel: 019-241 3131
www.kaupunginhotelli.fi
The 20 rooms here are done in pastel colours and have hardwood floors (ask for one with a seaside view). Also offers a tapas restaurant. €€

Fiskars

B&B Vanha Meijeri
Suutarinmäki 7, 10470 Fiskars
Tel: 044-594 1959
www.kahvilavanhameijeri.fi
The rooms upstairs from this quaint cafe used to house cow maids. They feature Dutch-tile stoves, and are made up in gorgeous colours and rustic furnishings. €€

Hanko

B&B Garbo
Esplanaadi 84, 10900 Hanko
Tel: 040-542 1732
www.pensionat-garbo.com
In this charming little house, each themed room features a diva from the silver screen. An unusual choice, with just 10 rooms. €

Villa Maija
Appelgrenintie 7, 10900 Hanko
Tel: 019-248 2900
www.villamaija.fi
This fine 19th-century villa is one of many on this attractive street. Rooms are simple, but pleasantly decorated, with those facing the sea having small verandas. Open all year. €€

Kotka

Hotel Leikari
Haminantie 261, 48810 Kotka
Tel: 05-227 8111
www.hotellileikari.fi
The 79 rooms in this hotel, set 15km (10 miles) east of Kotka towards Hamina, are very spacious, and many have balconies to take in the Baltic sunshine. €€

Santalahti
Santalahdentie 150, 48310 Kotka
Tel: 05-260 5055
www.santalahti.fi
The only five-star holiday village in southern Finland has lovely rustic cottages for couples, families and small groups. The perfect place to bed down in the summer months. €

Sokos Hotel Seurahuone
Keskuskatu 21, 48100 Kotka

Tel: 020-123 4666
www.kotkanseurahuone.info
This very central hotel has 168 superb rooms and a fine restaurant, as well as one of the best locations along the coast. €€

Loviisa

Hotel Degerby
Brandensteininkatu 17, 07900 Loviisa
Tel: 019-50561
www.degerby.com
The Degerby's several dozen rooms are done up in fairly standard modern hotel style, with browns, blues and whites. Great attached restaurant. €€

Porvoo

Haikko Manor
Haikkoontie 114, 06400 Porvoo
Tel: 019-57601
www.haikko.fi
This old manor house complex consists of nearly 400 rooms across several buildings. Be sure to ask for the ones in the old main building, whose lovely 1860s-era antique rooms have either sea or park views. €€

Pyhtää

NEXT Hotel Patruunantalo
Stockfors, 49270 Pyhtää
Tel: 05-343 2066
www.nexthotels.fi
The 18 rooms are decorated in rich woods, rustic prints and warm summery colours. One of the nicest places to stay in this area. €€

Ruotsinpyhtää

Krouvinmäki
Puistokuja, 07970 Ruotsinpyhtää
Tel: 0400-913 669
Set in a quiet town, this 1805-built hostel only has 7 rooms, so book ahead. €

WESTERN FINLAND

Järvenpää

Hotel Rivoli Järvenpää
Asema-aukio, 04400 Järvenpää
Tel: 09-27141
www.nexthotels.fi
The rooms in this downtown hotel are simple but some of the best in town. Large pool and three restaurants. €€

Naantali

Naantali Spa Hotel and Resort

Matkailijantie 2, 21100 Naantali
Tel: 02-44550
www.naantalispa.fi
Pampered luxury in this spa hotel, with spacious rooms and innumerable spa treatments. Also enquire about the 40 new de luxe suite apartments, with sea view balconies and full kitchens. €€

Tampere

Cumulus Koskikatu
Koskikatu 5, 33100 Tampere
Tel: 03-242 4111
www.cumulus.fi
Built in 1979, overlooking the city's rapids, the rooms in this chain hotel are surprisingly modern, and several are very spacious.

Also has a very good restaurant and bar. €€

Sokos Hotel Ilves
Hatanpäänvaltatie 1, 33100 Tampere
Tel: 020-123 4631
www.sokoshotels.fi
A large, modern hotel with views over the harbour and Tammarkoski rapids. Stylish rooms with access to pool and saunas. €€

Sokos Hotel Tammer
Satakunnankatu 13, 33100 Tampere
Tel: 020-123 4632
www.sokoshotels.fi
A tribute to Finnish Art Deco, set in a green, hilly part of the city. This hotel was entirely renovated in 2009. €€

Victoria
Itsenäisyydenkatu 1, 33100 Tampere
Tel: 03-242 5111
www.hotellivictoria.fi

This simple hotel set just next to the railway station offers clean and modern (but bland) rooms and a lively bar and restaurant in the basement. €€€

TRANSPORT

ACCOMMODATION

EATING OUT

ACTIVITIES

A – Z

LANGUAGE

Turku

Sokos City Börs
Eerikinkatu 11 (across the market square), 20100 Turku
Tel: 02-337 381
www.sokoshotels.fi
A slightly cheaper but excellent alternative to Hamburger Bors, located just opposite. €€

Sokos Hamburger Börs
Kauppiaskatu 6, 20100 Turku
Tel: 02-337 381
www.sokoshotels.fi

Centrally located on Market Square, with rooms that are brighter and spunkier than most chain hotels; excellent restaurants include French Fransmanni and German-style Hamburger Hof. €€€

Park Hotel
Rauhankatu 1, 20100 Turku
Tel: 02-273 2555
www.parkhotelturku.fi
This elegantly restored Jugendstil building (1902) was once a private mansion.

Each of the gorgeously furnished rooms is completely different; some have a park view. €€

Scandic Hotel Julia
Eerikinkatu 4, 20110 Turku
Tel: 02-336 000
www.scandichotels.com/julia
Popular hotel centrally located near Market Square with attentive service, comfortable rooms and a fitness centre on the top floor. Acclaimed restaurant. €€

Seaport Hotel Turku
Toinen Poikkikatu 2, 20100 Turku
Tel: 02-283 3000
www.hotelseaport.fi
One of the more imaginatively restored hotels in Finland, once a 19th-century warehouse. Its red-brick facade is in original neo-Gothic style with beautiful wooden beams inside. Views of harbour or castle. Modern bathrooms. €€

ÅLAND ISLANDS

Eckerö

Hotel Elvira
Sandmovägen 85, 22270 Eckerö
Tel: 018-38200
www.hotelelvira.eu
With just under two dozen individually furnished rooms, this rustic guesthouse is one of the most fetching in all the archipelago. €€

Geta

HavsVidden
Geta, 22340 Geta
Tel: 018-49408
www.havsvidden.com
Set at the northern tip of Åland, some of the several dozen rooms in this modern hotel are small, others (the suites) are much larger, with full balconies and views straight out to the sea. €

Godby

Godby Hotell
Engelsgränd 2, 22410 Godby
Tel: 018-41170
www.godbyhotell.ax
Built around an 1846 homestead, this red hotel's 90 rooms come in many shapes and sizes, and all have en suite baths. Also features an outdoor pool. €€

Kökar

Brudhäll Hotell and Restaurang
Karlby, 22730 Kökar
Tel: 018-55955
www.brudhall.com
On the remote isle of Kökar, this lovely old hotel has agreeable rooms with a rustic flavour and one of the best seafood restaurants on these islands. €€

Mariehamn

Hotel Arkipelag
Strandgatan 31, 22100 Mariehamn
Tel: 018-24020
www.hotellarkipelag.com
Åland's most "modern" hotel has fairly standard rooms in the expected colours of beige and green. Sea view costs €20 extra. Be aware that after hours, everyone in town heads to "Arken", the hotel's nightclub. €€€

Park Alandia
Norra Esplanadgatan 3, 22100 Mariehamn
Tel: 018-14130
www.vikingline.fi/parkalandiahotel
Situated between the city centre and the ferry harbour, this friendly hotel is a bit dated but generally a good deal. Check the website for frequent offers. €€

Strandnäs Hotell
Godbyvägen 21, 22100 Mariehamn
Tel: 018-21511
www.strandnashotell.ax
This mid-sized hotel feels somewhat dated, but its relatively low prices and good location keep it full for much of the summer. €

WEST COAST

Kristinestad

Houneistomajoitus Krepelin
Östra Långgatan 47, 64100 Kristinestad
Tel: 040-066 1434
www.oneistomajoituskrepelin.fi
The 7 simple rooms at this guesthouse have their own kitchen, TV and free wi-fi. €€

Oulu

Holiday Club Oulun Eden
Holstinsalmentie 29, 90500 Oulu

Tel: 020-123 4905
www.holidayclubhotels.fi
This hotel offers lovely spa facilities in the Hiehtasaari beach area. Well over 100 rooms, the newest of which offer wonderful views across the open sea and adjacent parkland. €€

Pori

Cumulus Hotel Pori
Yrjönkatu 24, 28100 Pori
Tel: 02-550 900
www.cumulus.fi

The 100 or so rooms at this chain hotel are fairly run-of-the-mill, but still some of the best offerings in town. Right in the city centre two blocks south of the market square. €€

Rauma

Hotel Vanha Rauma
Vanhankirkonkatu 26, 26100 Rauma
Tel: 02-8376 2200
www.hotelvanharauma.fi
A small, pleasant hotel in a renovated early 1800s

estate, with beautifully renovated rooms done in classic stylings. €€

Seinäjoki

Hotel Alma
Ruukintie 4, 60100 Seinäjoki
Tel: 06-421 5200
www.veturitalli.info
Set just next to the railway station in an early 20th-

century Jugendstil building, these 13 atmospheric rooms feature furnishings culled from antique stores around the country. €€

Vaasa

Astor
Asemakatu 4, 65100 Vaasa
Tel: 06-326 9111
www.astorvaasa.com

Set immediately across from the railway station, this classically styled hotel is a good option to the many chain hotels in Vaasa. Rooms have light antique accents, while bathrooms feature bevelled glazed glass – some have tubs. €€
Sokos Vaakuna
Korsholmanpuistikko 6–8, 65100 Vaasa

Tel: 040-066 8521
www.sokoshotels.com
The most central hotel in town, a colourful, modern affair with a very popular disco on the top floor. Rooms are spacious, and you may want to ask for one overlooking the market square because they have excellent night-time views. €€

LAKELAND

Imatra

Rantasipi Imatran Valtionhotelli
Torkkelinkatu 2, 55100 Imatra
Tel: 05-625 2000
www.rantasipi.fi
This imposing Art Nouveau castle, next to the Imatrankoski hydroelectric power station (with daily waterfall shows in summer) is one of the most notable hotel buildings in Finland. €€

Jyväskylä

Hotel Milton
Hannikaisenkatu 27–29, 40100 Jyväskylä
Tel: 014-337 7900
www.hotellimilton.com
This family-owned hotel is a better bet than the city's bland chain hotels, with rooms in bright and cheery colours. Free wi-fi for all guests. €€
Hotel Yöpuu
Yliopistonkatu 23, 40100 Jyväskylä
Tel: 014-333 900
Although Jyväskylä has many large hotels, this 26-room boutique hotel is one of the best choices, with an old-world ambience in each individualised room and a fine restaurant. €€

Kuopio

Scandic Hotel Kuopio
Satamakatu 1, 70100 Kuopio
Tel: 017-195 111
www.scandichotels.com
Though not much to look at from the outside, this large hotel on the waterfront is one of the finest in town. There is an indoor pool,

3 saunas and an excellent restaurant with lake views. €€
Sokos Hotel Puijonsarvi
Minna Canthinkatu 16, 70100 Kuopio
Tel: 017-192 2000
http://sokoshotels.fi
With 300 rooms that aren't half bad, this good-value hotel comes out ahead of other chains. Immediately east of the market square towards the water. €€
Hotelli-Kylpylä Rauhalahti
Katiskaniementie 8, 70700 Kuopio
Tel: 017-473 473
www.rauhalahti.fi
Set a few miles outside of town, this fine spa hotel includes a hostel wing with clean apartments for budget travellers. A smoke sauna bath is open for visitors on Tuesdays and Fridays – reputedly the largest of its kind in the country. A traditional dinner is also available on those evenings. €–€€

Lappeenranta

Scandic Hotel Patria
Kauppakatu 21, 53100 Lappeenranta
Tel: 05-677 511
www.scandic.com
This modern hotel is situated close to the harbour and the fortress area. There are 130 rooms, and several restaurants and saunas. €€

Parikkala

Laatokan Portti
Kuutostie 722, 59100 Parikkala
Tel: 05-449 282
www.laatokanportti.com

Set on Lake Simpele, you can actually look out to the Russian border from the small dock. Main building rooms are fairly standard; ask for those in the *aitta* ("granary") for some more atmosphere. €

Punkaharju

Punkaharjun Valtionhotelli
58450 Punkaharju
Tel: 020-752 9800
www.fontana.fi/punkaharju
Not far from Savonlinna, this is an opportunity to stay in Finland's oldest hotel. It's a wooden Russian-style villa with lots of atmosphere and 24 rooms. Cheaper cabin rooms also available. €€

Savonlinna

Perhehotelli Hospitz
Linnankatu 20, 57130 Savonlinna
Tel: 015-515 661
www.hospitz.com
Built in 1933 by architect Wivi Lönn, this cosy spot near Olavinlinna Castle is a well-run family hotel with a lovely garden on the waterfront. €€
Savonlinnan Seurahuone
Kauppatori 4–6, 57130 Savonlinna
Tel: 015-5731
www.savonlinnanseurahuone.fi
This 1950s-era hotel was completely renovated in 2007, with the bright new rooms being preferable over the older, slightly more forgotten rooms. €€€
Spa Hotel Casino
Kylpylaitoksentie, 57130 Savonlinna
Tel: 015-739 5430
www.spahotelcasino.fi

Helsinki

This large hotel complex has very clean rooms, a significant spa section and some inexpensive hostel beds available in summer. The hotel is located on an island opposite the central railway halt, access via a wooden bridge. €€

Valamo

Valamon Monastery
Valamontie 42, 79850 Uusi-Valamo
Tel: 017-570 111
www.valamo.fi
Possibly the most atmospheric place to stay in Finland. The austere and functional rooms at this monastery are perfect for getting some real peace and quiet. Not for partying types. €

PRICE CATEGORIES

Price categories are for a double room in high season:
€ = under €75
€€ = €75–150
€€€ = €150–225
€€€€ = over €225

KARELIA AND KUUSAMO

Joensuu

GreenStar
Torikatu 16, 80100 Joensuu
Tel: 010-423 9390
www.greenstar.fi
This great new environmentally-friendly concept hotel is the best place to stay in Joensuu. No reception; check in via computer. €

Sokos Hotel Kimmel
Itäranta 1, 80100 Joensuu
Tel: 020-123 4663
www.sokoshotels.fi
Set opposite the railway station in the lovely Sirkkala Park on the shore of Pielisjoki River, the renovated rooms here are bright and modern. A lively spot in the evenings. €€

Kaajani

Hotelli Kajaani
1 Onnelantie, 87100 Kaajani
Tel: 030-608 6100
www.hotellikajaani.fi
The riverbank rooms here are fairly basic, but the location gives great access to exploring Kajaani's environs. Special summer rates if you stay for more than one night. €€

Scandic Kajanus
Koskikatu 3, 87200 Kaajani
Tel: 08-61641
www.scandic-hotels.com
Set in leafy grounds right by Kajaaninjoki River, this excellently priced chain hotel is a great way to stay in Kajaani without having to stay in the downtown. €

Kuhmo

Hotel Kalevala
Väinömöinen 9, 88900 Kuhmo
Tel: 08-655 4100
www.hotellikalevala.fi
A few kilometres from the city centre, this lovely hotel with characterful rooms offers excellent views over the banks of Lake Lammasjärvi near the Russian border. One of the best places to relax – or base yourself for exploring – in this part of the country. €€

Kuusamo

Sokos Hotel Kuusamo
Kirkkotie 23, 93600 Kuusamo
Tel: 020-123 4693
www.sokoshotels.fi

Located a five-minute walk from downtown Kuusamo and half an hour from the ski slopes at Ruka. There is an indoor (non-heated) pool. €€

LAPLAND

Inari

Villa Lanca
Kittilän ratsutie 2, 99870 Inari
Tel: 040-748 0984
www.villalanca.com
This small guesthouse opposite the tourist office has some of the most charming owners you'll ever meet. Rooms are decorated in original furnishings and colours. €

Ivalo

Hotelli Ivalo
Ivalontie 34, 99800 Ivalo
Tel: 016-688 111
www.hotelivalo.fi
Though there isn't much reason to stay in Ivalo, if you're here this is really the only place to stay. Rooms are somewhat cramped, but it's set right next to a river. €€

Karigasniemi

Kalastajan Majatalo
99950 Karigasniemi
Tel: 016-676 171
www.hansabar.fi
Simple rooms and cabins set on a tree-lined lawn in one of Finland's northernmost villages, set

on the Norwegian-Finnish border. It doesn't get more remote than this. €

Lemmenjoki

Ahkun Tupa
Lemmenjoentie 1030, 99885 Lemmenjoki
Tel: 016-673 435
www.ahkuntupa.fi
This large restaurant also operates a number of modern cabin structures – each with modern bathrooms and sauna – around the banks of the Lemmenjoki River. €

Heikki Paltto
99885 Lemmenjoki
Tel: 016-673 413
www.lemmenjoki.com
An effervescent Sami couple rents out several rural cabins in the Lemmenjoki Park and further afield. A great way to get to know the rustic traditional life of northern Finland. €

Rovaniemi

Clarion Santa Claus
Korkalonkatu 49, 96100 Rovaniemi
Tel: 016-321 321
www.hotelsantaclaus.fi

If you can deal with staying in a place with a name such as this one, you'll be fine here. Tidy modern rooms right in the city centre, with a popular local restaurant on the ground floor. Excellent service. €€

Guesthouse Borealis
Asemieskatu 1, 96100 Rovaniemi
Tel: 016-342 0130
www.guesthouseborealis.com
Family-run guesthouse very popular with independent Inter-rail travellers. A few minutes' walk from the city centre in a quiet location that's well placed for the train station. €

Kakslauttanen Igloos
99830 Saariselkä
Tel: 016-667 100
www.kakslauttanen.fi
There are two types of igloo here: snow and glass. The first are traditional and basic; the latter let you sleep under the stars and enjoy views of the Northern Lights in comfort. €€

Rantasipi Pohjanhovi
Pohjanpuistikko 2, 96200 Rovaniemi
Tel: 016-33711
www.rantasipi.fi
This legendary and luxurious hotel underwent a thorough renovation in 2009. Located

on the quiet Kemijoki riverfront, it features a swimming pool, nightclub, casino, dance and concert events and a range of travel services and outdoor activities. €€

Sodänkylä

Hotel Bear Inn
Lapintie 7, 99600 Sodankylä
Tel: 0201-620 610
www.hotel-bearinn.com
A recent renovation has brought the 42 bright, spacious rooms at this roadside hotel – located off the main E4 road – up to snuff. €€

TRANSPORT
ACCOMMODATION
EATING OUT
ACTIVITIES
A – Z
LANGUAGE

E ATING OUT

RECOMMENDED RESTAURANTS, CAFÉS AND BARS

What to Eat

Finnish cuisine has improved dramatically over the past decade, as the back-to-basics cuisine trends sweeping the Nordic countries infuse Finland's menus. Organic and farm-to-plate practices are becoming quite widespread, and some produce once unheard of above 60° north latitude – such as Finnish-grown cucumbers and red tomatoes – can now be seen in the markets.

You'll also find that there are some excellent Finnish cooks, especially in the capital, who are preparing and serving excellent-tasting and healthy vegetable, meat and fish meals. Wild game dishes are a real treat and are usually served with exquisite mushroom and berry sauces. In summer, you are recommended to try Finnish crayfish, or *ravut (see page 128)*. If you choose to eat only in cafeteria-style restaurants, however, you may get bored with the monotony of the meat-and-potato offerings.

Many Finns eat a large hot lunch and then a smaller cold meal in the evening, although this is not to say that you can't have wonderful evening meals in Helsinki and other cities. Interest in international and fusion cuisine has crept in slowly over the years, and you'll now find French, Italian and Asian-style restaurants in almost all major towns. The best Russian cuisine outside of Russia is still found in a dozen-odd restaurants spread about Helsinki.

While on the whole Finns eat dinner rather early – around 7pm – it is not unusual to find restaurants serving food until as late as 10 or sometimes 11pm, especially in larger cities.

Drinking Notes

The sale of alcohol is strictly controlled in Finland; spirits and wine can be bought only from Alko (the state alcohol monopoly; Stockmann's department store in Helsinki has an Alko unit on the ground floor). Medium- and lower-alcohol beer can be bought in supermarkets. Most restaurants serve alcohol as long as they serve food. A restaurant marked *B-oikeudet* is licensed only to serve beer and wine.

The Finnish *tuoppi* is slightly smaller than the British pint, usually 0.4 litres. *Pieni ("small") tuoppi* is about two-thirds of that quantity. If you don't specify, you will be served a large, middle-strength beer (number III = 4.5 percent alcohol), which is known as *keski-olut*. You must specify if you would like a stronger beer (number IV = over 5 percent) or a weaker one that has under 3 percent

BELOW: Kappeli restaurant, Helsinki.

alcohol level and is known as *ykkösolut* (number I). If you prefer sweeter drinks try the Finnish cider, *siideri*, which comes in many flavours.

Wine in Finland is imported and costly in restaurants, but there is more choice in Alko these days. The range of prices begins with Eastern European wines (about €6 a bottle) and goes up precipitously.

Most bars and taverns are open until at least midnight in Helsinki; some stay open until 3 or 4am.

Choosing a Restaurant

It is not impossible to find a really cheap meal in Finland, and you can often find places where you will get good value for money – in other words, where portions are generous and quality is high. Fixed-price lunches are often very good deals and are usually advertised on signboards outside restaurants – you will often pay under €10 for the buffet. Nearly all places have menus in English.

For on-the-run, really cheap eats, go to a *nakki* (sausage) kiosk. Hot dogs, sausages and burgers are the main fare, and you can usually get French fries and drinks as well. Other slightly more expensive quick meals can be had at any one of the ubiquitous hamburger chains such as McDonald's, Hesburger or Carrols. Pizza is also very popular in Finland; Kotipizza is the biggest (and best) chain.

Many of the hotels in the three main cities of Helsinki, Turku and Tampere, and elsewhere, have rather good restaurants, ranging from gourmet to wine bars and cafés, including restaurants that specialise in particular ethnic cuisines.

RESTAURANT LISTINGS

HELSINKI

ABOVE: the Michelin-starred Chez Dominique.

Expensive

Chez Dominique
Rikhardinkatu 4
Tel: 09-612 7393
The first word in fine
Finnish dining, this superb
two-Michelin-starred
gastronomic goldmine is
rated among the top 20
restaurants in the world.
Chef Hans Välimäki has
taken Finnish cuisine and
virtually reinvented it from
scratch. If you've got the
budget, this is an absolute
must while in Helsinki.
€€€

Kasakka
Meritullinkatu 13
One of Helsinki's best
Russian restaurants –
make that best restaurants,
period – this old-world spot
serves traditional Russian
dishes. Service is
impeccable, and the decor
couldn't be more
authentically tsarist if it
tried. €€€

Moderate

Elite
Eteläinen Hesperiankatu 22
Tel: 09-434 2200
A restaurant classic from
the 1930s, traditionally
favoured by Finland's
cultural and artistic circles.
The international menu also
includes some Finnish
classics like fried Baltic

herrings with mashed
potatoes and sirloin steak
with creamed onion à la
Tauno Palo, who was one of
the most popular actors in
Finland from the 1930s to
the 1960s. There is also a
green outdoor terrace. €€

Gastone
Korkeavuorenkatu 45
Tel: 09-666 116
www.gastone.fi
Opened in 2003, this has
quickly become Helsinki's
best Italian restaurant.
Serves several unique
dishes as well as traditional
Italian *piatti*. Try the grilled
tiger prawn or the
parmesan-gratinated
chicken breast served with
pomegranate sauce. €€

Havis
Eteläranta 16
Tel: 09-6869 5660
Set down by the harbour,
this classic fine seafood
restaurant offers an
excellent collection of
seasonal fish and seafood
varieties, and seldom
disappoints. €€

Juuri
Korkeavuorenkatu 27
Tel: 09-635 732
This unique, central
restaurant serves "Sapas"
or Finnish tapas – some of
the most unusual dishes
you'll ever try in Finland. An
absolute must, if it's on the
menu, is the smoked
reindeer heart. €€

Kappeli
Eteläesplanadi 1
Tel: 010-766 3880
Classic Finnish dishes, from
reindeer to salmon, in a
building on Esplanadi dating
back to 1867. €€

Kolme Seppää
Mannerheimintie 14
Tel: 020-761 9888
This new restaurant may
have secured the best
location in the city –
overlooking the crossroads
of Salomonkatu and the
railway station. €€

König
Mikonkatu 4
Tel: 09-8568 5740
A solid lunch option right off
Esplanadi that is particularly
popular with local
businessmen and
politicians. Great steaks. €€

Kuurna
Meritullinkatu 6
Tel: 09-670 849
www.kuurna.fi
This restaurant offers
traditional home-style
meals. Specials include
poached pike perch and
beef roast, served with
polenta and *salsa verde*. €€

Lehtovaara
Mechelininkatu 39
Tel: 09-440 833
www.lehtovaararavintola.fi
Founded in 1916, this is
one of Helsinki's longest-
standing restaurants and an
excellent place to catch a
bit of Old Finland. The
Finnish meals are best
enjoyed on the glass
terrace. The wine list has
over 100 vintages. €€

Pääposti
Mannerheimintie 1
Tel: 020-729 6712
Located next to the railway
station. this weekday lunch-
only restaurant is a popular
stop for businessmen. Very
good menu of Continental
and Finnish dishes. €€

Rakuya
Eteläranta 14
Tel: 09-675 449
www.rakuya.fi

Hands down Helsinki's best
Japanese restaurant,
serving traditional sushi and
sashimi plates as well as a
good number of modern
concoctions. Set
immediately opposite the
harbour and next to the old
market hall. €€

Saaga
Bulevardi 34
Tel: 09-7425 5544
An authentic Lapland
experience as offered here
is a bonus when sampling
anything made of reindeer,
tasty fish, salted fungi and
exotic berries. Or do you
have the stomach for bear?
Try the Lappish plate to
savour a full range of
northern specialities. €€

Salve
Hietalahdenranta 11
Tel: 09-603 455
This unassuming
restaurant-pub is one of the
longest-standing in the city.
Serves very good traditional
Finnish meals in a distinct
maritime atmosphere,
though drinking is often a
more popular reason to
come here. Looks onto
Helsinki's world-famous
shipyards. €

Seahorse
Kapteenikatu 11
Tel: 09-628 169
This restaurant designed by
Alvar Aalto has entertained
such celebs as Dizzy
Gillespie and Pablo Neruda.
Surprisingly, the menu is
good value, even for the
not-so-famous. €€

Inexpensive

Bali-Hai
Iso Roobertinkatu 35
Tel: 09-179 904

PRICE CATEGORIES

Price categories are per
person for a starter and
main course, without drinks:
€ = under €15
€€ = €15–37
€€€ = over €37

Possibly Helsinki's hippest place to tuck into great salads, pastas and burgers. The original interior manages to feel strikingly similar to an early 1900s diner in middle America. Prices are low, but the celebrity-spotting factor is high. Their rödburger is the best burger in town. €
Vegemesta
Vaasankatu 6

Tel: 044-938 5212
www.vegemesta.com
This trendy vegetarian spot in the Kallio district does largely takeaway, but it's well worth it. Order their popular veggie burger, the Skipper, then take it to a nearby park to eat. €
Virgin Oil Company
Mannerheimintie 5
Tel: 010-766 4000
www.virginoil.fi

Located just around the corner from the railway station in the old student house, this popular American-style restaurant serves a vast selection of steaks and pasta dishes. It also has a good and varied wine list. There is a concert venue just upstairs, so it can get very busy on weekend evenings. €€

Vltava
Elielinaukio 2
Tel: 010-766 3650
www.vltava.fi
Ideally situated just next to the railway station, this Czech restaurant serves thick wursts and traditional sausages. They're also renowned for their beer selection, culled straight from the best areas of the Czech Republic. €

SOUTHERN FINLAND

Ekenäs

Knipan
Strandallén
Tel: 019-2411 1169
This atmospheric clapboard wooden summer restaurant is delicately placed at the end of a pier just outside of Ekenäs centre. €€

BELOW: delicious seafood.

Hamina

Tullimakasiini
Tervasaari Harbour
Tel: 05-344 7470
Set into the town's old customs house – Hamina was once a very active port – the Finnish meals here are some of the tastiest in Hamina. Given the fact there are few other restaurants anyway, you don't really have much choice. €

Hanko

På Kroken
Hangonkylä Harbour
Tel: 040-358 1815
Opened by a local

fisherman, this cosy family spot has comfy wooden chairs, views to a picturesque harbour and a delicious archipelago buffet spread. €

Kotka

Wanha Fiskari
Ruotsinsalmenkatu 1
Tel: 05-218 6585
www.wanhafiskari.fi
Situated immediately alongside Kotka's new Maretarium, there is no better place in town to come and enjoy the local catch of the day than in the two atmospheric halls at this cosy and popular restaurant. €

Luoma

Ravintola Hvitträsk
Hvitträskintie 166, 02440 Luoma
Tel: 09-297 6033
www.ravintolahvittrask.fi
Set in the Hvitträsk Museum's courtyard, this café and restaurant serves an inspired collection of Scandinavian dishes. Open during museum hours. €

Vantaa

La Famiglia
Flamingo
Tel: 09-8568 5850
In the Flamingo centre, the real draw here is the excellent pasta mains –the lasagne is excellent. €€

WESTERN FINLAND

Tampere

Astor
Aleksis Kivenkatu 26
Tel: 03-260 5700
www.ravintola-astor.fi
A popular white-tablecloth spot for food and drink with live piano music every night and an even livelier crowd. European dishes, reindeer meat and a good variety of fish available. €€
Eetvartti
Sumeliuksenkatu 16
Tel: 03-3155 5300
www.eetvartti.fi
This is the restaurant of the Pirkanmaa Hotel and Restaurant School, which means you can dine very well on high-quality fare

cooked by the students at extremely reasonable prices. €€
Näsinneula
Näsinneula, Särkänniemi
Tel: 03-248 8234
This revolving restaurant in the Observation Tower gets you dining 168 metres (635ft) above the scenic landscape of Tampere. Fine Finnish cuisine is a speciality. A very memorable experience. €€€
Plevna
Itäinen katu 8
Tel: 03-260 1200
Lively brewery and pub that serves good food too. Their speciality is steaks and grilled sausages. A variety of microbrewed beers are also

available – they serve some 50 types of beer in total. €
Salud
Tuomiokirkonkatu 19
Tel: 03-233 4400
www.salud.fi
Salud is a Spanish restaurant founded and run by a Finn who fell in love with Spain 20 years ago. This long-standing local spot is still one of Tampere's most popular place to wine and dine. €

Turku

Summer in Turku is incomplete without spending a lazy time in one of the dozen boat restaurants on Aurajoki

River. Most people stop for beer and a bite to eat.
Enkeliravintola
Kauppiaskatu 16
Tel: 02-231 8088
www.enkeliravintola.fi
Decorated with angels in all shapes and sizes, this fine restaurant serves good traditional Finnish and Scandinavian food in a tranquil atmosphere. €€
Samppalinna
Itäinen Rantakatu 10
Tel: 02-231 1165
Continental cuisine including roast mutton and a host of Finnish specialities such as salmon soup, all served in a splendid Victorian building. Open in summertime only. €€

ÅLAND ISLANDS

Eckerö

Jannes Bodega
Käringsund Harbour
Tel: 018-38530
This quiet harbour café is a good place to linger over a coffee as you watch the large passenger ships dock, unload and make their way off into the sunset. €

Föglö

Gästhem Enigheten
Degerby
Tel: 018-50310
www.enigheten.ax
A cosy farmhouse inn which offers a warm welcome and is a great place to come for classic home-cooked meals. Be sure to ask for the traditional Åland pancake, as well as the locally caught perch if they are serving it. €€

Mariehamn

Café Bönan
Sjökvarteret
Tel: 018-21735
A lunch-only restaurant pleasantly located in a grand old red wooden storage house. All the food served here is organic and vegetarian. Make sure you try some of their scrumptious homemade cakes. €

Indigo
Nygatan 1
Tel: 018-16550
This restaurant and lounge is set into a lovely old stone house situated by Lilla Torget. The main floor serves modern à la carte dishes, while more casual meals are served off a lower-priced bistro menu. In the summer, everyone eats on the outdoor terrace. €– €€

ABOVE: dining alfresco in summer.

Restaurang Nautical
Hamngatan 2
Tel: 018-19931
Located in the same building as the Åland Maritime Museum at the harbour, this is a popular business and family place to dine, with great local food. The svårtbröd, Åland's famed local black bread, is recommended. Also has a very well-stocked wine cellar. €€

Von Knorring
Österhamn
Excellent choice for an evening meal – fish, steak, burgers and kebabs – in the summertime. The restaurant is based in the bowels of a great old boat; the terrace above is for cocktails and sunset drinks. €€

WEST COAST

Kristinestad

Pavis
Korkeasaari
Tel: 050-554 1570
www.pavis.fi
This summer restaurant is the best place in town to come to sample Bothnian cooking. Things also tend to get quite lively once they start with their regular summer jazz events. €€

Pori

Raatihuoneen Kellari
Hallituskatu 9
Tel: 02-633 4804
www.raatihuoneenkellari.fi
Set into a lovely building constructed by national architect Carl Engel in 1841, this great restaurant is full of atmosphere. Three prix-fixe menus from €35 to €48 are a great way to sample the very best of Finnish cuisine without breaking the bank. €€€

Vaasa

Bistrot Ernst Café
Hietasaarenkatu 7
Tel: 06-317 8556
www.ernst.fi
Set just below the local Swedish-language Wasa Theatre, this casual but well-put-together spot has salads, sandwiches and a few more substantial steak dishes too. Also great late in the evening for a post-dinner drink. €

Faros
Kalaranta
Tel: 06-312 6411
www.faros.fi
This boat in Vaasa's harbour is easily the most memorable summer spot to dine in town. You can eat on board under the deck, then retire for a sunset drink upstairs on the terrace afterwards. €€

Gustav Wasa
Raastuvankatu 24
Tel: 050-466 3208
www.gustavwasa.com
This award-winning basement restaurant serves consistently excellent meat and fish dishes. The rustic dining hall served as a coal-storing cellar until 1967. €€

Kaffehuset August
Hovioikeudenpuistikko 13
Tel: 06-320 0555
www.kaffehusetaugust.fi
Looking onto the market square, this quaint Finlandsvenska café serves crêpes, salads and light fish dishes. €

PRICE CATEGORIES

Price categories are per person for a starter and main course, without drinks:
€ = under €15
€€ = €15–37
€€€ = over €37

BELOW: Faros, a restaurant moored in Vaasa's harbour.

TRANSPORT
ACCOMMODATION
EATING OUT
ACTIVITIES
A – Z
LANGUAGE

LAKELAND

Kuopio

The small *muikku* (whitefish) is a must in Kuopio, although more famous is the *kalakukko* (loaf of rye bread crust filled with fish and pork) that can be found at the market.
Musta Lammas
Satamakatu 4
Tel: 017-581 0458
www.mustalammas.net
A pleasant restaurant, considered by some to be Kuopio's finest. The vaulted dining hall is a great place to come on a summer evening for local fish after a tour of the Lake District. €€
Vapaasatama Sampo
Kauppakatu 13
Tel: 017-261 4677

Kuopio's most famous restaurant, formerly a "sailors' pub", serves excellent fish (*muikku* is the most popular dish) in what still seems to be a very informal pub. €€€
Wanha Satama
Matkustajasatama
Tel: 017-197 304
www.wanhasatama.net
This rustic and lively pub-restaurant by the passenger harbour serves very tasty *muikku* fish with garlic and mashed potatoes. Kuopio's largest and sunniest terrace is here. €€

Savonlinna

Prices tend to rise quite steeply during the opera festival *(see page 100)*.

ABOVE: sophisticated new Finnish cuisine.

Majakka
Satamakatu 11
Tel: 015-206 2825
www.ravintolamajakka.fi
This popular restaurant near the market serves tasty, fresh fish and meat. Also offers an extensive and eclectic wine list. €€

Sillansuu
Verkkosaarenkatu 1
Tel: 015-531 451
This pub near the market bridge is considered to be one of the best in Finland, with good food and an excellent selection of spirits. €€

KARELIA AND KUUSAMO

Joensuu

Sokos Hotel Kimmel
Itäranta 1
Tel: 020-123 4663
www.sokoshotels.com
The largest hotel in Joensuu, set just opposite the railway station, has a great collection of restaurants inside. It is also one of the liveliest spots to

drink and dine in the evenings. €€

Kaajani

Sirius
Brahenkatu 5
Tel: 08-612 2087
www.ravintolasirius.fi
Set into a building on the Kaajani River, the clean lines of this decidedly

Finnish restaurant was designed by Eino Pitkänen and has seen presidents of Finland and the former Soviet Union dine here. €€

Nurmes

Bomba House
Suojärvenkatu 1
Tel: 013-687 200
www.bomba.fi

A popular spot with tourists as the restaurant is well known for its buffet dinners serving traditional Karelian dishes – available from 11am to 7pm daily. There is also international fare on the à la carte menu here, and in the summer months lively regional music and other entertainment as well. €€

LAPLAND

Inari

Hotelli Inari
Inarintie 40
Tel: 016-671 026
www.hotelliinari.fi
One of the few places to eat in Inari, serving any number of Lappish delicacies, including broiled salmon, fried reindeer, and baked white fish, as well as fresh cloudberries. Views onto Lake Inarijärvi. €€
Sarrit
SIIDA, Inarintie 46
Tel: 0400-898 212/016-661 662
With a name meaning "blueberry" in Finnish, this restaurant-cafeteria is

very good, serving local fish and reindeer dishes as well as seasonal game. Located inside the Sami museum and Northern Lapland Nature Centre (SIIDA), the tastes are authentic; try the delectable hollandaise Lake Inari whitefish and trout platter. €€

Lemmenjoki

Ahkun Tupa
Tel: 016-673 435
www.ahkuntupa.fi
Situated inside a small and simple holiday village, the café-restaurant here deals almost exclusively in

fish dishes. As it sits right on a local river and near a lake, it's obvious where the fresh dishes come from. €

Rovaniemi

Cómico
Koskikatu 25
Tel: 016-344 433
www.comico.fi
Serving a large menu of steaks, Tex-Mex dishes (tacos, burritos, quesadillas and fajitas), burgers, meatballs, chicken and salads, this may very well be the best place to eat in town, especially if you want a change from fish. €€

Hydos
Kansankatu 10
Tel: 016-311 181
www.hydos.com
Though it might seem strange to come all the way to Rovaniemi to taste Turkish food, this is one of the better places to eat in town. They do an excellent, good-value lunch for an amazing €7. €

PRICE CATEGORIES

Price categories are per person for a starter and main course, without drinks:
€ = under €15
€€ = €15–37
€€€ = over €37

ACTIVITIES

THE ARTS, FESTIVALS, NIGHTLIFE, CHILDREN, SHOPPING AND SPORTS

THE ARTS

Museums

Finland is a country of small museums. The grandest in scale is the Ateneum in Helsinki, which could fit neatly into London's National Gallery at least three times over. Art, both contemporary and classic, dominates the museum scene, with the greatest variety of venues in Helsinki.

Admission prices are generally steep, but Helsinki sells the Helsinki Card (see box, page 303), which includes free entrance to many museums on presentation. Turku recently introduced a similar card.

Museum opening hours are almost always reduced in winter. Nearly all museums close on Mondays. Be prepared that many museums also close for public holidays.

Classical Music and Opera

Most larger cities have a steady itinerary of concerts throughout the year, but music festivals abound in Finland in summer, and many of these are held in stunning settings (see page 100). The most famous of these are held in July: the Savonlinna Opera Festival at Olavinlinna Castle in eastern Finland, the Kuhmo Chamber Music Festival, also in eastern Finland, and the Kaustinen Folk Festival in western Finland. The festivals feature Finnish and international performers.

Lahti, in Lakeland (see page 268), is home to Sibelius Hall, one of the best places in the world to hear classical music.

Theatre

Helsinki

The Finnish National Theatre and Svenska Teatern in Helsinki both enjoy long traditions of performance in, respectively, Finnish and Swedish. Unfortunately, there is no foreign-language theatre to speak of – except perhaps during the odd summer arts festival – but you may be interested in touring the theatre buildings themselves, or even going to a play you know well enough to overcome the language barrier.

The listings guides in Helsinki will list theatre events (see page 326). Equivalent guides in Turku and Tampere also carry listings.

Turku

Plays performed are of a high standard but rarely in languages other than Finnish or Swedish. In winter, there is the Turku City Theatre on the bank of the Aura River and the Swedish Theatre on the corner of Market Square – the oldest theatre in Finland still in use.

Tampere

Tampere rivals Helsinki for year-round theatrical events, but, again, the main difficulty is language. One exception is the Pyynikki's Outdoor Summer Theatre (see page 221), where you can see plays from early June to mid-August, with synopses in English. This is particularly worthwhile if you want to enjoy the setting at the edge of the Lake Pyhäjärvi. Booking is necessary, tel: 03-216 0300; www. pyynikinkesateatteri.com

The Tampere Theatre Festival in August includes many international companies who produce plays in their own languages.

Further information is available from **Tampere International Theatre Festival**, Tullikamarinaukio 2, 33100 Tampere, tel: 03-214 0992; www.teatterikesa.fi

BELOW: dinosaur on display at the Natural History Museum, Helsinki.

ABOVE: Finnish style is apparent everywhere.

Cinema

Finns do not dub foreign films, meaning that you can enjoy as good a selection of movies here as in any other European city of moderate size. The **Suomen Elokuva-arkisto** at the Orion Film Archive (Eerikinkatu 15–17, tel: 09-6154 0201; www.kava.fi) has endless stocks of older films, both Finnish and foreign. Helsinki has two main cinema megaplexes, **Kinopalatsi** in Kaisaniemenkatu 2 and **Tennispalatsi** at Salomonkatu 15. Smaller cinemas are dotted around the town, often showing a wider range of titles.

Film showings are generally held throughout the day. The kiosk outside the east entrance to Helsinki railway station has comprehensive listings, as do the newspapers; listings are also available at the tourist board. Box offices usually open 30–45 minutes before show time, but at some cinemas tickets may be purchased even earlier. Note that many film showings do sell out, so buying ahead of time is advised.

Tampere has a cinema centre, **Finnkino Plevna**, in the Finlayson area (Itäinenkatu 4). In Turku most cinemas are found in the Hansa Shopping Centre (see page 209).

FESTIVALS

Though Finland is well known for its quirky and off-the-wall yearly festivals (eg wife-carrying and air guitar), the summer months also see hundreds of arts, music and cultural festivals as well. Many of these make great venues for hearing classical music,

jazz or hard rock, depending on where your interest lies. The tango festival in Seinäjoki (www.tangomarkkinat.fi), east of Vaasa, has become one of the biggest festivals in Finland. From a weekend bluegrass festival in diminutive Loviisa (see page 199) to a grandiose, month-long opera festival held in Savonlinna's medieval castle, there is plenty to occupy your time. For more on festivals in Finland, see page 100.

Helsinki Events

Come late summer the capital hosts the Helsinki *Juhlaviikot* (festival weeks), featuring broad-ranging programmes with artists from Finland and abroad, set at different venues all over the city. Information from:
Helsinki Festival Office
Lasipalatsi, Mannerheimintie 22–24, FI-00100 Helsinki
Tel: 09-6126 5100
www.helsinginjuhlaviikot.fi

Also, try the weekday evening series of concerts at the unique Temppeliaukio (Church in the Rock) in Töölö, Helsinki (see page 172).

During the rest of the year, main events are at Finlandia Concert Hall, many by the Radio Symphony Orchestra and the Helsinki Philharmonic Orchestra. The National Opera House (and ballet) in Helsinki opened in 1993 (see page 172).

Turku Events

Turku is another lively musical city, with concerts given by the Turku City Orchestra, a series of concerts in the Sibelius Museum, and others in the cathedral and the castle. The Turku Musical Festival is one of the oldest in Finland and holds a variety of genres of classical music – from medieval music to debut performances of

modern compositions. Held in mid-August, it attracts visiting composers and international musicians.

Further information is available from the Turku Music Festival, Aninkaistenkatu 9, 20100 Turku, tel: 02-262 0814; www.turkumusicfestival.fi.

Tampere Events

Tampere has always had its share of Finnish music, including both classical and modern rock and jazz. Since 1975 the city has held an international choir festival each year and the Tampere Biennale, started in 1986, is a festival of new Finnish music, arranged in cooperation with the Association of Finnish Composers. For information contact:
Tampere
Tullikamarinaukio 2, 33100 Tampere, tel: 05-5656 6172; www.tampere.fi

Since the grand opening of Tampere Hall, the largest concert venue in the Nordic countries, interest in all types of musical forms has soared. The auditorium is one of the great concert halls of the world and the acoustics are acknowledged to be far better than those of Helsinki's Finlandia Hall. The small auditorium is used for chamber music, and the hall is also a conference venue. Tampere holds numerous concerts in its cathedral, churches and halls. More information at:
Tampere Hall
Yliopistonkatu 55, 33100 Tampere
Tel: 03-243 4111
www.tampere-talo.fi

NIGHTLIFE

Pubs, Bars and Clubs

Nightlife can be a difficult thing to get the hang of in Finland. In Helsinki, you will see hordes of revellers bar-crawling their way across town into the early hours; most are old acquaintances and work colleagues going out drinking together. There are several clubs which attract the best music acts, for example the university-owned Tavastia and the long-standing Kaarle XII. Often these days a great jazz or rock act will come to Helsinki as part of a larger European tour, and the music scene is also greatly added to by the growing number of solid Finnish indie, pop, rock and jazz groups.

The official drinking age is 18 and over but some clubs may have a minimum age limit of 21 or 24. Entrance fees can be anything from free to outrageous. Nightclubs can be expensive and good dance floors are hard to find. More easily found is the casual camaraderie of the few places that attract a sprinkling of foreigners, such as the pubs O'Malley's and Vanha.

A few of the better bars and night spots in Finland's three main cities are listed as follows:

Helsinki

Café Bar 9
Uudenmaakatu 9
Tel: 09-621 4059
Unlike many other bars, the interior of Bar 9 has remained almost the same since 1996. However, it is still trendy and popular with the artistic crowd. Very reasonably priced and tasty food such as large salads and good pasta.

Corona Bar
Eerinkatu 11
Tel: 09-642 002
This popular spot attracts a young, hip crowd who come to talk, drink beer and play pool. Downstairs is Dubrovnik Lounge and Lobby and next door to Corona is **Kafe Moskova**, a small, "Brezhnevian-style" bar which doesn't seem to have changed in the last 30 years – even the jukebox still plays speeches of former Soviet leaders. Both are owned by the Kaurismäki brothers, directors of such fine films as *Drifting Clouds* (see page 98).

Kaivohuone
Iso Puistotie 1
Tel: 020-785 0815
A popular club in the Kaivopuisto park that attracts the beautiful and famous

Jazz and Rock

The most famous of Finland's jazz festivals is *PoriJazz*, which has been going on for over 40 years. Big open-air concerts are held in the concert park by the Kokemäki River and evening venues vary between intimate clubs and large concert halls. For more information contact the **Pori Jazz Office**, Pohjoisranta 11 D, 28100 Pori, tel: 02-626 2200; www.porijazz.fi.

In Tampere there is an annual jazz festival called Jazz Happening. For information on dates and concerts, contact **Tampere Jazz Happening**, Tullikamarinaukio 2, 33100 Tampere, tel: 03-5656 6172; www.tampere.fi.

There is also Ruisrock on the island of Ruissalo in Turku, Finland's oldest and highly popular rock festival (see page 101).

of Helsinki nightlife during the summer. Extensive VIP areas and a terrace.

Lost and Found
Annankatu 6
Tel: 09-680 1010
A popular "hetero-friendly" gay club that stays open until 4am, this is a long-standing favourite after everywhere else in town has shut.

Molly Malones
Kaisaniemenkatu 1
Tel: 09-5766 7500
Easily the best Irish pub in the city, and a great place to speak English with locals and foreigners. Mellow and usually crowded, often with live music.

Storyville
Museokatu 8
Tel: 09-408 007
Jazz club featuring local and international musicians. A cosy spot to have a late drink. Cover charge. In the summertime there is a terrace outside to listen to the music.

Tavastia
Urho Kekkosenkatu 4
Tel: 09-7746 7420
This legendary rock club attracts some of Helsinki's best live music. Rocking atmosphere; downstairs is a usually packed self-service bar, waiter service upstairs.

Teatteri
Pohjoisesplanadi 2
Tel: 09-681 1130
An extremely popular and trendy post-work bar and restaurant in the centre of Helsinki with a terrace overlooking the Esplanade Park. Set inside the Swedish Theatre, meaning that it gets very crowded just before the curtains open.

We Got Beef
Iso Roobertinkatu 21
09-679 280
Possibly Helsinki's hippest club, started by a local in-the-know skateboarder and artistic type. Everyone – from office workers to some of Finland's best-known celebrities – come here to drink the night away until very, very late.

Zetor
Kaivopiha
Tel: 09-666 966
This "tractor-style" rock 'n' roll disco has to be seen to be believed. Experience the surrealism of the Finnish countryside in this restaurant founded by one of the Kaurismäki brothers.

Tampere

Tampere's nightlife is very evident on the town's main street, Hämeenkatu. Bar-hopping is very easy, and you will

also find a good number of traditional pubs as well as discos.

Doris
Aleksanterinkatu 20
The city's young and hip set comes here several days a week to chill out to DJ music until the wee hours.

Paapan Kapakka
Koskikatu 9
Tel: 03-211 0037
Great jazz bar with draught Guinness and a regular selection of bebop jazz groups who play on the small stage here.

Plevna
Itäinen katu 8
Set in the Finlayson factory area, this downstairs spot serves good local beer – brewed on-site.

Turku

Blanko
Aurakatu 1
Tel: 02-233 3966
Extremely trendy bar with good cocktails (as well as food). On the sofas you're likely to meet some unusually talkative Finns.

Edison
Kauppiaskatu 4
A good after-work bar popular with young professionals and students. Tends to close rather early though, so make this your first stop out.

Panimoravintola Koulu
Eerikinkatu 18
Tel: 02-274 5757
Just next to Market Square, this old former school building is the largest brewery restaurant in Finland. Excellent selection of beers.

Puutorin Vessa
Puutori
Tel: 02-233 8123
This unusual pub was once a public toilet. Now it is frequented by a small collection of locals who guard their bar very closely, but rarely speak.

Uusi Apteekki
Kaskenkatu 1
Tel: 02-250 2595
Literally "new pharmacy", this pub is set in an old chemist shop and sells over 20 different beers.

CHILDREN

Attractions

Helsinki

Helsinki has many attractions for families, for example the **Korkeasaari Zoo** (see page 180), **Linnanmäki Amusement Park** (see page 172), and **Sea Life Helsinki** (tel: 09-565 8200; www.sealife.fi) with more than 30 displays from the tropics to the Baltic and a walk-through underwater glass tunnel. **Serena Water Park** (tel: 09-887 0550; www.serena.fi) in Espoo can easily be reached by bus from Helsinki. It is open throughout the year and there is plenty to do for the whole family. Just a 15-minute train ride from downtown Helsinki is an ideal spot for engaging children and grown-ups: **Heureka**, the Finnish Science Centre in Vantaa-Tikkurila, has a range of permanent and temporary "hands-on" exhibitions, a planetarium and an IMAX theatre. Tel: 09-85799; www.heureka.fi.

Tampere

In Tampere the **Särkänniemi Amusement Park** is another popular family destination, comprising seven different attractions (*see page 220*). Near Turku, in Lieto, is the zoo and activity centre **Zoolandia** (tel: 010-423 4140; www.zoolandia.fi). There are around 200 animals in the zoo, but its biggest attraction, literally, is Finland's only elephant, called Vanni.

Turku and Around

In Naantali, **Moominworld** (Muumimaailma; *see also page 214*) is open from June to August (charge). It is a theme park – consistently rated as one of the best in the world – with characters from Tove Jansson's books very much in evidence. Tel: 02-511 1111; www.muumimaailma.fi.

Lakeland

There are several good spots in the Lakeland region for travellers with children. At **Messilä Vacation Centre** in Hollola near Lahti, there are all manner of supervised activities for children, including horse- and pony-riding. In winter, there are skiing activities (Alpine and Nordic) for children and adults. Tel: 03-86011;

www.messila.fi. A bit north from Hollola, towards Hartola, is the fascinating little **Musta and Valkea Ratsu Dollhouse and Puppet Theatre** on Road 52 (signposted), holding some 300 figures: 19230 Onkiniemi, tel: 03-718 6959; www.sci.fi/~kinnunen. A bit further east, **Tykkimäki Outdoor Centre**, outside Kouvola, is a family holiday and amusement resort in the green landscape. It has Finland's third-biggest amusement park, a reptile zoo, a dance pavilion and a popular campsite beside a lake. The campsite also has cottages for hire, as well as a traditional sauna and recreational facilities. For more information and opening times tel: 05-778 700; www.tykkimaki.fi. Mikkeli has the **Visulahti Travel Centre** (tel: 015-18281; www.visulahdenmatkailu.fi), including a dinosaur theme adventure and water park, waxworks and a motor park with 10 different tracks. Furthermore, you can rent a hotel-style bungalow right in the centre of everything. Meanwhile, further from Mikkeli is an arboretum which includes a small menagerie. Contact **Mikkeli Tourism**, tel: 020-370 071.

Åland

When in the **Åland Islands**, you might want to check out the amusement park by Mariehamn's west harbour, the *Pommern* ship museum (at the west harbour), and Lilla Holmen bird park on the east harbour. Here you will be able to catch a glimpse of peacocks, ducks and beautiful angora rabbits.

Lapland

Rovaniemi, near the Arctic Circle, is where you will find possibly the most perfect attraction for children in the entire world – **Santa Claus Village** (*see box below*).

Santa's Home

For better or worse, Rovaniemi has become best known not for its Arctic Museum or its Aalto architecture but for the Santa Claus Village that lies just north. This large wooden cabin is filled with kitschy Christmas goodies, reindeer paraphernalia and lots of winter cheer. Rumour has it that Father Christmas stays here when he is visiting from his secret hideaway in Korvatunturi-fell. There is a post office as well as a shopping centre which stocks gifts from Lapland. The Santa Park inside has a number of small amusement park

rides. To get there, take the Santa Claus Express train at Rovaniemi and get off at Napapiiri (a 10km/6-mile journey). Open daily year-round. While the kids are hanging out with Santa, adults can head over to cross the actual Arctic Circle – a man-drawn line in the concrete just nearby. Many tour operators offer Christmas tours that package together reindeer, husky and toboggan rides with a visit to Santa during the holiday season. One of the best is Cosmos (www.cosmos-holidays.co.uk).

SHOPPING

What to Buy

Finnish Design

If people know anything at all about Finnish design, it is often the fact that Finns apply the smooth contemporary lines often associated with Finnish architecture to jewellery, woodwork, clothing, glassware and sculpture. To see the best of the design, you might want to go first to the Design Museum in Helsinki (Korkeavuorenkatu 23, 00120 Helsinki; tel: 09-622 0540; www.designmuseum.fi).

Lapponia, Aarikka and Kaleva Koru jewellery are expressly Finnish, the first being a mainly contemporary collection and the second a collection based on designs from the Finnish epic poem *Kalevala*, rendered in silver, gold, and also in more affordable brass.

Aarikka also puts out some of the finer woodwork products, including chopping boards, Christmas decorations, toys, wooden jewellery and a range of great northern-style gift items.

The most impressive ceramic work is commissioned by Arabia, one of the older Finnish firms. Their factory (about 25 minutes' tram ride from downtown Helsinki) has a small museum upstairs, and first- and second-quality goods on sale downstairs.

Pentik is known for its ceramics as well as beautifully designed textiles. Iittala (*see page 223*) makes beautiful glassware at its factory, from drinking glasses to candle holders. Iittala items can also be found at the Arabia factory in Helsinki.

Marimekko is the quintessential Finnish clothing designer, with items made of brightly coloured fabrics for men, women and children, as well as textiles for home use.

All these companies can be found both in their own stores and in department stores in most Finnish towns of any size, including Stockmann's in Helsinki.

Shopping Areas

Helsinki

Apart from mainstream department stores and boutique shopping in Helsinki, there are several market squares that sell both fresh food and a range of other consumer goods of greatly varying quality, from second-

Department Stores

The king of department stores in Finland is Stockmann's; it is the place Finns go to when they want to hunt down some elusive item, or some exotic gift. To the outsider it will probably seem merely a large, pleasant place to shop, but to Finns it is something of an institution; branches are also in Tampere, Turku and Tapiola (Espoo). Stockmann's also owns the Akateeminen Kirjakauppa, Finland's best-known bookstore. Another good department store to look out for throughout Finland is Sokos, with its fine food hall.

hand clothes and records to designer jewellery, Lapp mittens and fur hats.

Kauppatori is the main Helsinki market, followed by Hietalahdentori and Hakaniementori, all near the centre. Note that markets have extended hours in summer and are open until about 8pm, but close briefly from about 2pm.

Otherwise, the **Esplanadi** and **Aleksi** are the hub of shopping delights in Helsinki. You'll find relatively few foreign retail outlets in Finland, but in recent years a few have managed to establish themselves, such as Hennes & Mauritz (H&M), IKEA, Body Shop and Benetton.

Tampere

Tampere has most of the medium-sized department stores found in Helsinki and Turku. This area also has a host of interesting smaller boutiques. A good collection of handicrafts, design items and clothing is at **Keräsaari Boutique Centre**, Laukontori 1, Keräsaari, in a converted brick textile mill. Visit also the **Verkaranta Arts and Crafts Centre** at Verkatehtaankatu 2, for a good selection of handicrafts and toys.

The main Tampere Market Hall is at Hämeenkatu 19, open Monday to Saturday.

Turku

Turku has its own Stockmann's at **Yliopistonkatu** 22. Also on Yliopistonkatu are **Pentik** (No. 25), famous for ceramics, and **Aarikka** (No. 27B), for handmade wooden crafts and decorations.

For more crafts, look into **Sylvi Salonen**, at Yliopistonkatu 26, specialising in linens and decorative objects.

Check locally for market days at the lovely main market (the market opens in summer from 4–8pm). The **Hansa Shopping Centre** is also in Turku (see page 209).

SPORTS

Participant Sports

Finland is a sporting nation, and devotion to training is constant; it is not unusual on a hot summer's day to see squadrons of muscular youths out on roller-skis ensuring they stay in shape for the coming winter. Whether your goal is to keep fit, meet other travellers or locals or just to get out and see the countryside, there are dozens of athletic ways to move about the country.

For more information, contact:
Suomen Liikunta ja Urheilu (Finnish Sports Federation)
Radiokatu 20, 00240 Helsinki (Ilmala), tel: 09-348 121; www.slu.fi

Birdwatching

Finland is one of the best places in Europe to come twittering. The country's multiple national parks, sanctioned preserves and open wilderness areas – not to mention its unique geographic location – are natural habitats for a large number of migratory birds, which stop on their way here before their yearly mass migrations. For more information, visit **Bird Life**, Annankatu 29A, 00101 Helsinki, tel: 09-4135 3300; www.birdlife.fi

Boating and Sailing

The Finnish coast, combined with its vast network of inland waterways,

allows for umpteen opportunities in boating. The country's alluring coastline of islands, bays and inlets can make for some extremely adventurous sailing, while the thousands of lakes offers unequalled relaxation in a gorgeous setting. These waters can be enjoyed from any type of boat – from one-man dinghy to a full-on sailing yacht or cruiser. Most harbours have guest marinas where one can dock for reasonable overnight fees. Renting a large sailboat isn't the easiest of prospects, though it is not unheard of. Check with **Finlandia Sailing**, Sparbacka 5, 25900 Taalintehdas, tel: 0400-421 050; www. finlandiasailing.fi.

Canoeing and Kayaking

Finland's waterways are perfect for canoeing and kayaking, offering a variety of levels. For the calmest of paddles, try the Lake region, while for something occasionally more choppy, go for the many islands off Finland's southern and western coasts. Meanwhile, if it's rapid shooting you are looking for, there are also a number of exciting rapids all over the country. For comprehensive information, contact:
Finnish Canoe Federation
Olympiastadion
Eteläkaarre, 00250 Helsinki
Tel: 09-494 965; www.kanoottiliitto.fi

Cycling

Bicycling is big in Finland. The countryside is ideal for cyclists, dead flat on the west coast leading to gently rolling hill areas; for suggested cycle routes, contact:
Finnish Youth Hostel Association
Yrjönkatu 38B, 00100 Helsinki, tel: 09-565 7150; www.srmnet.org

BELOW: Finland's ice hockey team won silver in the 2006 Winter Olympics.

ABOVE: be a rally driver for a day in northern Finland.

Fishing

On account of its endless waterways – both lake and river – Finland offers some of the best angling and fly fishing opportunities to be found anywhere on the continent. To do any kind of fishing (ice-fishing aside) in Finland, however, you must have a licence. These are inexpensive, costing under €10 for a week, and can be picked up from a tour operator or, alternatively, at a post office. Several regions of the country (ie Lapland) maintain their own proprietary licences, which will cost extra, and certain "owned" waterways will require the permission of the owner – though this can be done more or less on the spot. For more information, contact the **Federation of Finnish Fisheries Association**, Malmin kauppatie 26, 00700 Helsinki, tel: 09-684 4590; www.ahven.net

Hiking, Trekking and Snowshoeing

Hiking is extremely popular all over the country. In some areas, you can go on a guided hike with a well-informed local who really knows the area. For a guided hike around Kilpisjärvi, for example, contact Harriniva, Käsivarrentie 14703 (tel: 0400-396 087; www.harriniva.fi) or Kilpissafarit, Tsahkalluoktantie 14 (tel: 040-516 1952; www.kilpissafarit.fi). For winter walking in snowshoes, one of the best places to go is the Koillismaa region. A number of companies offer winter adventure packages with rental. Contact **NorthTrek** , Erkkorannantie 1, 93825 Ruka, tel: 040-418 2832; www.northtrek.net

Rally Driving

Some of the most successful racing-car drivers in the world are Finns. There are a few places in the country where you can get to grips with this exciting, adrenalin-producing activity. In the north of Finland, for example, there is a track that remains one of the best places in Europe to get behind the wheel of a finely tuned, high-performance rally car.
Visit **Juha Kankkunen Race Track**, Kuusamo, tel: 050-305 5755; www.juhakankkunen.com

Skiing

In addition to a strong reputation as long-distance runners, Finns are also famous as cross-country skiers and ski-jumpers. You'll find excellent facilities for these sports; in most major urban areas there are maps of paths specifically set aside for such pastimes. Ask for the *Ulkoilukartta* (outdoor map) from tourist boards.
    You can ski cross-country nearly anywhere in Finland, but Lapland is a favourite spot for this very Nordic sport, as it is for downhill skiing (try to avoid school holiday weeks). Unlike Norway and even Sweden, Finland has very few true mountains, except in the far north, where the Lappish hills *(tunturi)* scatter the otherwise flat, tundral landscape. The highest rises to over 1,400 metres (4,000ft). There are also a large number of cross-country ski events and competitions you can participate in; information is available from **Suomen Latu (Finnish Ski Trek Association)**, Radiokatu 20, 00240 Helsinki, tel: 09-4159 1100, www.suomenlatu.fi.

Snowkiting

Snowkiting (also known as kite skiing) combines kitesurfing with snowboarding, employing inflatable kites that allow kiters to travel uphill. The sport has become very popular in recent years in Finland, where small hills have often failed to challenge hardcore downhill skiers or snowboarders. Popular areas include Saariselkä and Lake Kallavesi. For more information, contact the **Finnish Boardsailing Association** (www. purjelautaliitto.fi) or try ProWind (040-508 4000; www.prowind.fi).

Summer

One of the biggest sailing events of the year is the Hanko Regatta, which takes place in early July off Finland's south coast. Kotka also sponsors a yearly Tall Ships event.
    The biggest inland sailing regatta is on Lake Päijänne, also in July. Details are available from the **Finnish Yachting Association**, Westendinkatu 7, 02160 Espoo, tel: 020-796 4200; www.yachting.fi
    Before mid-June is the **Finlandia Canoeing Relay**, held in the Lakeland region – the venue changes annually. It lasts five days and covers over 545km (350 miles).

Winter

The three Olympic-sized ski jumps at Lahti, about 105km (65 miles) north of Helsinki, is the best place to watch ski-jumping.
    For winter spectator sports, the **Finlandia Ski Race** in mid-February is one of the top events. This 60km (37-mile) event attracts the best Finnish skiers and has ample spectator opportunities. Another great event to see is the week-long Marjanpäivä festival in Enontekiö in Lapland, where the Sami hold a great collection of reindeer races and snowmobiling competitions.
    Contact **Finlandia Ski Race Office** Urheilukeskus, 15110 Lahti, tel: 03-816 813.

A – Z

A HANDY SUMMARY OF PRACTICAL INFORMATION, ARRANGED ALPHABETICALLY

Admission Charges

Few bars charge admission fees per se, but many places in Finland have a "wardrobe" charge of €2, which you'll have to pay whether or not you have a coat or jacket on. Clubs may charge anywhere between €7 and €10 for entry, while tickets for music concerts can cost upwards of €10 or €15 – sometimes double that if the band is fairly well known.

Age Restrictions

Most bars will not admit anyone under the age of 18, while some have a limit of 21. The age restriction for clubs is generally 21, though occasionally this may be either 24 or, rarely, 26. Note that while many bars and clubs in Finland have their age limits posted loud and clear on the front door, this does not mean that the limits are necessarily strictly upheld. While most hostels do not impose an age restriction, this may not be the case when the establishment has a bar on the premises. Both the Viking and Silja line ferries do not allow

unaccompanied youth under 23 to board their cruises on Fridays or Saturdays. On other nights the age limit is 20, while it is 18 for travellers not on same-day-return tickets.

Budgeting for Your Trip

Compared to other countries in Europe, Finland is expensive. A hotel

BELOW: taking a break in Helsinki.

room in most cities is likely to cost upwards of €100 per night, though cheaper ones can be found. Meals are similarly high priced, with an average two-course meal for two plus wine at a mid-level restaurant costing upwards of €75. Museums average around €5. Groceries tend to be around the EU average for items, while very late at night you can get some fairly inexpensive food items at the ubiquitous *grilli* kiosks in larger cities (for example a €3 hamburger).

Business Travellers

Doing business in Finland is comparatively straightforward compared to other countries in Europe. For one, nearly every Finn speaks superb, near-native English – and many are rather eager to speak it to show you this fact. But Finns are also quite easy to get along with when it comes to business issues, and rather straightforward when it comes to contract negotiation and deal signing. Otherwise, you probably won't notice too much different from business practices in other Western

CLIMATE CHART

Helsinki

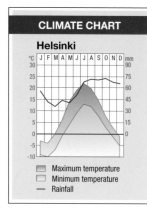

- ▢ Maximum temperature
- ▢ Minimum temperature
- — Rainfall

European countries – with the exception that you'll probably be spending more time in the sauna talking about the finer points of your business, somewhat more so than in other countries, anyway.

Business Hours: Everything is done earlier. Lunch is earlier (as early as 11am, with 1pm generally being the outside limit), and many offices operate 8am–4pm as opposed to 9am–5pm; in summer offices often close as early as 3pm, even 2pm on Fridays.

Business Style: There is a marked lack of bombast. Finns tend not to dress anything up, but rather present things as they are, warts and all. In other words, they are terribly honest, and do not go in much for exaggeration of any kind, whether it relates to a person or a business deal. Hence, their way of selling things might seem a bit subdued compared to other countries. But Finns are also more likely to be sympathetic and reserved than aggressive and braggart – especially in business matters. As Bertolt Brecht famously once put it, "Finns are silent in two languages."

Business Entertaining: You are as likely to be invited on a ski outing or sailboat ride as on a night out on the town. These days, Finns tend not to drink at lunch, but after-hours drinking is still de rigueur, and as people on business accounts are about the only ones who can afford long spells of drinking, if you get an invitation, enjoy it while you can. If you are invited to visit a sauna with a Finn, by all means accept the invitation, as it is likely to work in your favour in business dealings.

Business Etiquette: It is ill-advised to be late for business meetings; Finns tend to be very punctual and courteous, though quite formal. Handshakes are used for meeting business as well as casual

acquaintances; most people have business cards (hand the card to the other person so that they receive it facing in their direction). All have mobile phones, which they are delighted to use – it is often printed on their business card – so do not be put off by the fact that office hours seem short; there is almost always a mobile phone link to the person in question.

Holidays: Finally, try to avoid business in July and early August. The Finnish summer is short and sacred, and you'll find some offices nearly deserted of staff at these times. (Conversely, this is a good time for tourists, who can often benefit from the many hotel discounts offered to compensate for the lost business trade.) Other blackout periods are the spring skiing break in late February (southern Finland) or early March (northern Finland), plus two weeks at Christmas and a week at Easter.

C hildren

Overall, Finland is a family- and child-orientated society, and hence one that is generally safe for children. Public conveniences usually include baby-changing areas and most restaurants can provide high chairs. Children are almost always accepted in all hotels. In Helsinki, the Tourist Board can provide a list of qualified child-minders. In the cities, public transport is geared for use by those with prams, as well as wheelchairs, and getting around with children is easier than in almost any other country.

Climate

What to Bring

The best advice on packing for Finland is to bring layers of clothes,

BELOW: Helsinki-Vantaa airport is well connected to the capital.

regardless of the season. While it is famous for frigid winters – when gloves, long underwear, hats, woollen tights and socks, and several layers of cotton topped by wool and something waterproof are recommended – Finland also has very sunny and temperate summers. As a result, sun block and a sun hat are as essential at these times as warm clothes are in the winter.

In winter, bring heavy-duty footwear not only to keep out the damp but also to avoid damage to good shoes ruined by salt and gravel put down to melt ice on the pavements. Spring and autumn are rainy, and summers are usually pleasantly dry and sunny, but occasionally wet.

Crime and Safety

Finland is one of the safest countries in Europe. You may find in the larger cities a number of very drunk people wandering around after hours, but they will mostly be harmless to others. Vandalism is the only real noticeable sign of crime – often perpetrated by young teenagers trying to act cool. Occasional pickpocketing has been known on the Helsinki metro and at the main railway station; again, this is often attributed to either young kids or alcoholics, on the hunt for money for successive drinking bouts. Be on your guard in these places.

Customs Regulations

Goods from EU countries destined for personal use can be taken freely in and out of Finland by EU citizens, although importing tobacco products from the member states that joined in 2004 (Czech Republic, Slovenia, Slovakia, Hungary, Poland, Lithuania, Latvia and Estonia) is restricted during the transformation period. Note that a person has to be 20 years or over in order to possess or transport strong alcohol (drinks containing more than 22 percent by volume of ethyl alcohol) and at least 18 years to possess or transport mild alcohols. For enquiries about goods or changes in regulations contact the Customs Information Service, tel: 09-6141; www.tulli.fi/en. The following items are permitted to be brought into Finland from non-EU countries.

Cigarettes/Tobacco

Any visitor over 16 years of age may bring in 200 cigarettes or 250g (½lb) of tobacco products duty free.

Emergencies

National emergency number:
112
Police: 10022
Helsinki house-call doctors:
010-850 4743
Emergency dental services:
09-310 47450

Alcohol

Any visitor aged 20 or over can bring in 1 litre of strong alcohol (spirits) or 2 litres of mild alcohol (max 22 percent); in addition to that, 2 litres of wine and 16 litres of beer; 50g of perfume or 250ml of eau de toilette. For visitors 18–19 years of age, the quantity limit is the same, but must not include strong alcohol.

In addition, visitors can bring in up to €175 worth of gifts or items intended for one's own use.

Animal Quarantine

Pets vaccinated against rabies are in most cases allowed into Finland (pets must have been vaccinated at least 30 days and less than 12 months before entry). Double-checking these requirements and your vaccination certificates is crucial because Finland is sometimes rabies-free, sometimes not, and these rules change from year to year.

D isabled Travellers

For disabled people, travelling should not pose tremendous problems in Finland. Most newer buildings have access for disabled people, in terms of ramps and lifts. Check the *Finland Hotel* guide, which indicates by symbols which hotels have access and facilities for disabled people. With careful planning, transport should also go smoothly; when ordering a taxi, specify your needs (wheelchair is "*pyörätuoli*"). Helsinki metro is accessible for wheelchair-users, but other forms of public transport may be a bit more problematic, although some city buses "kneel", making it easier to board. If you have any queries related to disabled travel in Finland, contact:
Rullaten
Pajutie 7C, 02770 Espoo
Tel: 050-579 5335
www.rullaten.fi

E lectricity

Finland uses electricity at 220 volts AC (two-pin plug).

Embassies and Consulates

Helsinki has embassies for most large European nations. The following is a list of English-speaking embassies in the capital. Canada, Pohjoisesplanadi 25B (tel: 228 530; www.canada.fi); Ireland, Erottajankatu 7A (tel: 646 006); UK, Itäinen Puistotie 17 (tel: 2286 5100; http://ukinfinland.fco.gov.uk); US, Itäinen Puistotie 14B (tel: 616 250; www.usembassy.fi). Australia has a consular office at Museokatu 25B (tel: 4777 6640), but its nearest embassy is in Sweden.

Etiquette

In general, Finns are courteous, particularly to foreign guests. However, they do not squeak "Sorry!" any time they brush past you on the street, not even if they tread on your toes; they do not use the Finnish term for "Sorry" or "Excuse Me" *(Anteeksi)* in such situations. Rather, this term is used for graver offences or extreme politeness. For minor offences, a simple "Oops" is usually enough. If you spend time in a Finnish sauna with locals, be aware that nearly every Finn will attend a sauna session naked. There is no sexual assocation with the sauna ritual whatsoever – it is much more about being close to nature and feeling free and uninhibited. If you are going to a Finn's house for dinner, bringing a plant or flowers for the host or hostess and, if you plan to drink, a bottle of wine, is the norm. However, if you are out with Finns at a bar, be aware that buying rounds is not an aspect of Finnish culture. If you offer to buy rounds for a group of Finns, your generosity will be looked at with some bemusement. More importantly, however, your new Finnish friends will not buy you a round in return – it just isn't done.

BELOW: buying tickets for public transport is easy.

G ay and Lesbian Travellers

Finland has progressed leaps and bounds over the past decade when it comes to gay and lesbian visitors. Homosexual lifestyles are thus readily accepted in the country's larger cities and towns, though somewhat less so in smaller communities. The gay community in Helsinki has a number of nightlife venues, as do several other Finnish cities. For more information, contact the organisation for gay and lesbian equality, Seksuaalinen tasavertaisuus (tel: 09-681 2580; www.heseta.fi). *Z Lehti* (www.z-lehti.fi) is a gay and lesbian magazine.

H ealth and Medical Care

You'll have little to worry about healthwise in Finland. However, you may have an uncomfortable time if you coincide with the mosquito season, which descends on the northern and central parts of the country in July and into August. Enquire in Finland about the most effective mosquito repellents from chemists, who know their own brand of insect best.

If you need medical treatment in Finland, it is generally free, or dispensed at a nominal charge (a hospital visit will be charged at €22, or €26 if an overnight stay is required). Almost any *Terveysasema* (health clinic) or *Sairaala* (hospital) will treat you; you can also schedule regular appointments at a *Terveysasema* (listed as such in telephone directories). The Emergency section is generally called *Ensiapu*.

Visitors needing hospital care in Helsinki should contact:
Meilahti Hospital, Haartmaninkatu 4, Helsinki, tel: 09-4717 2432 (for

ABOVE: Lifesaver record store in Helsinki, a treasure-house for fans of vinyl.

surgery and medicine); **Helsinki University Hospitals' Töölö Hospital**, Topeliuksenkatu 5, tel: 09-4718 7383 (orthopaedic specialists). Visit www.hus.fi for more information on other hospitals in the Helsinki region; there are 32 individual hospitals in the area. In other cities, consult hotels for hospital emergency numbers.

Pharmacies *(Apteekki)* charge for prescriptions, but not outrageously. There is usually at least one pharmacy open in larger towns on a late-night basis. In Helsinki, the Apteekki at Mannerheimintie 96 is open 24 hours; tel: 020-320 200 for around-the-clock on-call numbers.

Internet

Finns are the second-most active internet users in the world – over 50 percent of the country uses the internet on a daily basis. Moreover, Helsinki's technological infrastructure ranks among the most sophisticated in the world, and Finnish firms such as Kone, F-Secue, Rocla and Nokia – one of the world's most valuable and pre-eminent brands – now vie for office and R&D space in the city with foreign subsidiaries and research units from groups such as ABB, 3M, Hewlett-Packard, Siemens and Accenture. As a result of all this interest and expertise in high technology, there is excellent internet connectivity all around the country. Finland's hotel internet services, for example, are the most developed of anywhere in the world, with nearly every hotel offering free wi-fi and, at the very least, ethernet connectivity in every

room. Many cities, the capital included, even offer municipal-wide, password-free networks that anyone can log into at any time.

Maps

Maps of Finland and its cities and towns are readily available in most tourist offices. For maps that are more detailed – for example, hiking or kayaking maps – visit Karttakeskus (tel: 020-577 7580; www.karttakeskus.fi) in Helsinki at Vuorikatu 14.

Media

Newspapers and Books

No one has yet been able to come up with a good explanation as to why papers published in Europe cannot arrive in Finland on their day of publication. But, with the exception of the *International Herald Tribune*, which arrives on the afternoon of its publication date, you'll have to wait a day and a half for British newspapers to get to Helsinki. The papers are sold at Helsinki railway station, in at least two bookstores (Suomalainen Kirjakauppa at Aleksanterinkatu 23, and Akateeminen Kirjakauppa at Pohjoisesplanadi 39, where you can also get books in English), and at the larger hotels in other cities, as well as at main airports.

Radio and Television

The Finnish national broadcasting service offers 24-hour world radio that broadcasts news in English as well as Finnish language-learning programmes. English-language programmes are often in the early evening or during the night. Visit

www.yle.fi/ylemondo for specific schedules or to listen online. Otherwise, tune into Capital FM (97.5 FM) throughout much of southern Finland. This broadcasts hours of programmes in Spanish, French and Russian, but mainly English, using relays from American, Canadian, Australian and South African stations as well as the BBC and Ireland's RTE. The news in English is broadcast daily on YLE Radio 1 (87.9 FM in the Helsinki region) weekdays at 7.30am and 8.55am. For up-to-date schedules, visit YLE at www.yli.fi. The BBC's World Service and other English-language television channels are usually available in hotels.

Money

Since early 2002, Finland, in common with numerous other EU member states, has used euro (€) notes and coins. Finns themselves have had longer to get used to the change, with salaries and prices being displayed in both marks and euros for some time prior to the official changeover.

There are 100 cents (Finnish: *sentti*) to the euro. Coins come in denominations of 1, 2, 5, 10 and 50 cents, and 1 and 2 euros. Controversially, Finnish shops and businesses are not obliged to accept 1- or 2-cent coins, and prices are rounded off to the nearest factor of 5. Notes come in denominations of 5, 10, 20, 50, 100, 200 and 500 euros; the lowest amount withdrawable from a cash machine is €20.

Credit Cards and Travellers' Cheques

Credit cards are widely accepted in Finland. MasterCard/Access, Visa, Diner's Club and American Express are accepted in all but the most humble establishments.

Travellers' cheques and common currencies can be exchanged easily in banks.

Most cash machines (ATMs) marked OTTO will give euros if you have a bank card with an international PIN number (Visa, Cirrus, Plus, MasterCard, Maestro, and so on).

Opening Hours

Shop opening hours are fairly straightforward in Finland. Generally shops are open from Monday to Saturday, except small food stores which are allowed to stay open on Sunday also. However, what can sometimes be confusing is that there is selected Sunday opening

Public Holidays

1 Jan New Year's Day
6 Jan Epiphany
Mar/Apr Good Friday, Easter Sunday, Easter Monday
1 May May Day
May Ascension (40 days after Easter)
May Whitsun (50 days after Easter)
A Fri/Sat between 20–26 June Midsummer Eve/Day
Early November All Saints' Day
6 Dec Independence Day
24 Dec Christmas Eve
25 Dec Christmas Day
26 Dec Boxing Day

during the summer and on certain weekends during the rest of the year. Shops are generally open between 9am and 5pm; on Saturday some close earlier, especially in the smaller towns and villages. In Helsinki many larger stores are open until 9pm on weekdays and until 6pm on Saturday. Supermarkets – such as K-Citymarket – are often open until 9pm on weekdays and 6pm on Saturday in Helsinki and elsewhere. However, it is best to be aware that in smaller towns and rural areas shops might close earlier. The only really late-opening places are in the tunnel under the Helsinki railway station, open Monday to Saturday 7am–10pm and Sunday 10am–10pm. Larger shopping outlets, such as Stockmann's department store and the shops in the Forum shopping mall diagonally across from it on Mannerheimintie in Helsinki, are open weekdays 9am–9pm, Saturday 9am–6pm and Sunday noon–6pm.

Banking hours are Monday to Friday 9.15am–4.15pm. Some exchange bureaus open later, particularly at travel points such as airports and major harbours, as well as on international ferries.

Postal Services

Post offices are generally open 9am–5pm. Services include stamps, registered mail and *poste restante*. The *poste restante* address in Helsinki is Mannerheimintie 11, 00100 Helsinki. It's on the railway square side of the post office and is open Monday to Friday 9am–6pm.

When post offices are closed, there are stamp machines outside and in the railway station. Insert the necessary coin and you get the equivalent in stamps. The machines

are orange and mounted on the walls, as are the post boxes.

Religious Services

The Lutheran Church is the state Church of Finland, with 84 percent of Finns counted as Lutherans. There is a small Greek Orthodox population, and just two Catholic churches in Finland.

In Helsinki, services in English are held at the Temppelinaukion church, the Church in the Rock on Lutherinkatu (see page 174); there are both Lutheran and ecumenical services here. There is also one synagogue and one mosque in Helsinki, for those of Jewish or Muslim faith.

Smoking

Health-conscious Finland has jumped on the growing global bandwagon of anti-smoking. Smoking is not permitted indoors in public buildings and other places open to the public, except in designated smoking zones. Such areas do not exist in facilities expressly made for children or other persons under 18. Additionally, smoking is heavily prohibited on trains, trams, buses and, of course, aircraft. It is also outlawed at all schools and other educational institutions, all offices and other places of work. You must be 18 years or older to buy cigarettes or other tobacco products in Finland.

Telephones

Callers from outside Finland should dial the international code (00 in Europe; 011 in the US), then the country code (358) followed by the

BELOW: Åland Island postage stamps.

local area code and phone number, omitting the initial zero (0). Due to the proliferation of mobile phones, coin-operated phoneboxes have become very rare in Finland – they are due to be phased out over the next several years – and the few that still exist can be operated with credit cards. There are two call centres in Helsinki, at Hämeentie 23 and Vuorikatu 8 (near the Sörnäinen and Kaisaniemi tube stations). To make a normal direct call to abroad dial 00, 990, 996 or 999 to get a line outside Finland, then the country code and number (for example, 00-44 for the UK; 00-1 for US numbers). If you want to reach an operator in your own country to make a reverse-charge call (call collect), ask for the *Finland Direct* pamphlet, which lists the numbers. For the UK operator, dial 9-800 1 0440; for the US, 9-800 1 0010/ATT. Dial 02 02 08 for overseas call assistance from a Finnish (English-speaking) operator. For Finnish number enquiries dial 02 02 02 or 118. The front of the White Pages telephone directory also has directions for foreigners. Don't forget that hotels usually add surcharges for telephone calls made from your room.

Mobile Phones

Finland is a nation of mobile phone users, and the easiest and most inexpensive way to make calls while in Finland is by using a mobile phone. If you use your own mobile phone from home, you will usually be charged a surcharge (often around €0.25 per minute for the privilege of calling – or receiving calls – abroad). A more inexpensive way, however, is to purchase a Finnish SIM card with a local mobile provider. In order to do this, you will need to make sure that your phone is unlocked before you leave home; this can be done quite easily either through your home provider or at any number of mobile shops. In Finland, there are several mobile providers to choose from, including **Sonera**, **Saunalahti** and **DNA**. The country is covered by GSM900 mobile technology. DNA offers some of the best rates of any Finnish provider. For €20 you can get a SIM card with a Finnish number and around 100 minutes of talk time. The cards (and their refills) can be picked up at any R-Kioski shop. Note that US mobile phone operators do not use GSM at all, so to use your phone in Finland, the chip has to be removed and replaced with a GSM chip – enquire at your local phone store for more information.

International Dialling Code

358.

Toilets

In Helsinki there are public toilets placed in various locations throughout the city. Several central places include beside the Old Market Hall, in Esplanade Park and in Sibelius Park. The price of entry is €0.50 per visit. Otherwise, you could visit the public toilet on Sofiankatu, which is suitable for wheelchairs. The fee here should be paid to the attendant.

Tourist Information

Finland has over 50 main tourist information offices, marked with an "i" for information. Summer tourist offices spring up along harbours and lakes where need dictates.

Information on travel for the entirety of Finland is available from the **Finnish Tourist Board**, but as they no longer have an office in Helsinki, you should either contact them before you leave your home country or try to go through the Helsinki City Tourist Office. In Helsinki, you can book hotels through the Hotel Booking Centre at the railway station (tel: 09-2288 1400; www.helsinkiexpert.fi). A full listing of all tourist offices can be obtained at the Helsinki offices.

Main Tourist Offices

Finnish Tourist Board
www.visitfinland.com (no public office)
Helsinki Tourist and Convention Bureau
Pohjoisesplanadi 19, 00099 Helsinki
Tel: 09-3101 3300
www.visithelsinki.fi

VisitRovaniemi
Maakuntakatu 29–31, 96200 Rovaniemi
Tel: 016-346 270
www.visitrovaniemi.fi
GoTampere
Rautatienkatu 25A, 33100 Tampere
Tel: 03-565 6680
www.gotampere.fi
Turku Touring
Aurakatu 4, 20100 Turku
Tel: 02-262 7444
www.turku.fi

Tourist Publications

Useful publications in Helsinki include *The Helsinki Times*, an English-language newspaper that lists cultural and tourist events, available in shops all over the city; *City*, a weekly newspaper featuring a calendar of cultural events and restaurant listings; *Helsinki This Week*, and brochures put out by the Tourist Board.

The Tourist Board also has an excellent website (www.visitfinland.com) that allows you to search for accommodation by region and by type among other things.

Tour Operators and Travel Agents

Finland doesn't always lie directly on the map when it comes to tour operators. Many groups that specialise in Scandinavia often leave Finland off itineraries – it is, after all, technically not a Scandinavian but a Nordic country. Or, if it is included at all, is generally put as an "add on" destination after everyone has seen the other countries. It is occasionally a jumping-off point for trips to Russia. However, some groups do offer good coverage of Finland when

Time Zone

Greenwich Mean Time (GMT) + 2 hours; Eastern Standard Time (EST) + 7 hours.

it comes to guided, bespoke or personalised tours:
Emagine UK
Tel: 01942-262 662
www.emagine-travel.co.uk
Go2Lapland
Tel: 0871-222 0736
http://go2lapland.com
Inghams
Tel: 020-8780 4400
www.inghams.co.uk
Intrepid Travel
Tel: 020-3147 7777
www.intrepidtravel.com
Kuoni
Tel: 01306-744 222
www.kuoni.co.uk
Nortours
Tel: 0870-744 7315
www.nortours.co.uk

V isas and Passports

Citizens of most Western countries do not need visas to travel to Finland; a valid passport will suffice. Finland is also a member of the Schengen countries. The Nordic countries only stamp you in once for a three-month tourist stay, so if you arrive via, say Sweden, you won't need to be stamped at the Finnish border.

It is difficult for non-EU citizens to work in Finland; if you want to work, though, contact a Finnish Embassy or Consulate outside Finland well before you go. An employer's letter is usually needed in advance of the work permit being granted.

BELOW: spacious bar at Helsinki-Vantaa airport.

L ANGUAGE

UNDERSTANDING THE LANGUAGE

Getting By

Hello *Päivää or terve*
How do you do? *Kuinka voit?*
Good morning *Hyvää huomenta*
Good day *Hyvää päivää*
Good evening *Hyvää iltaa*
Goodbye *Näkemiin or hei hei*
Yes *Kyllä or Joo*
No *Ei*
Thank you *Kiitos*
How do I get to...? *Miten pääsen...?*
aircraft *lentokone*
bus/coach *bussi/linja-auto*
train *juna*
Where is...? *Missä on...?*
right *oikealla*
left *vasemmalla*
straight on *suoraan or eteenpäin*
What time is it? *Paljonko kello on?*
It is (the time is)... *Kello on...*
Could I have your name? *Saisinko nimesi?*
My name is... *Nimeni on...*
Do you speak English? *Puhutko englantia?*
I only speak English *Puhun vain englantia*
Can I help you? *Voinko auttaa sinua?*
I do not understand *En ymmärrä*
I do not know *En tiedä*

Eating Out

breakfast *aamiainen*
lunch *lounas*
dinner *illallinen*
to eat *syödä*
to drink *juoda*
I would like to order... *Haluaisin tilata...*
Could I have the bill? *Saisko laskun?*
Cheers *Kippis (Swedish: skål)*
toilet *vessa*
gentlemen *miehet (Swedish: herrar)*
ladies *naiset (Swedish: damer)*

vacant *vapaa*
engaged *varattu*

Shopping

to buy *ostaa*
money *raha*
How much does this cost? *Paljonko tämä maksaa?*
It costs... *Se maksaa...*
Free, no charge *LImainen or LImaiseksi*
clothes *vaatteet*
blouse *pusero*
jacket *takki*
jersey *neulepusero or villapusero*
shoes *kengät*
skirt *hame*
suit *puku*
shop *kauppa*
food *ruoka*
grocers *ruokakauppa*
handicraft *käsityö*
off licence *alko*
launderette *pesula*
dirty/clean *likainen/puhdas*
entrance *sisäänkäynti*
exit *uloskääynti*
no entry *pääsy kielletty*
open *avoinna, auki*
closed *suljettu, kiinni*
push *työnnä*
pull *vedä*

Days of the Week

Monday *Maanantai*
Tuesday *Tiistai*
Wednesday *Keskiviikko*
Thursday *Torstai*
Friday *Perjantai*
Saturday *Launantai*
Sunday *Sunnuntai*
today *tänään*
tomorrow *huomenna*
yesterday *eilen*

Numbers

1 *yksi*
2 *kaksi*
3 *kolme*
4 *neljä*
5 *viisi*
6 *kuusi*
7 *seitsemän*
8 *kahdeksan*
9 *yhdeksän*
10 *kymmenen*
11 *yksitoista*
12 *kaksitoista*
13 *kolmetoista*
14 *neljätoista*
15 *viisitoista*
16 *kuusitoista*
17 *seitsemäntoista*
18 *kahdeksantoista*
19 *yhdeksäntoista*
20 *kaksikymmentä*
30 *kolmekymmentä*
40 *neljäkymmentä*
50 *viisikymmentä*
60 *kuusikymmentä*
70 *seitsemänkymmentä*
80 *kahdeksankymmentä*
90 *yhdeksänkymmentä*
100 *sata*
1000 *tuhat*

Useful Words

doctor *lääkäri*
hospital *sairaala*
chemist *apteekki*
police station *poliisilaitos*
parking *paikoitus*
phrase book *turistien sanakirja*
dictionary *sanakirja*
to rent *vuokrata*
room to rent *vuokrattavana huone*
Could I have the key? *Saisko avaimen?*

FURTHER READING

History

Finland in Europe by Matti Klinge. A well-illustrated book with emphasis on Finnish history under Russian rule and after independence.

The Sami People: Traditions in Transition by Veli-Pekka Lehtola. An excellent illustrated history of the Sami people that details the lives of these traditional herdsmen, increasingly caught between their nomadic past and their settled present.

A Short History of Finland by Singleton & Upton. As the name suggests, this book covers Finland's history in brief, and is perhaps the best-written account of the past two millennia.

Art and Architecture

Alvar Aalto by Richard Weston. A very well-informed introduction into the life and work of Finnish architect Aalto, documented with excellent photographs.

Golden Age: Finnish Art 1850–1907 by Markku Valkonen. Includes works by Edelfelt, Gallén-Kallela and Schjerfbeck.

A Guide to Finnish Architecture by Kaipia & Putkonen. A fascinating town-by-town guide to individual buildings, with plenty of photos and illustrations.

Helsinki: An Architectural Guide by Arvi Ilonen. Features the capital's most important architectural landmarks and details on individual buildings.

Fiction

The Egyptian by Mika Waltari. The novel that made Finnish writer Waltari's name – a great epic of Sinuhe, the Egyptian.

Harjunpää and the Stone Murders by Matti Joensuu. Set in modern-day, war-ridden Helsinki, this detective novel is by one of Scandinavia's most esteemed and popular crime writers.

Seven Brothers by Aleksis Kivi (Finnish American Translators Association). The cornerstone of

Finnish literature and first novel ever written in Finnish.

The Summer Book by Tove Jansson. Jansson's bestselling children's book following the lives of the beloved Moomins.

Troll: A Love Story by Johanna Sinisalo. This heralded debut novel concerns a photographer who one day comes upon a magical troll who ends up changing his life and that of the people he knows and loves.

Under the North Star by Väinö Linna. A quintessential Finnish novel by one of the country's most outstanding writers, this is volume one in a trilogy that depicts the development of Finnish society from the late 19th century to the years just following World War II.

The Year of the Bull by Oscar Parland. This engrossing story follows the life of a young boy during the post-war society of Finland c.1918.

The Year of the Hare by Arto

Paasilinna. A great example of a contemporary Finnish novel, with Finnish satire throughout.

Specialist

Finnish Sauna, Design, Construction and Maintenance (the Finnish Building Centre). Among the many books on Finnish sauna, this one is the most practical, and is popular among home-builders.

Pure Finland by Jyrki Sukula (Tammi). Recipe guide from Finland's finest celebrity chef.

Under the Midnight Sun by Liisa Rasimus (Gummerus). An excellent guide to Finnish food and the Finnish way of life.

Other Insight Guides

Other Insight Guides which highlight destinations in this region include Denmark, Russia, Norway and Sweden.

Insight Guide: Norway takes readers on a compelling journey through the Land of the Midnight Sun, from the fjords and mountains to the forests and lakes.

Sweden is one of Europe's last green lungs. Apa Publications assembled expert writers and talented photographers to produce **Insight Guide: Sweden**, which tells you what is and what is not worth seeing from the vibrant cities of Stockholm and Gothenburg to distant, snowy Lapland, home of the Sami.

Send Us Your Thoughts

We do our best to ensure the information in our books is as accurate and up-to-date as possible. The books are updated on a regular basis using local contacts, who painstakingly add, amend and correct as required. However, some details (such as telephone numbers and opening times) are liable to change, and we are ultimately reliant on our readers to put us in the picture.

We welcome your feedback, especially your experience of using the book "on the road". Maybe we recommended a hotel that you liked (or another that you didn't), or you came across a great bar or new attraction we missed.

We will acknowledge all contributions, and we'll offer an Insight Guide to the best letters received.

Please write to us at:
   Insight Guides
   PO Box 7910
   London SE1 1WE
Or email us at:
   insight@apaguide.co.uk

ART AND PHOTO CREDITS

INDEX